ESCORT CARRIER

ESCORT CARRIER

HMS VINDEX AT WAR

by

Kenneth Poolman

LEO COOPER
in association with
SECKER & WARBURG

ISBN 0 436 37705 5

Printed in Great Britain by
Richard Clay Limited, The Chaucer Press, Bungay, Suffolk

Frontispiece
Flight deck. Aboard *Vindex* in Scapa Flow, with
Swordfish and Sea Hurricanes parked, the fixed-
wing fighters on outriggers to keep them clear of the
flight path, with two Swordfish ranged for take-off.

CONTENTS

ILLUSTRATIONS

ACKNOWLEDGEMENTS

I owe my thanks for their kindness in helping me with information and/or photographs to the following: Lieutenant-Commander P. B. Austin, VRD, RNZNVR (Rtd); Commander John I. Baker, RN (Rtd); Captain V. G. Battle, MN (Rtd); Captain H. T. T. Bayliss, DSO, RN (Rtd); Mr Gordon Bennett; Mr J. M. Blair; Mr B. Brown; Mr David Brown; Mr Jack Bryant; Mrs Olive Burnett; Mr John A. Calvert; Mr Eric Clark; Mr Len Compton; Mr S. T. Conway; Mr Peter Couch, DSC; Mr Simon Cox; Mr P. E. Cumberland, DSC; Mr A. P. Cumming; Mr M. Dale; Mr John Darby; Mr J. S. Daymond; Mr E. B. Everett; Mr Alan Francis; Rear-Admiral P. D. Gick, CB, OBE, DSC and Bar, RN; Mrs Jean Gittins; Mr S. J. Guise; Lieutenant-Commander A. J. D. Harding, DSC, RN (Rtd); Captain H. J. Holdrup, MN; Commander Paul R. House, OBE, RN (Rtd); Mr P. J. Humphreys; Lieutenant-Commander JW Isaacson, RN (Rtd); Lieutenant-Commander Gareth Jenkins, VRD, RNR; Commander E. R. A. Johnson, RN; Mr R. Johnson; Lieutenant-Commander Norman Lauchlan, RN (Rtd); Lieutenant-Commander John T. Leech, RN (Rtd); Mr H. C. Lovell; Mr W. A. Mackay; Mr Kenneth Mason; Commander G. A. K. McCombe, VRD, RNR; Mr Malcolm McPhee; Mr P. A. Milne; Lieutenant-Commander G. E. Milner, MBE, RNR; Mr John E. Moore; Commander C. G. Palmer, DSC, VRD, RNZNVR; Mr J. Palmer, MBE; Mr F. Portman; Mr E. W. H. Rodgers; Lieutenant-Commander Norman L. Sharrock, RN (Rtd); Colonel F. O. J. Shaw, MRCS, LRCP; Mr Ronald Sired; Mr K. S. Smith; Mrs Felicity Spear; Mr R. A. W. Strong; Lieutenant A. E. Suggitt, RN (Rtd); Mr I. G. Taylor, MB, BS, VRD; Mr D. C. Trussell; Captain Desmond Vincent-Jones, DSC, RN (Rtd); Mr C. A. Waldram; Mr A. A. Walker; Mr E. J. Ward; Commander H. N. Weir, DSC, RNR; Mr T. White; Mr Chris Williams; Commander J. D. L. Williams, DSC, RN (Rtd); Lieutenant-Commander M. Wilson, RN (Rtd).

Mrs Jean Gittins kindly allowed me to draw upon the chapter 'My Years In Stanley' from her memoirs, originally published by *The South China Morning Post* in 1969, and upon part of another autobiographical manuscript, both of which are to be published by the Hong Kong University Press.

I am also grateful for help in obtaining contacts and information to: British Shipbuilders; Cunard Brocklebank; the Fleet Air Arm Officers Association; *Flight Deck*; Historical Branch, Ministry of Defence (Navy); *MMSA Reporter*; *Navy News*; *Sea Breezes*; Smith's Dock Company Ltd; Smiths Shiprepairers North Shields Ltd; Swan Hunter Shipbuilders Ltd; the Telegraphist Air Gunners Association

GLOSSARY

(A)   Affix to RN, RNR or RNVR rank denoting an Air Branch officer.

A25   Fleet Air Arm accident report form.

A-Branch   Flying officers who had transferred their Short Service commissions from the RAF to the Fleet Air Arm of the Royal Navy shortly before World War 2 formed what was familiarly known as the A-Branch. They wore the straight rings of the Royal Navy on their sleeves but, unlike regular, long-service Royal Navy officers who had specialised in aviation, bore the letter A in the curl of the highest ring, which also affixed their rank in the Navy list, e.g. Lieutenant-Commander (A) Stovin-Bradford, RN, but Lieutenant-Commander Gick, RN.

ADDL   Aerodrome Dummy Deck Landing. A preliminary to a practice landing on an actual flight deck, using part of an airfield dimensioned like a flight deck.

Air Direction Room   Office from which the movement of a carrier's aircraft is controlled by voice radio.

Amatol   Explosive used in depth-charges, composed of a mixture of ammonium nitrate and molten TNT (Trinitrotoluene) high explosive. Originally invented in World War I to make supplies of TNT go further. Also cheaper than pure TNT.

Ar 196   German Arado Ar 196 seaplane.

Armed Merchant Cruiser   Allied merchant ships previously 'stiffened' to carry guns, converted to auxiliary cruisers, and most frequently used to intercept blockade runners or German raiding cruisers. (v. 'Stiffening')

A/S   Anti-Submarine.

Asdic   ASDIC, for Anti-Submarine Detection Investigation Committee, set up by Britain and France in 1918 which gave its name to the apparatus for locating a submerged submarine with a sound wave and calculating its range and bearing. The American 'sonar' is more descriptive.

ASO   Air Staff Officer, otherwise Lieutenant-Commander or Commander (Operations). Responsible for the planning of flying operations.

ASV   Air to Surface Vessel radar installed in aircraft.

ATS   Auxiliary Territorial Service, the British women's army organisation in World War II.

BABS   Blind Approach Beam System. A short-range radio beacon system used to guide an aircraft on to the correct glide path in bad visibility. (v. 'YE beacon')

Banana boat   Refrigerated cargo ship mainly used for the carrying of bananas.

Barrier   The crash barrier, resembling a wire-stranded tennis net, was raised by moving a lever on the catwalk just before aircraft landed on, to provide a last-ditch means of stopping them. The actual contact was also known as a 'barrier'. (v. 'Jesus Christ wire')

Bats   (1) The implements, shaped like ten-

	nis *bats*, used by the Deck Landing Control Officer or 'batsman' to guide aircraft down on to the deck.
	(2) 'Bats', the familar term for the 'batsman' or DLCO. (v. DLCO)
Batsman	Familiar term for the Deck Landing Control Officer (DLCO).
Beriberi	Dietary deficiency disease caused by lack of vitamin B1 (thiamin, aneurin), resulting from too exclusive a diet of polished rice, from which the germ and bran, containing the vitamin, have been extracted by milling. (v. 'Thiamin tablets')
Blip	The indication of a target thrown up on a Plan Position Indicator (PPI) type radar screen. (v. 'PPI')
Bogey	R/T procedure code for an unidentified aircraft
Bollards	Pair of metal stump posts for making fast a rope.
Bottle	Slang for a reprimand, the tearing off of a strip.
Box	The space left inside the convoy, open at the rear, for the escort carrier to manoeuvre when operating aircraft.
BPF	British Pacific Fleet, operated as Task Force 37 or 57 of the US Pacific Fleet.
Brake horsepower	The mechanical output of an engine, turbine or motor available at the shaft, so called because a common method of measuring mechanical output is by the use of a Pony brake.
Brocks Benefit	Brocks Ltd were well known firework manufacturers.
Butts	The ends of metal plates used in the sides of ships.
Buzz	Slang for rumour, as US Navy 'scuttlebutt'.
Bv 138	Three-engined Blohm und Voss Bv 138G-1 reconnaissance flying boat. A tough, armour-plated customer, in

	spite of its comparatively slow speed (177 mph maximum, at sea level, 146 mph at 3,280 feet), able to carry six 110 lb or four 331 lb bombs over a maximum range of 2,670 miles, sometimes extended by refuelling from U-boats at sea.
Cable	As a measurement, eight shackles, i.e. 100 fathoms. (v. 'Shackle')
Calibration trials	Tests to calculate the irregularities of the ship's compasses.
Cambered	Curved.
CAM ship	Catapult Aircraft Merchant Ship, a cargo vessel fitted with a catapult on her bows, from which a Sea Hurricane fighter could be launched to drive off an enemy aircraft reconnoitring or attacking the convoy. CAM ship air contingents were mostly drawn from the specially formed Merchant Service Fighter Unit of the RAF, and the pilots were volunteers for a job which could often mean ditching or baling out in the sea after combat, as the fighter could not return to its parent ship, and land was usually out of range.
Carley float	Life raft in the form of a large oval tube of canvas painted to make it watertight and stuffed with kapok or granulated cork, with a light wooden grid inside the oval, and hand lines on the outer circumference, so that a large number of men could be supported, both inside and outside. A big Carley float could support fifty men.
Catalina	American Consolidated Catalina flying boat loaned in quantity to RAF Coastal Command by the Lend-Lease bill.
Catwalk	The gallery running round the edge of the flight deck in a carrier. (v.

'Goofers')

Cheese down Coil down the tail of a rope into a neat circular pattern on the deck. The end of the tail is in the centre and the remainder coiled flat round it in a tight spiral.

Circuits and bumps Practice touch-downs without actually landing.

Cobra search An aircraft patrol round a convoy at a specified distance, e.g. Cobra 12 (miles).

Commander (Flying) Officer in a carrier responsible for the carrying out of flying operations. Commonly shortened to Commander (F). Office often held, as in HMS *Vindex*, by a Lieutenant-Commander.

Commander (Operations) v. 'ASO'.

Compressors Air compressors, from which the compressed air was pumped via valves into the cylinders of a diesel-engined ship's main engines for starting purposes.

Condenser Machinery in a ship's engine room which reconverted the steam used in the main engines into feed water for the boilers.

CS10 10th Cruiser Squadron and, by association, its Commanding Officer.

Cutter Large (30–34 foot) ship's boat fitted with one mast, or pulling eight to fourteen oars. (v. 'Whaler')

CVE Escort carriers in US Navy service were initially designated AVGs, then ACVs, and finally, on 20 August 1942, CVEs (CV = aircraft carrier, E = escort). In 1943 US Navy CVEs joined British escort carriers in the North Atlantic, and the RN adopted the same code. Most of the RN-manned CVEs were US-built.

Dan buoy Small buoy normally used by mine-sweepers to mark the boundary of a swept channel.

DC Depth charge.

Deck hook The hook lowered from a Swordfish or a Sea Hurricane's fuselage before landing on to catch an arrester wire was of the simple, rigid V-frame type fitted outside the fuselage. A Wildcat's deck hook was of a more sophisticated type located when not in use inside the fuselage further aft.

Degaussing Once the polarity of German magnetic mines had been discovered from a captured specimen, Allied warships were fitted with an encircling degaussing ring through which an electric current was passed to counteract or reverse the ship's magnetic field, which could otherwise trigger off a magnetic mine.

Demobbed Demobilised from the armed forces.

DEMS Defensively Equipped Merchant Ship. A term defining the gun and the Royal Navy or Army gunners supplied to merchant ships for defence against U-boats or aircraft.

Derrick A single spar, pivoted at the lower or inboard end and used aboard ships like a crane for hoisting boats, cargo and other heavy weights. From the name of a 17th-century Tyburn hangman.

DLCO Deck Landing Control Officer or, in common usage the 'batsman'—from the 'bats' or paddles he wielded to guide the pilots down on to the deck. A carrier's batsman was always an experienced pilot himself.

(E) Affix to RN, RNR or RNVR rank denoting an Engineering Branch officer.

Echo Strictly the result of an Asdic sound

wave bouncing off an object below the surface of the sea, but used to describe a contact by radar pulse. (v. 'Trace')

Eight bells   Time is denoted on board HM ships by striking the bell every half-hour, with one stroke at half-past four, half-past eight and half-past twelve, and the addition of one stroke for each half-hour until eight strokes of the bell (Eight Bells) are reached at four, eight and twelve o'clock.

EG   Escort Group.

Enigma   German secret naval code, intercepted by Allied listening posts and passed to the Government Code and Cypher School at Bletchley Park in Buckinghamshire for decyphering. The resulting secret information was known as Ultra.

ERA   Engine Room Artificer, a noncommissioned rank.

Evaporator   Machinery which made distilled water for cooling a ship's main engines or for drinking.

Executive Officer   In a major warship the officer who ran the ship, leaving the Captain free to fight her.

Fathom   A measurement of six feet.

FDO   Fighter Direction Officer, later renamed Air Direction Officer, who controlled the actions of a carrier's aircraft on voice radio from the ship.

Finmark   Inclusive name for the Scandinavian countries.

Fix   The establishment of another ship's position at the intersection of two bearings of her obtained at different times.

Flagiolet   Small wind instrument like a recorder, with six main holes.

Flame float/marker   Container full of calcium carbide with an activating string at the top, kept in a bag in the rear cockpit of a Swordfish for dropping by the observer in darkness.

Fleet Train   Mobile logistics task force of tankers, supply ships and replenishment aircraft carriers which accompanied the US Pacific Fleet.

Flyco   Flying Control. Lieutenant-Commander (Flying)'s position on the bridge overlooking the flight deck during flying operations.

Focke Wulf Condor   Four-engined, long-range, land-based anti-shipping German bomber developed from the pre-war Focke Wulf airliner after the failure of the advanced Heinkel 177 Greif maritime bomber. The heavily armed military Condor, a *Gruppe* of which (KG40) operated from Bordeaux-Mérignac airfield, could carry five 250 kg (551 lb) bombs over a range of 2,000 miles, and was frequently used for the reconnaissance of Allied convoys, though its airliner's basic structure made it vulnerable to the strain of combat manoeuvres and to determined anti-aircraft gun and fighter attack.

FOCT   Flag Officer, Carrier Training.

Foul berth   A mooring ground made unsafe by uncharted wrecks lying on the bottom.

Four-piper   A four-funnelled ship.

Foxers   An Allied countermeasure to the 'Gnat' acoustic torpedo. A Foxer consisted of two steel pipes mounted in parallel in a metal frame. Escorts towed two Foxers, one on each quarter. The pipes vibrated against each other, sending off air bubbles which set up a facsimile of propeller cavi-

	tation effect. The Germans replied by shielding their Gnats against noises from the side. The Allies countered with single Foxers towed right astern.
Galley	Ship's kitchen. In British-built warships food was normally issued to the day's 'cooks of the mess', prepared by them, then returned to the galley to be cooked.
Gas	Petrol, aviation spirit.
Gnat	German version of the acoustic torpedo, which homed on the sound of a ship's propellors. (v. 'Foxers')
Goofers	'The Goofers' was the catwalk or gallery round the edge of the flight deck of a carrier, where many of the ship's company not on watch came to *goof* at aircraft taking off or, more especially, landing on.
Gremlin	Mischievous goblin said to harass airmen.
Griped to	A ship's boat was secured when hoisted at the davits by pieces of matting called *gripes*.
Grub screw	Small screw with no head, resembling maggot or *grub*.
Grumman Martlet	US-built Grumman Wildcat shipboard fighters on loan to the Royal Navy were at first renamed Martlets in British service, but later reverted to their original name. They were rugged aircraft, well armed with four 0.5-inch Colt-Browning machine guns, and specially designed for carrier operation, unlike the British Sea Hurricane or Seafire. A Martlet's narrow-tracked undercarriage, though much more resistant to the shocks of deck landing than the frail underpinning of the Seafire, allowed it to rock uneasily in rolling conditions.
Gunner (G)	A warrant officer specialising in gun-

	nery, differentiated by the affix (G) from the equivalent torpedo specialist, who was called a Gunner (T).
Gyro compass	The older compass activated by magnets points to the earth's magnetic north pole, but a gyro compass, which is electrically driven, indicates the true north pole, relying on a spinning wheel, which maintains its axis and plane of rotation relative to space.
Hawsepipe	The channel in a ship's bows through which the anchor cable passes.
Heat exchanger	Apparatus in a ship's engine room for re-cooling the coolant water which had circulated round the main engines and thus absorbed heat from them.
Hedgehog launcher	Type of mortar firing missiles forward of the carrying ship's bows as she headed towards a U-boat target. This enabled the ship to maintain Asdic contact with the target, whereas depth-charges were dropped amidships or astern, and the attacking ship then lost contact as she steamed over the U-boat's position. However, Hedgehog missiles only exploded on hitting the target, and the precision of attack required was difficult to achieve at any speed.
Hellcat	The American Gruman Hellcat F6F-3/5 fighters, successors to the Wildcat, bigger, some 40 mph faster (above 20,000 feet), with a wide-tracked undercarriage for more stability on a carrier's flight deck. Also in RN service as the F Mk I and II, the latter fitted for bombs and RPs, and some with radar as night fighters. (v 'Wildcat')
HF/DF	High Frequency Direction Finding. The interception of U-boat radio sig-

nals, the object being to fix the submarine's position by the plotting of two intersecting bearings from separate interceptions. Known familiarly as Huff-Duff.

HMCS His Majesty's Canadian Ship.

Homing beacon Radio transmitter in a ship beaming a signal to guide a returning aircraft.

Hook Anchor.

Huff-Duff Slang for HF/DF apparatus. (v.)

Hydrophone Listening device for picking up the sound of an enemy vessel's engines and propellers.

IFF Identification Friend or Foe. A small transmitter fitted in an aircraft transmitted a signal which could be picked up on the radar screen of a friendly warship.

Indicator unit Part of a radar set incorporating the display screen.

Intercom Intercommunication system between members of an aircrew in the aircraft. Usually radio, but in earlier British naval aircraft a 'Gosport tube', a simple voicepipe between pilot and observer.

Jack Union Jack.

Jackstay Wire or hemp rope or pendant secured firmly between two points and used as a support for lifelines, for a breeches buoy or a refuelling hose between ships, or for an awning, etc.

Jesus Christ wire If an oncoming pilot missed the first main arrester wires on a flight deck, which had hydraulic retardation, the only means of stopping, short of a barrier crash, was by hooking one remaining single wire. As this wire was not fitted with hydraulic retardation, contact with it produced a short, very sharp shock. Thus, both the anticipation and the actual con-

tact could produce a fervent 'Jesus Christ!' from the unfortunate pilot.

Ju 88 Junkers Ju 88A-6 fighter bomber. Junkers Jumo 211G engines. Maximum speed 281 mph at 19,780 lbs weight, 248 mph at 24,350 lbs weight. Climb 1,370 feet/minute at 19,780 lbs, 700 feet/minute at 24,350 lbs. Bomb load 3,986 lbs normal, 5,510 lbs maximum.

Jump wire Also 'jumping' or 'jumper' wire. A serrated wire leading from the stemhead of a submarine to the forward edge of the bridge casing above the conning tower, and from the after edge of the bridge casing to the stern, used for cutting a way through defensive nets when submerged.

Junk Chinese sailing vessel.

Kamikaze 'Divine Wind', the Japanese aircraft, carrying bombs, which were deliberately crashed into Allied warships, causing major damage to the US Pacific Fleet.

Korvettenkapitän German equivalent of Commander Royal Navy.

Lend-Lease The US Lend-Lease Act, finally passed on 11 March 1941, enabled the USA to lend or lease arms and supplies, with repayment in cash not required, to any country considered vital to her defence. By the time the Act was terminated on 20 August 1945, this had amounted to some £5,049 million's worth of materials delivered to the USA's allies.

Liberty boat A boat, either from their own ship or from shore, taking men on leave (liberty men) ashore or bringing them back.

Liberty ship Type of war programme American merchant ship mass-produced with prefabricated sections and welded

	seams instead of the traditional rivetted construction.
Lighter	A 'dumb' vessel, built like a barge, without propulsion of its own, towed by tugs for the transport of cargo between ship and shore.
Loud-hailer	Megaphone.
Macra	RN air station, Macrihanish, Scotland.
MAC ship	Merchant Aircraft Carrier. Nineteen grain ships and tankers, i.e. vessels which could be fitted with flight decks and still carry their cargoes, piped aboard through trunk hoses, were converted into MAC ships. They carried three or four Swordfish, but flew the Red Ensign of the Merchant Navy, and remained in convoy. Distinct from escort carriers.
Matelot	Colloquial Royal Navy term for a sailor, quoted in this book in its original French form, but sometimes printed phonetically as 'matloe' or 'matlow'.
Mess-decks	Spaces in British-built warships where the ship's company lived when not on duty, with meals taken there, and hammocks slung for sleeping. In US-built escort carriers sleeping spaces (with metal bunks) and eating spaces were separate.
Messenger	A small rope attached to the eye of a hawser (heavy rope or small cable) to haul it in.
MO	Medical Officer.
MOWT	Ministry of War Transport.
NAAFI	Navy, Army and Air Force Institutes. These included canteens ashore and stores aboard ships supplying consumer goods.
Nelson's Blood	Traditional slang term for rum in the Royal Navy derived from the preservation of Lord Nelson's body in a cask of rum on board HMS *Victory* for her return to Portsmouth after Trafalgar.
NKVD	Narodny Komitet Vnutrennih Del, or People's Commissariat of Internal Affairs, an earlier version of the KGB.
Ocker	Slang for the mythical average Foster's Lager-swilling Australian male.
Ops Room	Headquarters for the planning and conducting of an operation, containing a surface plot and a PPI (v.).
'Outrageous' class	The aircraft carriers HMS *Courageous*, *Furious* and *Glorious* were originally built as Light Battlecruisers, *Courageous* and *Glorious* with four 15-inch, *Furious* to carry two huge 18-inch guns, to form part of Lord Fisher's projected fleet for the invasion of the Baltic. They were all regarded as freaks, and this operation, never carried out, very dubious.
Packet boat	Originally a vessel plying regularly between two ports carrying mail as well as goods and passengers.
Pancake	R/T procedure code for an aircraft landing.
Paravane	Torpedo-shaped device streamed from the bows of a ship at a depth regulated by its vanes or planes, to cut the moorings of submerged mines.
Pellagra	Dietary deficiency disease caused by lack of nicotinamide (P-P vitamin), endemic especially among maize eaters, producing dermatitis and cracking of the skin, diarrhoea, and often insanity.
Ping	A contact by Asdic, from the sound which this makes. (v. 'Asdic')
Pole	Slang for the joystick or control column in an aircraft cockpit.
Pom-pom	Multi-barrelled long-range Maxim

	automatic quick-firing anti-aircraft gun.
Poop deck	Merchant Navy term for the after deck or quarter-deck.
Pooped	A ship was 'pooped' when a big following sea broke aboard her *poop* or quarterdeck.
POSH	'Port out, starboard home', the *posh*. way to travel to avoid the sun aboard the steamships of the P and O Line carrying the British Colonials to and from The Old Country.
Poteen	Whisky distilled privately, i.e. illicitly, in Ireland.
PPI	Plan Position Indicator. The display on the screen of the advanced type of radar which used a scanner revolving through 360 degrees. (v. 'Indicator unit', 'Scanner', 'Trace'.)
Puffer	Small Scottish coastal steamer.
Purifier	Apparatus purifying either a ship's fuel oil or lubricating oil of impurities, e.g. water.
Quarter	The part of a ship's side towards the stern.
Querencia	Spanish term for the area in the bull ring which a bull selects as his own territory, from which he will mount his attacks on the matador.
Radio altimeter	Electronic instrument measuring height in terms of the transit time of a radar pulse between aircraft and land or sea surface.
RATOG	Rocket Assisted Take-Off Gear.
Ready Room	Or Crew Room, for aircrew on standby.
Reciprocal	The course directly opposite to the one desired, obtained by carelessly reading off the opposite bearing on the compass card.
RNR	The British naval reserve officer branch formed from professional Merchant Navy officers, who served full-time with the Royal Navy for the duration of hostilities only.
RNVR	The British naval reserve officer branch composed of civilians serving full-time for the duration of the war only.
Round-down	The after end of the flight deck, curved downwards to avoid snagging the undercarriage of a landing aircraft.
Rounds	Daily inspection of the ship in the evening by the Officer of The Watch, with a special Captain's Rounds on a Sunday morning.
RP	Rocket projectile, $4\frac{1}{2}$ feet long, weighing 66 lbs, with a 25 lb armour-piercing warhead. Fired electrically by a button in the pilot's cockpit via a cordite propellant charge. Usually launched in pairs from both wings of an aircraft to prevent the latter from yawing.
R/T	Radio Telephonic voice communication between ship and ship and ship and aircraft.
Salthorse	A non-flying naval officer. Sometimes a term of contempt, used by flying officers for those with an entrenched, old-fashioned bias against the flying 'dirty-fingernailed' types, and a blinkered attachment to the gun and the torpedo tube.
Sampan	Small, light oriental boat propelled either by a single scull over the stern (harbour type) or by a junk-type sail on a single mast (coastal). From Chinese *san*, thin, and *pan*, board.
SAP	Semi-Armour-Piercing.
SBT	Submarine Bubble Target. This device, called *Pillenwerfer* by the Germans, ejected special chemical 'pills' which were activated by sea water,

	creating an asdic echo like that of the U-boat herself. The pill began to work two minutes after release, and its effect lasted for some six minutes.
Scanner	The rotating arm of the type of advanced radar installation which provided automatic continuous 360 degree coverage, as in the Mark XI ASV radar fitted to Swordfish Mark I, IIs and IIIs, in which the scanner was housed in a bulge underneath the forward fuselage. The action of the scanner was copied by a rotating line of light, called the trace, on the screen, and a target showed up as a *blip* (v.) there when the scanner beam struck it. (v. 'PPI', 'Trace')
Schnorkel	Tube through which later types of U-boats could suck in air from periscope depth and thus run the diesel engines underwater, which could be used to recharge the electric batteries in greater safety than before.
Seaboat	In a warship of the Royal Navy two boats, called seaboats, were kept ready for rapid lowering at sea, one on either side, for rescue or other emergencies, and were fitted with special Robinson's Disengaging Gear for slipping the boat smartly from the falls while the ship was still travelling through the water. The seaboat was usually a whaler. (v.)
Seafire	The naval adaptation of the Spitfire for use in carriers, some with folding wings.
Sea Hurricane IIC	Fixed-wing fighter converted from the Hurricane Mark IIA. Maximum speed 336 mph at 20,000 feet. Climb 9.1 minutes to 20,000 feet. Range 460 miles normal, 970 miles with auxiliary tanks. Service ceiling 35,600 feet. Armament four 20-millimetre cannon, four RPs.
'Secure'	'Stop work'.
Senior	Senior Engineer.
Shackle	A U-shaped iron closed with a pin across the jaws, used, for example, to join the standard $12\frac{1}{2}$-fathom lengths of chain cable, hence also used to denote a length of $12\frac{1}{2}$ fathoms. (v. 'Fathom')
Smoke float	Small cylinder-shaped sea marker which emitted smoke on contact with the water and was dropped by aircraft during daylight hours.
SOE	Senior Officer, Escort.
Special Sea Dutymen	Senior hands who relieve the ordinary watchkeepers on regular standing jobs for entering and leaving harbour. The chief quartermaster takes the wheel, quartermasters man the chains (the platform on the side of the ship from which the leadsman 'swings the lead'), the telegraphs are manned by special ratings usually detailed from the galley's crew, special signalmen close up, etc.
Split circuit	Breaking off from an orthodox complete circuit of the carrier round the bow to make a sharp turn-in over the round-down instead of a long approach from astern.
Sponson	Platform projecting from a ship's side.
Square-rigged	Propelled by square sails, set on yards hoisted on the masts. Technically, a *ship* has square sails on all her masts, whereas in *barques*, *barquentines*, *brigs* and *brigantines* there is a mixture of square and fore-and-aft sails, and *schooners* are usually fore-and-aft rigged.
Squeegee	Straight-edged rubber rake with a long handle for pushing the water

used in scrubbing decks into the scuppers.

Squid launcher The Squid forward-firing shipborne mortar, though a bigger and heavier installation, was more accurate than the Hedgehog, which had to hit to score, because Squid missiles were set to explode at the target depth indicated by special depth-finding asdic.

Standard Displacement The weight of water displaced by a ship, less the weight of fuel and reserve feed water.

Starshell Shell fired at a high elevation with a fuse timed to burst the shell and release a pyrotechnic flare suspended on a small parachute to illuminate briefly an enemy ship or fleet at night.

Stiffening Before World War II fifty British merchant ships were fitted with extra 'stiffening' in the appropriate places so that they could be fitted with guns and used as Armed Merchant Cruisers in the event of war, e.g. HMS *Jervis Bay* and *Rawalpindi*. Bulkheads were of greater strength, 'gun' decks were double-plated, sometimes steel packing rings to take gun pedestals were actually fitted to the deck and covered with teak planking, extra portable pillars stored.

Stringbag Familiar term, often affectionate, for the Fairey Swordfish aircraft.

Stone frigate A shore-based naval establishment.

TAG Telegraphist/Air-Gunner in the Fleet Air Arm.

Thiamin tablets Pills to prevent beriberi (v.).

Torpex The most powerful of all non-atomic military explosives, a cast mixture of RDX (a mixture containing TNT), TNT and aluminium, used in World War II in torpedo warheads.

Trace The line of green fluorescent light, fixed and horizontal or sweeping through 360 degrees, on the screen of radar sets. Sometimes used loosely to mean the screen itself. A target registered as a kink or a 'blip' in the line. (v. 'Echo' and 'Blip')

Trials carrier Aircraft carrier used mainly for breaking in new squadrons or aircraft. HMS *Pretoria Castle*, converted from an Armed Merchant Cruiser, was so employed.

Tropical rig White shoes, stockings, shorts and shirts (called 'flannels' in the case of ratings) with white cap covers for officers and white caps for ratings.

TT Teetotal, abstaining from alcohol. When coming of age, at twenty, to draw his tot of rum, a teetotal rating could opt for 3d a day in lieu.

T124X articles Special articles signed by Merchant Navy personnel serving in HM ships with RNR rank.

Ultra v. 'Enigma'.

Vector Alteration of course.

Very cartridge Not 'very' but 'Very', the name of the inventor of this large signal cartridge which, fired from a special Very Pistol, produced either a red or green flare in the sky. Used frequently by aircraft.

Viper patrol Code for a patrol round a convoy at visibility distance, usually flown by day in poor weather conditions and in variable visibility when U-boats were known to be in the vicinity, also in general use at night.

Walrus Homely, single-engined amphibious flying boat built by Supermarine from a design by Frank Mitchell, creator of the Spitfire. Launched from catapults aboard battleships and cruisers, and

	valuable for air/sea rescue work. Familiarly known as the 'Shagbat'.
Wardroom	Officers' dining quarters.
Whaler	A 25-foot or 27-foot boat with a drop keel, for pulling or sailing, based on the design of the original whaleboats used in whaling ships. It pulls five oars, and when sailed is yawl-rigged, with a mainmast for'ard and a small mizzenmast aft which is controlled by a separate tiller. Smaller than a cutter (30–34 feet) or a gig (30 feet), larger than a dinghy ($13\frac{1}{2}$–16 feet).
Wildcat VI	American Grumman shipboard fighter. One Wright R-1820-56 engine. Maximum speeds 332 mph at 28,000 feet, 306 at sea level. Cruising speed 164 mph. Landing speed 76 mph. Climb 3,650 feet in one minute. Range 900 miles normal, 1,310 miles maximum. Service ceiling 34,700 feet. Armament six 50-calibre Colt-Browning machine guns.
'Wings'	Lieutenant-Commander or Commander (Flying).
Wolf pack	A number of U-boats operating as a team to attack a convoy. The first boat to sight the convoy acted as contact keeper and homed in the others by radio.
Woolworth carrier	An escort carrier, particularly one converted from a merchant ship or a merchant hull in the USA. A derogatory term for an excellent type of warship.
W/T	Wireless telegraphy, or signalling in Morse code.
X, Y and Z doors	Painted letters governed the securing of watertight doors thus marked. To open an X door at sea permission had to be obtained from the ship's Damage Control headquarters, when in harbour from the Officer of the Watch, the door to be closed and secured again immediately after passing through. A Y door could be opened without permission but must be closed immediately after passage. A Z door could be left open except when the ship was at action stations or in an emergency.
YE Beacon	Radio homing beacon for the long-range control of aircraft, also code-named HAYRAKE.
Y-Scheme	An arrangement whereby a volunteer for war service with the Royal Navy was granted deferment from service for one year to complete the preliminary stage of a programme of higher education while receiving part-time naval training, e.g. in one of the Naval Divisions formed for the purpose at Oxford or Cambridge Universities.

Many of the illustrations are enlarged from contemporary snapshots culled from the albums of members of *Vindex*'s crew, acknowledged on p. *viii*. Some of the photographs show evidence both of their age and the conditions under which they were taken, but no attempt has been made to retouch them: what they may lack in clarity they more than gain in immediacy and atmosphere.

1

No. 4698, HMS *Vindex*

AT A FEW MINUTES before twelve on the still summer night of 25 July 1981, at Hill Farm, near Wymondham, Norfolk, the home of orthopaedic surgeon Ian Taylor, four men gathered round a ship's bell. There was enough light from the waning moon to see the name HMS VINDEX engraved on the bell, which had rested silently for some years in the Taylors' barn. As the last minute of eleven o'clock passed, Eddie Ward, former Swordfish pilot, raised the bell from the ground, and John Darby, once his observer, took hold of the white, plaited clapper toggle, and rang eight bells, four pairs of sharp metallic notes which resounded through the quiet Norfolk countryside as they had often echoed round the decks of the aircraft carrier whose name was on the bell, and aboard which all three men had served together. The voice of the old ship died away, and the three figures from her wartime days of hard seatime and struggle went their separate ways again after the brief reunion, leaving the author, the fourth man present, to record something of those memorable days, and to tell this story ...

... Forty years before this meeting, on 2 October 1941, the Port Line of London, which traded with Australia and New Zealand, placed an order for a fast twin-screw diesel-engined refrigerated cargo liner of their *Port Napier* class, to carry general cargo outwards and fruit and dairy products homeward, with the Wallsend-on-Tyne firm of Swan Hunter & Wigham Richardson. As in most of the Line's ships, she would have comfortable accommodation for 12 passengers, the maximum number allowed by the Board of Trade in this category of vessel.

There was at this time a pressing need for aircraft carriers to join the escort of Allied convoys bringing essential weapons, fuel and food from the Americas to Britain. There had never been enough of the big Fleet carriers to sail with the convoys, and with the beginning of the Battle of the Atlantic in the autumn of 1940 the Admiralty adopted the conception of the converted merchant ship, which could be put into service comparatively quickly.

The pioneer ship was the small HMS *Audacity*, converted in six months, January–June 1941, from the 5,537-ton captured German 'banana boat' *Hannover*, after she had been originally allocated for use as an Ocean Boarding Vessel. The British Ministry of War Transport would not release any merchant ships for use as carriers unless they had already been selected

HMS *Vindex* at Swan Hunter's yard, Newcastle-on-Tyne at the time of commissioning. The V-shaped exhaust trunking in lieu of the merchant ship funnel can be plainly seen, and the ship's merchantile anchors, which proved inadequate. Her pennant number (15) has not yet been painted on her side.

for warship conversion of some kind, so in April 1941, while *Audacity* was still in dockyard hands, the Admiralty asked the United States government for the loan of six of the new auxiliary carriers being converted from merchantmen in American yards, and were promised the first six to be completed.

Audacity had no hangar and, as the Focke-Wulf Condor maritime bombers seemed a bigger threat at the time than U-boats, operated only fighters, just six American Grumman Martlets, from her flight deck, but she had given such a good account of herself, against both bombers and submarines, before she was sunk by a U-boat on 21 December 1941, that more 'escort carriers' were ordered from the USA, and the MOWT grudgingly reserved several new merchant ship hulls on the stocks in Britain for conversion.

The first of these was an 11,800-ton ship under construction in the yard of the Caledon Shipbuilding Company at Dundee, Scotland. Originally named *Telemachus*, she was launched as HMS *Activity* on 30 May 1942.

On 21 July the keel of the fast cargo-liner ordered by the Port Line from

Swan Hunter's nine months earlier was laid in the yard on the north bank of the Tyne.

On 20 October she was acquired by the Ministry of War Transport under the Defence (General) Regulations, 1939, by Licence No. 600, and allocated for conversion to an auxiliary aircraft carrier.

Two ships building at John Brown's, Clydebank, and Harland & Wolff's, Belfast, were chosen for similar conversion at the same time. The prototype was the John Brown ship, which had also been on order for the Port Line and was a sister of the Swan Hunter ship. The Admiralty sent the original plans for the fitting-out to Clydebank, where copies were made and sent to Swan Hunter's and Harland's.

On 12 December Admiralty Job No. 4698 at Swan's, which was to have been christened *Port Sydney* after a previous ship which had been a trooper in World War I, was allocated the name HMS *Vindex*. There had been a Royal Navy ex-merchantman aircraft carrier of that name in the very infancy of naval aviation, an Isle of Man passenger steamer acquired by the Admiralty in 1915 and converted to have hangar space for five seaplanes and two landplane fighters, with a deck above the forward stowage hangar from which the fighters could be flown off. From her flight deck on 3 November 1915 a Bristol Scout made the first operational take-off by a fighter from a British warship. The old *Vindex*, renamed *Viking*, was still running her original service to the Isle of Man.

The Latin name, meaning Avenger (not to be confused with HMS *Avenger*, the second of the US-built escort carriers to reach British waters) was a reference to the ring in the form of an asp and containing poison worn by Hannibal, the scourge of Rome in bloody battles like Cannae in 215 BC. When threatened with inevitable capture he swallowed the poison, and the Romans called the ring Cannarum Vindex. It is not known which classical scholar in the Admiralty suggested the name.

The John Brown carrier was named *Nairana*, after another packet boat converted to a carrier in 1917, with a large hangar abaft the funnels for the stowage of seaplanes, and a smaller hangar for'ard, aircraft having to be partially dismantled for stowage. The third sister of the trio, the Harland & Wolff ship, was named *Campania*, after a conversion from the Cunard liner of 20,000 tons, completed in 1916 as the first large seaplane carrier in the British Grand Fleet, with a complement of ten seaplanes. In a gale off Rosyth she had fouled the mooring cable of the battleship *Ramillies*, was holed and sank rapidly.

The hull and engine room machinery of the new *Vindex* remained as specified by the Port Line. The hull was rivetted in the traditional way. This was considered by the Admiralty to be stronger than the all-welded construction of US-built escort carriers, which, particularly if sloppily done by wartime labour, could open up, it was thought, under the stresses of heavy seas and violent combat manoeuvring.

On 4 May 1943 HMS *Vindex* was christened and launched down the ways.

Another view of *Vindex* alongside the fitting-out wharf showing clearly the side exhaust vents, her twin 4-inch mounting right aft, and some of her four quadruple 2-pounder pom-poms and sixteen 20-millimetre Oerlikon guns in sponsons along the edge of the flight deck.

The launch of a big ship from Swan's Wallsend yard across the narrow stream of the 'Queen Of All The Rivers' was always a close-run thing, but the yard had long since perfected the drill, and chains pulled the heavy ship up short of the Jarrow bank. Her engines were then fitted as she lay alongside the wharf. *Nairana* was launched on 20 May, *Campania* at Belfast on 17 June.

Vindex's engine room contained two massive five-cylinder vertically-opposed Doxford main propulsion diesel engines capable of 10,700 brake horsepower; three diesel generators; two Cochrane vertical boilers; compressors; evaporators; purifiers; pumps; heat exchangers and other normal merchant ship installations and fittings. There were also two separate generator rooms, each with an Allen diesel generator and sub-station switchboard, and emergency electric motor-driven pumps located outside the engine room. *Nairana* had similar machinery, *Campania* had Burmeister & Wain diesel engines. All three ships had twin screws, better for manoeuvring than the single screws of the first classes of American-built CVEs.

Thus far the growing vessel was indistinguishable from the merchantman she was originally meant to be. Instead of cargo holds, however, she was fitted

out with mess-decks, petrol stowage compartments with the combined capacity for 52,000 gallons of aviation gas, with buoyancy compartments, consisting of void spaces fitted with empty 40-gallon drums in racks, and magazines. The main deck contained officers' cabins, galley, offices and Aircraft Direction Office.

Above this was the hangar, with a clear height of 17 feet 6 inches and a stowage capacity for 18 aircraft. On top of the hangar was laid the flight deck, 503 feet long overall, with an effective length of 495 feet between the tops of the round-downs fore and aft, and 77 feet wide, over 30 feet narrower than that of a contemporary American-built escort carrier of the class of the USS *Bogue* and the HMS *Attacker*, and steel-plated in contrast to the US carriers' decks of Oregon pine planking.

To starboard, and well for'ard, rose the bridge 'island', containing compass platform and charthouse, captain's sea cabin and Flying Control, with lattice mast and radar antennae. Let into the flight deck aft was the ship's one massive 45 by 35-foot aircraft lift, with a working load limit of 15,000 lbs. American escort carriers had two 'elevators' and an 'accelerator' (catapult), which these three British-designed ships also lacked. Suspended athwart the flight deck were the aircraft arrester wires, with the stout wire 'barrier' forward of them to check any aircraft which had missed all the wires. Round the edge of the deck was the gallery deck, otherwise known as the catwalk, or 'Goofers', which would become the most popular place in the ship whenever flying was in progress.

Overall, from stem to cruiser stern, HMS *Vindex* was 524 feet long, 68 feet in the beam at her widest point, underwater, with a draught of 24 feet 9 inches for'ard, 25 feet 6 inches aft, fully loaded, and displaced 13,445 tons standard, 16,830 tons with full load. Her sister ship *Nairana* was the heavier vessel at 13,825 tons standard, 17,210 tons deepload.

Some time before completion, specialists and key men appointed to the ship began to arrive at Wallsend. One of the earliest to join was *Vindex*'s new Executive Officer. Not many officers had reached commander's rank in the Royal Naval Volunteer Reserve, drawn entirely from civilian life ashore, by mid-1943, but Commander George Alan Kenneth McCombe, RNVR, had served in the Mersey Division for some time before the war. He had been Secretary to the Mersey Docks and Harbour Board, but had spent several weeks each year at sea with the Royal Navy as part of his Reserve training and had closely identified himself with the regular Service to the extent that he was 'more RN than the RN', as was often said of him.

He was a big man with a red fleshy face and a loud voice which earned him the nickname of 'Boom'. In his hectoring but seamanlike manner he threw himself into the fitting out of the ship and the establishment of an efficient organisation to run her. Previous to *Vindex* he had been Senior Watchkeeper in the old cruiser *Capetown* as a lieutenant-commander. He had travelled widely and was a proficient linguist, and all kinds of tall tales began to circulate about him, including the buzz that he had taken a tug down the Danube just ahead of the Gestapo, while on leave from *Capetown*. He was a first-class organiser and a hard driver who could not tolerate slackness, and was slightly lacking in the human touch.

McCombe was determined that *Vindex* should be the most efficient and best appointed ship of the three new British sister carriers. To accomplish this he had to circumvent the Admiralty Overseer and his rule book, but this was made easier by the support and encouragement of Sir Oliver Swan, who gave his personal nod to the fitting of many necessary extras, and some luxuries, which My Lords had not specified or would have frowned upon.

The contract said nothing, for example, about notice boards, cupboards, shelves and the dozens of items of woodwork that were essential for the smooth running of a ship's routine. McCombe himself had 'never thought of asking the yard to do them until one day I was waylaid by the foreman carpenter who told me that his Manager was not allowed to suggest these things to me but he—the foreman—thought it was about time I did something about it. One of the things I asked for was a mailbox in which the ship's company could put their letters for censoring. I expected a square wooden box—the final result was a very nice replica of a Post Office pillar box painted red, with a slot head, "Mail Closes" and changeable ivorine tablets for every hour of the day.' Sir Oliver also presented a grand piano to *Vindex*'s wardroom.

McCombe was helped in his work considerably by the famous naval aviator Richard Bell Davies, VC. The latter's career already spanned the history of British Naval aviation from its beginnings. He had won one of the Royal Navy's Victoria Crosses in World War I by landing in a Nieuport and rescuing another RNAS pilot who had crashed behind the Turkish lines. Retired before the war as a Vice-Admiral, he had returned to serve as a Captain, and was finishing off the commissioning of the new trials carrier HMS *Pretoria Castle*, which had undergone her second conversion from the Union Castle liner of the same name. 'PC' as she was familiarly known, had been one of the merchantmen stiffened before the war to carry 6-inch guns, and had served for some time as an Armed Merchant Cruiser.

Vindex's new Chief Engineer, Commander H. N. Weir, RNR, had met Captain Bell Davies before, when both had been involved in taking over the first American-built escort carriers for the Royal Navy. Hector Weir was a Geordie, born in Tynemouth of Scottish parents. Both his father and grandfather had served in the Port Line. Hector served his time as an apprentice at the Wallsend Slipway & Engineering Company and at Swan Hunter's, was torpedoed twice in World War I, and joined the Line. Between the wars he became their Guarantee Chief, sailing with each new ship on her maiden voyage and checking her engine room performance against contract specifications.

In 1939 he was standing by the new *Port Napier*, name ship of her class, which included the two cargo liners to be built at Swan's and John Brown's. The Admiralty took over the *Port Napier*, and Chief Engineer Weir, as a minelayer. She joined a squadron at Lochalsh, but the night before they were due to sail she dragged her anchor in a gale and drifted towards the Isle of Skye. A fire started in her engine room and with 600 mines aboard the ship was abandoned. These exploded, and *Port Napier* rolled over and sank.

Weir joined the armed merchant cruiser *Antenor*, then was sent to New York to look after the engines of the first batch of Lease-Lend escort carriers being converted from merchantmen for Britain in American yards. The American Sun-Droxford diesel engines were poor copies of British engines and were unreliable. He stood by HMS *Biter*, and brought HMS *Dasher* home, but had luckily left the ship to go to *Vindex* before *Dasher* blew up on 27 March 1943, with heavy loss of life.

Amongst the last equipment to be fitted to *Vindex* was the ship's defensive armament. Right aft on the quarterdeck, under the round-down of the flight deck, two 4-inch quick-firing Mk XVI high-angle guns were located in a twin mounting. Sixteen 2-pounder pom-poms in four quadruple mountings and sixteen 20-millimetre Oerlikon quick-firing cannon in twin mountings were sited at points all round the catwalk. This department was presided over by the ship's tough Gunner (G) Mr W. M. J. Lacey, RN.

Also appointed to *Vindex*'s staff was Lieutenant (A) J. I. Baker, RN. Baker was a pilot who had started his military life in the Inns of Court Regiment of the Territorial Army, then had taken a Short Service Commission in the Royal

Air Force and volunteered for transfer to the new Air Branch of the Royal Navy in 1938. He had spent most of his time in seaplanes and Walrus amphibians, in the cruisers *Enterprise* and *Edinburgh*, the battleship *King George V*, the battlecruiser *Renown*, and ashore in North Africa. As Air Gunnery Officer of *Vindex* he had as yet very little to do and inevitably became involved with the ship's armament as well.

Baker had a room in Whitley Bay, the holiday resort further up the coast, and travelled in to the dockyard by train every day with Lieutenant-Commander Percy Gick, *Vindex*'s bustling Commander (Flying), and Lieutenant-Commander G. E. Milner, RNR, the ship's Navigating Officer.

'Wings' Gick very soon acquired the nickname of 'Press On Percy'. He was a go-getter and a slasher of red tape, and a technical innovator. As an airman he had been a torpedo training instructor and had served in the *Ark Royal*. In six months of operations in the Mediterranean commanding No. 815 Squadron the convoys they were protecting did not lose a single ship. One reason for this success was Gick's use of flares for illuminating submarines at night from sea level.

On 24 May 1941 he was in command of a sub-flight of Stringbags in Eugene Esmonde's 825 Squadron which, only partially formed and not properly worked up, were in the carrier *Victorious* trying to stop the *Bismarck*. That evening the Squadron's nine aircraft took off in a rain squall. After an hour and a quarter's flying through murky weather they picked up the great battlewagon. They lost her again, were redirected by the cruiser *Norfolk*, and attacked, right into the fire of 50 guns. Gick, not satisfied with his approach, went round again. Sub-Lieutenant Lawson's torpedo hit the enemy. Three of the pilots had never made a night landing before, but all managed to land on *Victorious* again.

When Gick was appointed Commander (Flying) of the new escort carrier *Vindex*, he saw his opportunity. He had long thought that the only effective way to sink U-boats was to fly at night. *Vindex*, therefore, had to be a night-flying carrier.

With this objective in mind he roamed the Admiralty, lobbying. To anyone who might have some influence, particularly Admiral Sir Dennis Boyd, former Captain of the *Illustrious*, who chaired the relevant committee, he said, 'Have you heard of my new job? Isn't it marvellous? *Vindex*, the first night-flying anti-submarine carrier.'

He carefully checked the list of those down to attend the next meeting and made sure he met them beforehand, in their offices or clubs or in the Admiralty corridors. At the end of the meeting, which Gick attended, the names of all operational or near-operational carriers were brought up and their roles reviewed. Suddenly up came the name *Vindex*.

Dennis Boyd said, 'Oh yes. Isn't she going to be the first night-flying carrier?'

No-one said 'No.' *Vindex*'s future role was fixed.

Navigator Geoffrey Milner had served as a deck officer in Elder & Fyffe banana boats. On going ashore in 1937 to join the sales side of the firm, he had to leave the active list of the RNR, as he was no longer following the sea as a profession, and he found it difficult to re-join it for active service when war broke out, but discovered that with an extra-master's ticket he could turn over to the navigation branch, his only chance of a seagoing appointment. He went out to the South Atlantic to join the old cruiser *Dunedin*, which had captured the German cargo-liner *Hannover*, later converted into HMS *Audacity*, the RN's first escort carrier.

Having dodged the French battleship *Jean Bart* off Freetown, *Dunedin* was hunting a raider one fine afternoon when she was torpedoed and sunk, taking many men with her. The rest were left swimming in shark-infested water, the lucky ones like Milner in Carley floats, but with no water or food. Four days later, the few survivors from sharks and other predators were rescued by an American freighter.

Milner went to North Atlantic convoys in the destroyer *Highlander*. There were not enough escorts, and especially no aircraft, in mid-Atlantic. *Vindex*, he hoped, would put things right.

On 8 September *Vindex*'s new Commanding Officer, Captain H. T. T. Bayliss, RN, arrived at the yard. Horace Temple Taylor 'Bill' Bayliss was a heavy-set, solidly built man of 43. At first he seemed rather grim and taciturn and McCombe thought he was 'a wee bit staggered to find that he had been given an RNVR Commander as Executive Officer...' Bayliss was in fact a man preoccupied with the problems of taking over a new ship still very much in the builder's hands.

The Captain wore an observer's gold wings above the four shiny rings on his left sleeve. He had joined the Navy in the year before the Great War broke out. RN College Osborne was followed by Dartmouth, two years as a midshipman in the battlecruiser HMAS *Australia*, then destroyers in the Dover Patrol until the war ended. He went up to Pembroke College, Cambridge, on one of the special six-months courses and read English Literature and the Natural History of the Sea. As a lieutenant he served in the destroyer *Whitshed* and volunteered for the Observer's Course, doing his first job as an observer in HMS *Pegasus*, converted from a cross-Channel steamer to a seaplane carrier, and assisting in an aerial survey of Jahore, Singapore and Hong Kong.

Bayliss' next ship was the carrier *Furious*, which had started life as one of Lord Fisher's 'Outrageous Class' cruisers, with two 18-inch guns, but was modified, and joined the Fleet in 1918. Deck landing was very much in its infancy then, and *Furious* was fitted with fore-and-aft arrester wires. He joined the *Eagle*, a converted battleship, then the pioneer *Argus*, high, narrow and ugly, known as The Flat Iron, for service in Chinese waters against Chiang Kai-shek. Bayliss took photographs and rushed them down to a scruffy little dark room in the slums of Shanghai to develop and print them, and was very glad of a gallop on a little Chinese pony before breakfast. In June 1928 he had a bad crash, convalesced in Ireland, found the hunting there better and cheaper than in England, and made his home there.

Eagle and *Furious* again, the cruiser *Norfolk*'s catapult flight, preceded promotion to Commander, and the China sloops *Folkestone* and *Sandwich* in command. At the outbreak of war in 1939 he went first to Donibristle, which was mainly an aircraft repair yard, then as Chief Staff Officer to Rear Admiral, Naval Air Stations. Promoted Captain, he was given the escort carrier *Archer*.

HMS *Archer* had been the first of the Lease-Lend escort carriers from the USA to join the Royal Navy. This small 9,000-ton ship, with a hangar, one lift and a catapult, and capacity for 15 aircraft, was plagued with mechanical troubles. Then on Sunday 23 May 1943 she partially redeemed herself when one of her Swordfish became the first aircraft to sink a U-boat with the new rocket projectiles.

She was a single-screw ship and Bayliss found her 'not very nice to handle'. In July 1943, when the offensive against U-boats in the Bay of Biscay was at its height, she was sent with an escort group to work there. With eight Swordfish and four Martlet fighters, she was within easy range of Condor bombers and Ju 88s in France. Thick weather and low winds hampered her patrols, and when Ju 88s approached she was forced to withdraw out of range. After five abortive days and nights the operation was abandoned. In the post-mortem it was thought that 'escort carriers might be usefully employed in waters outside the range of shore-based aircraft, as separate hunting units, and in co-operation with a hunting group of anti-submarine vessels.' *Archer*'s group had intercepted plenty of signals from U-boats at night, but her Swordfish were not equipped or trained to attack in the dark.

It was precisely the latter type of operation that Bayliss would be asked to pioneer with his new, British-built carrier, for which he had been earmarked, and to which, *Archer*'s engines having broken down for good, he was now free to go.

Bayliss' first impressions of his new ship were 'confused in the clatter of riveting and dockyard noises generally, but I soon realised that I would have a ship as well constructed as any in the world'. In the yard he shared an office with Geoffrey Milner and Percy Gick. He relied heavily on the ebullient Commander (F) for some time as he eased his way into command, and was, Boom McCombe discovered with some relief, 'agreeably pleased to find that the routine side of the ship's organisation was well up to date'. The Captain's original image as the stern martinet changed and he was seen as a firm but rather fatherly figure. He never wasted words, and never needed to, and these came out in clipped tones, often spiced with dry humour. Soon it got round the ship that he was the only skipper who could smoke his pipe and drink a gin at the same time.

Bayliss had been with his new ship only a short time when he received further valuable support in the person of Lieutenant (Supply) J. W. Isaacson, RN, a paymaster and Captain's Secretary, whose job it was to organise the ship's office, start a filing system and supervise all the paperwork, including the Captain's correspondence. He was an important backroom boy in the running of the ship. 'Peter' Isaacson had taken a Special Entry Cadetship from King Edward VI School, Norwich, in the summer of 1938, and was accepted as a Paymaster Cadet, with an eyesight fault preventing entry to any other branch. He had seen action in the cruiser *Cumberland* against the Vichy French Fleet, and on the second convoy to Russia, before the appointment to *Vindex*.

He worked at first from a desk in a little hut in the yard. When it came to the time for the ship's cabin space to be allocated, the Principal Ship's Overseer, whom Isaacson had got to know quite well, came into the hut and said, 'Where are you having your cabin? There's a good space between the Captain's day cabin and the embarkation space.' Bayliss agreed that he could have this billet, which was bigger than his rank normally allowed, but it was obviously convenient from the Captain's point of view to have his Secretary near at hand in harbour, when so much paperwork would have to be coped with.

Shortly after joining the ship, Isaacson became involved in the first of many problems which a new captain was bound to have. This involved a difficulty peculiar to an escort carrier. *Vindex*'s hull was that of the original cargo-liner, and this included her hawsepipes and small merchantile anchors. Captain Bayliss was sure that these would be inadequate to hold the ship as she now was, with all a carrier's extra tophamper, especially against the strong south-westerly fetch in the Clyde, where she would be spending much time at anchor.

Vindex was due for her acceptance trials in less than a month, but Bayliss said he would not accept the ship with the anchors as fitted. He went down to the Admiralty to register his objections, but to install the heavy hooks he wanted would have meant cutting into the bows and strengthening them to take the heavier cables, and My Lords insisted that he make do with what he had. The best that Bayliss could do was to compose a letter, with Peter Isaacson's help, to record officially his raising of the matter.

Sir Oliver Swan continued to give him and his officers every possible help and encouragement. The Chairman always presided over the senior staff luncheon, and regularly at twelve o'clock *Vindex*'s Captain would receive an invitation to visit the Board Room. Sir Oliver, who liked the good things of life, would then carefully lock the door, go to a corner cupboard, and produce a measure of something extremely fortifying. Swan Hunter's was a 'family firm', with a long tradition of loyalty and craftmanship which seemed to extend to all grades.

More men were joining the ship all the time and life began to stir in her, although she would not come fully alive until the day her squadron flew aboard and her hangar filled up with aeroplanes.

Greenhorns and veterans, aviators and salthorses, they came up the gangplanks, wandered round the vast emptiness of the hangar and bumped apologetically into the dockyard mateys still thronging the narrow passage-ways. There was young Sub-Lieutenant Kenneth Mason RNVR. He had always loved the sea and the idea of flying about equally, and logically volunteered for the Fleet Air Arm. He read an Admiralty Fleet Order asking for volunteer Fighter Direction Officers, and found himself directing, from a blacked-out room, a flight of Wrens orbiting outside on converted Walls Icecream trolleys specially fitted with radio. Both he and Sub-Lieutenant Don Moore, RNVR, were appointed to *Vindex*. When they joined the ship at Swan Hunter's they found the Chief Aircraft Direction Officer, Lieutenant Keith Brading, RNVR, and the rest of the ADR staff already there, and the Air Plot set up.

There was Norman Lauchlan, a regular, the ship's very experienced staff Chief Petty Officer Telegraphist/Air-Gunner. Norman had joined the Navy as a boy seaman in 1926 and had volunteered for life in the wild blue yonder with the FAA. After 12 months of W/T, gunnery and bomb-aiming he went to *Furious* with No. 811 Squadron, flying in the elephantine Blackburn Baffin, 'a peculiar looking beast', he thought.

Three months later they were re-equipped, with the 'new' Fairey Swordfish TSR biplanes, then he was converted to Walruses and saw a lot of ocean in the cruiser *Berwick* and the little carrier *Hermes*. *Hermes* was sunk by the Japanese, and Lauchlan arrived home at the end of October 1942, spent a year training new TAGs in Swordfish and Albacores at Crail in Scotland, and reported to Waxing, Dunfermline, for draft. There he was given both Arctic and tropical kit, and told 'You're going to Job No. 4698. She's at Wallsend—Newcastle.' He reported aboard *Vindex* next morning and met famous characters like Percy Gick and his own boss Lieutenant-Commander Stovin-Bradford, the Air Staff Officer, a short, energetic, already rotund young man.

Freddie Stovin-Bradford had, among other jobs, played in a dance band in London before taking an Air Branch commission in the RN. He had been the observer in one of three Swordfish under Captain Oliver Patch, Royal Marines, which had taken off on the morning of 22 August 1940 from amongst the bomb craters of Sidi Barrani and attacked Italian warships in Bomba Bay, Cyrenaica, Italian North Africa. Captain Patch torpedoed a big ocean-going submarine four miles from shore in the centre of the bay, and she blew up. The other two Swordfish flew on towards a group of three ships, a submarine, a destroyer and a submarine depot ship, lying alongside one another, with the destroyer in the middle. The Swordfish of Lieutenant Welham and Petty Officer Marsh aimed its torpedo at the depot ship. As Lieutenant Cheesman, with Stovin-Bradford in the back seat, prepared to attack on the other flank, Stovin-Bradford noticed that they were over shoal water, and just in time saved his pilot from leaving his torpedo in the sand. Cheesman bored in to 350 yards and let go in deep water. The torpedo hit the submarine, which exploded and set fire to the destroyer. Three seconds later Welham's torpedo hit the depot ship, which began to blaze furiously. By the time the three Stringbags returned to Sidi Barrani in mid-afternoon the wrecks of all four ships were on the bottom.

Gick and Stovin-Bradford had already formed themselves into a hard-driving team, the latter to plan operations, 'Press-On Percy' to carry them out.

'Ops' and 'Wings'. Lieutenant-Commander (A) Freddie Stovin-Bradford, RN (left) and Lieutenant-Commander Percy Gick, RN.

Stovin-Bradford was short and tubby, Gick tall and slim, sometimes wearing a monocle. Norman Lauchlan commuted to the yard from Whitley Bay, and learned that he would be responsible to the ASO for briefing, instructing and generally chasing the Squadron TAGs and for control of the ship's homing beacon. Further, 'I shall require your presence' said Stovin-Bradford, 'on the gallery deck at all times aircraft are flying.' It looked like a busy schedule, but the immediate and urgent job for the Staff Chief TAG was to prepare the space for a radio workshop, get it fitted out with as much of the necessary test equipment as he could scrounge or steal, and arrange for power supplies of 220, 22 and 12 volts to be available from the ship's storage batteries. And there were the voice trainer and Morse trainer for instructing TAGs to rig, with commissioning almost on them ...

Peter Humphreys had done a three-year Senior Engineering Student's course at W. H. Allen's at Bedford, where they made diesels, turbines, pumps, generator sets, switchboard and other equipment, mostly for the Admiralty, before he joined the Service. As he was an uncertificated engineer, he was commissioned as a Sub-Lieutenant (E), RNVR, whereas most of the other engineering staff he met on joining Vindex were RNR on T124X articles. He had 'never really been aboard a ship before', and it was 'all rather amazing'— especially when he was told by Geordie Dan Shields, the Senior Engineer, that he was to be Flight Deck Engineer, responsible for maintaining the arrester gear and the aircraft lift machinery, all vital to the operation of aircraft. He still had not seen an aeroplane at close hand.

As in all her escort carrier predecessors, Vindex's wardroom was filled mainly with RNVR former civilians and Merchant Navy engineers with RNR commissions on T124X articles. On joining the ship, Peter Isaacson had been surprised to find that the only RN officers aboard were Captain Bayliss, Percy Gick, Stovin-Bradford, John Baker and himself. Some of the deck officers, like Geoffrey Milner and Lieutenant F. W. Willett, Mate of the Upper Deck, were RNR. Instead of non-commissioned Engine Room Artificers, there were a large number of Sub-Lieutenants (E) RNR, who carried out all the dirty jobs, such as being slung over the side in a bucket on the end of a crane to clean out the diesel exhaust pipes. They usually preferred to be known, MN style, as Junior Engineers, and most of them did not like messing in the wardroom. One of them demonstrated his feelings by sitting down to lunch in his overalls, and on being given a sound rollicking by long-service Warrant Gunner Bill Lacey, said, 'Why don't you call us ERAs and give us a mess on the lower deck?'

There was the same preponderance of T124X former Merchant Navy men on the lower deck, among the engine room ratings, cooks and stewards. More than once Executive Officer Boom McCoombe was faced with a man who justified the disobedience of an order by quoting a clause in his Board of Trade Agreement. A short time before they were due to get the final list of ratings to be drafted to the ship, McCoombe himself went down to Portsmouth, Vindex's manning port, and persuaded 'Draftie' to include a few long-service men as stiffening for what would otherwise be a green ship's company.

Young Temporary Surgeon-Lieutenant Ian Taylor, RNVR, late of St Mary's Hospital, Paddington, had had a rather unsatisfactory war so far, having spent nearly all of it in a new River-class frigate, HMS *Nith*, which persistently ran her main bearings during working-up and finally returned to Yarrow's yard with 'Any Old Iron' playing over the loudspeakers. Then one very dark night he found himself in Swan Hunter's yard. Bumping into a sentry he asked him, 'Can you tell me which is HMS *Vindex*?' 'Right in front of you, chum,' said the man. Looming up a few feet in front of his nose was a dark cliffside of steel. He stumbled along the jetty, found a gangway and went aboard. One of the first men he met was his Senior Medical Officer, Surgeon-Lieutenant-Commander C.A. 'Charlie' Kilpatrick, RNVR, an amiable, trombone-playing Scot from Glasgow. The general atmosphere on board was lively and friendly, and he soon settled down.

The ship's commissioning date was set for 15 November. Just before the day, Captain Bayliss had to take to his bed ashore with a bad dose of flu and a temperature of 104°, and Commander McCoombe presided over the ceremony, which he planned and carried out with his usual efficiency, helped by the ship's Master-at-Arms.

A bleary draft arrived by special train in Swan's yard at 6 am and were unbelievably treated to an egg, bacon and sausage breakfast in their vast canteen, where the matelots remained afterwards for sorting into the system of messes and watches arranged by their very methodical Executive Officer.

At 12 noon Job No. 4698 was officially commissioned into the Royal Navy as HMS *Vindex*. In peacetime the White Ensign would then have been hoisted, but the ensign staff at the after end of the flight deck remained bare for the time being, for fear of indicating to the enemy reconnaissance or Intelligence that the ship was nearing completion. The staff was an extra which McCoombe had wheedled out of Mr Lythgoe, Swan Hunter's very co-operative Yard Manager. Under austerity contracts, ensigns were flown from the mast, but McCoombe's argument was that *Vindex* and *Nairana* would be operating from the same base and would look like two peas in a pod. It would be a very good thing if people could say: '*Vindex* was built by Swan Hunter—you can tell by the ensign staff.' Lythgoe gave him the staff but was adamant that it would be impossible to provide an ornamental crown for the ensign and jack staffs. However, McCoombe had not given up hope of these, and kept on dropping hints.

Immediately after the ceremony the normal routine of one of His Majesty's ships at war began. At five o'clock 'Secure' was piped, 'Darken ship' at 5.30, 'Close X and Y doors' at 8.30. Rounds by the Officer of the Day were declared correct at 9.15, and at ten o'clock it was 'Pipe down' at the end of HMS *Vindex*'s first day at war.

The next five days were occupied by cleaning and storing ship. Decks were scrubbed regularly and the debris left by the dockyard mateys finally swept away. On 18 November a rather shaky Bayliss left his wife, who had also been stricken with the flu, at their lodgings, and rejoined the ship, regretting by this time that he had not defied doctor's orders and gone aboard for the commissioning. That morning he cleared lower deck and addressed his new ship's company for the first time.

At mid-day on 20 November the Bishop of Newcastle conducted the Dedication Service in the hangar. The whole ship's company sang the hymn 'Lead us, Heavenly Father, lead us o'er the world's tempestuous sea'. Captain Bayliss led them in the Bidding ...

'Bless our ship.'

'May God the Father bless her,' answered the men.

'Bless our ship.'

'May Jesus Christ bless her.'

'Bless our ship.'

'May the Holy Spirit bless her.'

'What do ye fear, seeing that God the Father is with you?'

'We fear nothing.'

'What do ye fear, seeing that God the Son is with you?'

'We fear nothing.'

'What do ye fear, seeing that God the Holy Spirit is with you?'

'We fear nothing.'

'May the Almighty God, for the sake of His Son Jesus Christ, through the comfort of the Holy Ghost, the one God who brought the Apostle Paul, with his ship, and the crew, out of the great tempest and out of the fierce storm, save us, and sanctify us, and carry us on with favouring winds, and comfort, over the sea and into the harbour, according to His own good Will; which things we desire from Him.'

Then, as so many men had done before them, they prayed as 'They that go down to the sea in ships; and occupy their business in great waters' to their god, at whose word 'the stormy wind ariseth; which lifteth up the waves ...' so that 'They reel to and fro, and stagger like drunken men; and are at their wits' end ...' so that He 'maketh the storm to cease; so that the waves thereof are still ...'

After the service there was a party for ship's officers and dockyard officials, and a young officer's baby was christened in the ship's bell. The yard resumed its hammering and clattering and an oiler came alongside *Vindex* to pump fuel oil into her tanks, which could hold 1,655 tons. Then, the following forenoon, 21 November, hands were closed up to shift ship under her own power for the first time. With the aid of tugs she slipped, and Tyne Pilot Duncan took her slowly down to the Tyne Commissioner's Quay at North Shields, where she secured at mid-day.

The next two days were spent storing and ammunitioning ship. 569 tons of fresh water were taken on board, and large quantities of 4-inch, 2-pounder and 20-millimetre shells were lowered into the magazines. Storing and cleaning ship continued, exercises with guns' crews and at Fire Stations. Early in the forenoon of 30 November there was a service in the ship's chapel, and after dinner 'Secure for sea!' was piped.

Trials. HMS *Vindex* shows her paces.

At 4.15 pm *Vindex* hoisted the White Ensign for the first time at her new ensign staff, then slipped from the wharf and proceeded to sea under her own power, with the tugs *Robert Redheart* and *Empire Leon* to port and starboard, and the *George V* and *Great Emperor* off her quarters. Half an hour later she slipped the tugs and steamed alone past the breakwater, increasing speed. She clipped past Tyne 1 and Tyne 2 Buoys at twelve knots, nosed into the North Sea for the first time, and altered course almost due north up the north-east coast.

After Rounds, at eight o'clock, Captain Bayliss increased speed to 15 knots, then to 17, getting the feel of the ship. Just after midnight he altered course west and rounded the North Rathlin buoy, and shortly after 1 am on 1 December *Vindex* entered Rosyth Harbour and in the pitch dark let go her puny mercantile anchor in ten fathoms. Bayliss brought the ship to at five and a half shackles, then hands secured from cruising stations and all but the duty part of the watch got their heads down thankfully. These included some Swan Hunter men who had come up with her for the acceptance trials.

'Wakey-wakey, lash up and stow!' came all too early, and at 8.15 *Vindex* weighed and proceeded to sea. An hour later, two and a half miles off May Island, she began preliminary full power trials, though Captain Bayliss already knew unofficially what speed she could do. At the same time he piped 'Action stations!' and began gunnery trials as they ran over the degaussing range. At 10.30 full power trials were judged complete as the ship passed No. 23 Buoy, and she commenced manoeuvring and astern trials. Just after six o'clock she was back in harbour, letting go her starboard anchor in 15 fathoms and coming to at six shackles. That evening 19 members of the new Flight Deck Party joined.

Next day *Vindex* steamed through her final full power trials. In the afternoon the Captain signed an agreement that the trials had been satisfactorily carried out, with a qualifying reference to the letter previously composed recording his objections to the ship's anchors, and signalled the acceptance to Admiral, Contract Built Ships, with repeats to all authorities concerned.

A few minutes before six o'clock *Vindex* passed under the Forth Bridge and anchored in B3 Berth below the bridge. Ship's officers and dockyard officials assembled in the wardroom for the latter's final dinner on board. After dinner Mr Lythgoe gave Commander McCoombe as a parting gift the ornamental crowns for jack and ensign staffs. To Captain Bayliss he presented two large ship's badges displaying the crest inherited from the old HMS *Vindex* seaplane carrier of World War I, one for the ship, one for Captain Bayliss himself.* On a field of gleaming white was the curled green asp, Cannarum Vindex, enbowed, biting its tail. With the large badge came a set of boat badges. Another personal gift to Captain Bayliss was a beautiful wooden cigarette box, a souvenir of Swan Hunter craftsmanship. With the crest the

---

* In later years the *Vindex* crest decorated the wall of the dining room in the Bayliss home in Ireland.

new *Vindex* also inherited the motto *Diu noctuque: mari colloque*, translated as 'By day and by night: by sea and by sky'.

That weekend of 4/5 December was spent in further ammunitioning, and young Ordinary Seaman Worsfold gave the Sick Bay a job when he got his fingers crushed in a winch. Fog closed down over the anchorage on Monday while the lighters were still alongside. Next day 'Away seaboat's crew!' was heard for the first time aboard the carrier, and she lowered her No. 1 whaler for practice, while torpedoes and Mark XI aircraft depth-charges were being lifted aboard from the lighters. Finally, on Friday 10 December, *Vindex* left for the Clyde.

North she steamed, west through the Pentland Firth between Scotland and Orkney, past Cape Wrath and across the mouth of North Minch to leave the Butt of Lewis to port and head south to seaward of the Outer Hebrides, round Tiree and set course for the Skerryvore Light and Rathlin Island off northern Antrim, into the North Channel, past the Mull of Kintyre, round to port and up into the Firth of Clyde. Ailsa Craig was passed abeam at seven o'clock on the morning of the 11th. At 10.53 the starboard anchor was let go in the Clyde, which *Vindex* was to come to know too well, and the ship brought to at five shackles in 14 fathoms at B5 Berth.

In the afternoon a petrol lighter came alongside, and a strong buzz went round the ship that the aircraft were coming. The next day, Sunday 12 December, the new American-built escort carrier HMS *Emperor* passed the anchored *Vindex* on her port quarter, wreathed in the thickening fog. The following morning 61 members of *Vindex*'s air squadron joined the ship. Heading this advance party were Sea Hurricane pilot Sub-Lieutenant W. D. McDonald, RNVR, and Swordfish observer Sub-Lieutenant Peter Couch, RNVR.

Two days went by with nothing but calibration trials to excite the blood. The ship went across into Rothesay Bay. Next morning she steamed out into the broad Firth, and at ten o'clock stopped engines to await aircraft.

At 11.30 she was still waiting, circling the rendezvous point at slow speed, and it was not until half-past two in the afternoon that a solitary aircraft was sighted approaching the ship.

This aircraft turned into the bulky, powerful shape of a Grumman Tarpon torpedo bomber, a modern Lease-Lend machine being supplied to the Fleet Air Arm by the USA, where it was called the Avenger. This was not what the lower deck had expected. Were they going to get Tarpons, not the old Stringbags after all? *That* was a turn-up for the book.

The Tarpon was being piloted by Lieutenant A. Whatley, RN. For two and a half hours he flew on and off *Vindex*'s virgin flight deck, testing her arrester wires and giving Commander (F) and DLCO (Deck Landing Control Officer) Lieutenant (A) L. J. Polwin, RNVR, and Flight Deck Officer Sub-Lieutenant Mansfield and his wind-blown warriors of the deck-handling party some vital practice in flying off and landing on aircraft.

Vindex was out in the Clyde again next day. She waited all day, steaming round in circles, burning up oil fuel. There were plenty of naval planes about, but the ones she was expecting never showed up.

She tried once more next morning, weighing from Rothesay at 9.42 and arriving at the rendezvous point eight miles off Cumbrae Light at eleven o'clock. A few minutes later a flight of aircraft was seen, identified as six Sea Hurricane fighters, all heading for *Vindex*. Captain Bayliss turned the ship into wind, Commander (F) ordered the affirmative flag, a white cross on a red ground, hoisted to indicate the ship's readiness to receive them, and soon the aircraft of No. 825 Squadron, Royal Navy, were touching down on the new carrier's narrow flight deck, the Sea Hurricanes being followed by twelve Swordfish. The new *Vindex* was easy to identify, with her pennant number, 15, painted on both sides of the hull and the broad 'V' in dark-shaded camouflage amidships on the port side.

2

Notice for Steam

IN 1936 THE FLEET AIR ARM was still part of the Royal Air Force. The RAF provided all its administration, equipment, air stations, ground crews and air gunners, and 30 percent of all its pilots. Other pilots and all observers were from the Royal Navy, which had operational control whenever the FAA went to sea in its carriers. Career-minded pilots did not like it because it was a blind alley for promotion to senior rank, in either Service.

It was also a poor relation when it came to aircraft, with the land-based squadrons of the Air Force being given all the best and most modern machines, and it came as no surprise to the FAA when in July of that year they received new equipment in the form of a slow, fabric-covered biplane with a fixed undercarriage and open cockpits with an aft-firing Western Front type Lewis gun and Scarff ring. All other major air forces were scrapping the biplane and re-equipping with fast metal monoplanes, but it was all right for the FAA to have the Fairey Swordfish.

The first to get it were the lucky lads of No. 825 Squadron. They found it a pleasant machine to fly, with no vices, robust in the dive and very easy on aircrew in a rough deck landing. In fact they grew to like their Stringbags, and in *Glorious* in the Mediterranean under the fiery and ferocious Captain A. St G. Lumley Lyster became very proficient in dummy torpedo attacks by night, when the Swordfish would be less vulnerable to fighters and ack-ack fire. They tried out Lyster's battle plan for a night strike against the modern Italian battle fleet in their main anchorage in Taranto harbour, a plan which was brilliantly put into action by Nos. 815 and 819 Squadrons flying from HMS *Illustrious* on the night of 11 November 1940, crippling the Italian fleet.

In Swordfish, 825 Squadron, motto *Nihil obstat*,* attacked U-boats and E-boats by night in the English Channel, and enemy guns, tanks and trucks round Calais in May 1940, losing eight machines. They were re-equipped and sent in *Furious* to do the same in Norway. They had only just re-formed under Eugene Esmonde and were not worked up when they were packed off in the *Victorious*, and flew their hazardous mission against the *Bismarck*. The Squadron supported Malta convoys from *Ark Royal*, sent some of its aircraft to help No. 830 Squadron's Stringbags at Hal Far, Malta, in their attacks on

---

* Usually translated as 'Nothing stops us'. 'The real meaning,' recorded a World War II Senior Pilot of the Squadron, 'is "There is nothing to prevent it" (from happening). Not so encouraging, but more suitable.'

No. 825 Squadron badge and crest.

Italian convoys to North Africa, and lost most of its machines when the *Ark* was sunk by a U-boat on 13 November 1941.

Young Gordon Bennett from Derbyshire was a metallurgist and a representative for an alloy steel firm of Sheffield when war broke out. He got his calling-up papers almost immediately and opted for the Navy. In early 1940 he reported to the stone frigate HMS *Collingwood* in Hampshire for basic training. Towards the end of this he volunteered for telegraphist/air-gunner in the Fleet Air Arm and was sent to the FAA's initial training depot HMS *St Vincent* at Gosport, where he got a chance to transfer to pilot training.

After completing ground subjects and a navigation course he went to Elmdon airport for initial flying training. Advanced training at Kingston, Ontario, followed, leading to wings and one wavy gold stripe on the sleeve and return to England for the officers' course at Greenwich College, then torpedo school at Crail, Arbroath, and, at Christmas 1941, to his first operational squadron, No. 825, which was forming up again, after the *Ark Royal* disaster, at Lee-on-Solent under Lieutenant (A) E. 'Winkle' Esmond, RN.

At the beginning of February 1942, the two battlecruisers *Scharnhorst* and *Gneisenau* and the heavy cruiser *Prinz Eugen* were believed to be nearly ready to leave Brest for Germany. Esmonde was ordered to prepare his six aircraft to operate against the three powerfully armed ships. The Squadron had not long landed from formation flying on the 12th when the alarm came. There were six aircraft and seven pilots. Bennett and Peter Bligh were of exactly equal seniority. Out on the airfield Esmonde tossed a coin. Peter Bligh won the toss and took the aircraft.

Officers of No. 825 Squadron at the time of joining *Vindex*, 18 December, 1943. Back row, left to right: Sub-Lieutenants (A) RNVR, J.A. Darby (observer), P.S. Couch (observer), J. McIlwraith (observer), N.L. Sharrock (pilot), N.D.G. Mountford (observer) and M.G.O. Varley (pilot). Front row (standing): Sub-Lieutenants (A) RNVR, P.T. Calcutt (observer), J.E. Ward (pilot), Lieutenant (A), RNVR, G. Bennett (Senior Pilot), Lieutenant-Commander (A) S.G. Cooper, RN, (Commanding Officer), Lieutenant (A) P.R. House, RNVR (Senior Observer), Sub-Lieutenants (A), RNZNVR, D. Webb (pilot) and C.R.I. Webb (pilot). Sitting: Sub-Lieutenants (A), RNVR, H. Broadley, (observer), D.G. Trussell (pilot), B.L.G. Jones (observer) and H. Burns (observer).

The signals from Air-Sea Rescue, Ramsgate, started to come in about 4.30 p.m., and were sent on to Bennett, now Senior Officer of what was left of 825 Squadron. About an hour later he realised that the six Swordfish would not be coming back. Next day he drove the Squadron van to Dover and picked up Sub-Lieutenant Edgar Lee, one of the five survivors of the 18 men who had taken off from Manston.

In September Esmonde's successor, Lieutenant (A) Stan Keane, took three Swordfish, with four more pilots (Winterbottom, Bennett, Mike Varley and Taff Evans), four observers and six TAGs, aboard the US-built escort carrier HMS *Avenger* to give air cover to Convoy PQ18, the first Russian convoy to have its own local air support. The main effort was to be against air attacks and *Avenger* carried 12 Sea Hurricane fighters, with six more spares. Her Captain, Commander Colthurst, did not want the Stringbags on board. They flew through snow and biting cold, shepherding stragglers and keeping U-boats down, and the 825 crews thought that they had done rather well, but Colthurst let them leave without so much as a 'Cheerio'.

In December, with a new CO, Lieutenant-Commander (A) S. G. 'Zeke' Cooper, RN, and six Stringbags doped black all over, they went minelaying at Le Havre. One crew was lost, and Taff Evans and his observer Dan Timms were taken prisoner.

Sub-Lieutenant Peter Seymour Couch, a teacher from north London, had been one of the replacements for the aircrews lost in the attack on the German warships in the Channel. He flew with Bennett, who developed an individual method of landing on a carrier, involving a split turn on to the after end of the flight deck instead of the normal straight approach from astern, to avoid the Swordfish's embarrassing difficulty in overtaking the ship, and would sometimes put his observer in difficult theoretical positions in the air to test his reactions. 'Quick, your pilot is dead,' he would say, 'What are you going to do about it?'

The Squadron flew aboard *Furious* early in March 1943, and at the end of May went with her on Arctic searches and patrols. When they came ashore from her they expanded to become a Composite Squadron, with the addition of six Sea Hurricanes under Lieutenant (A) A. N. D. Gough, RN. This meant that they were going to an escort carrier, and the buzzes flew round. The Squadron then spent over three months in intensive anti-U-boat training.

A move to a carrier came when they were at Sydenham, near Belfast. The ship was the newly converted *Pretoria Castle*, on a brief trip up to Iceland, carrying American personnel to the island base, and flying a few routine anti-submarine patrols on the way. At Kaldadarnes airfield, east of Reykjavik, they collected six redundant Swordfish for return to Britain, and while in the circuit waiting to land on *PC* next morning one of the newer 825 pilots got into a mock dogfight with a US Air Force fighter. The Swordfish used her party trick, well tested against Me 109s over Norway, of drawing a fighter in, then turning sharply, as only a Stringbag could, so that the enemy went plunging on past. The American plane not only overshot but plunged into the sea. The

The Hurricanes land on first. A Sea Hurricane's deck hook has picked up an arrester wire and the aircraft is being brought to a stop.

Squadron flew off *PC* to Sydenham on 4 November and ten days later went down to Inskip near Blackpool in Lancashire. There they spent a month on intensive night exercises, in the course of which Gordon Bennett contrived to fire a rocket projectile at Blackpool Tower. 'Force On' or 'Blitz' Gough, the 825 Fighter Leader, was constantly experimenting to improve aircraft performance. One of his modifications was the moving of the Hurricane's firing button to a position where the old R/T button had been. Soon after this he went to call up his flight, forgot the mod, and bounced cannon shells off the dinner plates in a local hospital. Being in wartime these crimes went unpunished. Gough also got the idea of accelerating take-off by tying down the aircraft with a cable, linked to the machine by a piece of string, revving up against the cable, and cutting the string with a pair of scissors. The first test resulted in Gough's Hurricane going through a brick wall.

For the most part, however, 'Life consisted', wrote TAG 'Buzz' Brown, 'of flying, sleep, exercises, practice, lectures, in a continuous cycle ... We became so good at night attack on surfaced subs, that once they had been contacted by ASV, we were immediately screaming down to the attack, leaving our stomachs behind temporarily, using "flare illumination", "moonlight silhouette", "low wavetop run-in", working together in a flight of three aircraft, or independently, giving the subs (ours) little chance of submerging in time to avoid us ... we chose to ignore the fact that when the real thing occurred there would be heavy flak to contend with. We were good, we knew it, were proud of it, in fact over-confident, and when the move came we were eager to go.' The day was calm and sunny but hazy when they took off on the morning of 18 December 1943 to join *Vindex* in the Clyde. Blackpool Tower remained long in the backward-facing TAGs' vision, until eventually disappearing in haze.

The visibility was bad enough for Blitz Gough's six Sea Hurricanes virtually to scrape Blackpool Tower. They then rapidly outdistanced the Stringbags, and soon sighted the carrier. As they approached they saw her wake curve as she turned into wind. Then she hoisted the Affirmative flag. The fighters circled the ship, and Gough broke off to make his approach. The batsman, Lieutenant Polwin, gave him the cut, and the first aircraft of *Vindex*'s squadron was aboard. All the remaining five landed safely, though New Zealander Sub-Lieutenant Alister E. 'Ali' Martin only just caught the last or 'Jesus Christ' wire, with his hook, and his machine bucked violently as it was wrenched to a stop. After that it was great relief and pink gins in the wardroom.

Meanwhile the Stringbags were chugging up from Inskip. Presently they appeared. Orbiting the ship in sub-flights, the aircraft then separated into line astern, and flew past the ship to starboard. The ship flashed a green light, and Zeke Cooper turned to port ahead of her, losing height all the time, swooped along the port side at some 200 feet, giving those on the Goofers a good view, lowered his deck hook, made a shallow turn to port to line up with the stern, then put himself in the batsman's hands, and made *Vindex*'s first Swordfish landing. The other eleven machines followed him down. She looked small, after *Pretoria Castle*. Her narrow, steel-plated flight deck was ten feet less welcoming in width than *Avenger*'s American pine-planked one, and seemed bleak and unwelcoming. To Buzz Brown, craning over the side from his back seat, it looked as if 'the Powers ... had undersized the flight deck ... This impression remained when we found our wings seemed to overhang each side, and the length of the deck was frightening in its shortness.' In fact, after *Avenger*, Bennett found that '*Vindex*, though narrower, was much better for deck work, being longer and rather faster and had a more rounded round-down, *Avenger*'s being more or less a shear-blade for tail wheels.'

But only one aircraft got into trouble. At 11.54 the Swordfish of Sub-Lieutenant (A) P. E. Cumberland, RNVR, with Midshipman (A) F. R. Jackson as his observer, approached, coming in very slowly from dead astern. It was young Lancastrian Frank Jackson's first deck landing, and Peter Cumberland, not very long since a Merchant Taylor's schoolboy, with most of his flying done shore-based in Egypt, had made only six previous deck landings, on the training carrier *Argus*. The Swordfish made a heavy landing on the round-down, short of the first wire, and smashed its undercarriage. Mike Varley, approaching next, was planning an urgent dash to the heads when he landed, but was forced to fly several more increasingly painful circuits while the crash

Sea Hurricane pilot. Sub-Lieutenant (A) A. 'Al' Martin, RNZNVR, drowned at sea.

Sea Hurricane pilots. Sub-Lieutenant (A) J.E. 'Johnny' Moore, RNZNVR (left) and Sub-Lieutenant (A) W.D.D. McDonald, RNVR.

was cleared off the flight deck. He made Cumberland stand him a pink gin when he had got down and was comfortable again.

But now the Squadron was all on board and the ship really came to life. The wardroom suddenly seemed very crowded, with 31 new air officers added to the some 60 already crowding the bar.

Of the Swordfish section of the Composite 825, pilots, headed by the CO, were Lieutenant (A) Gordon Bennett, now Senior Pilot, Lieutenant (A) M. G. O. 'Mike' Varley, and the seven sub-lieutenants RNVR, Peter Cumberland, Eddie Ward, Norman Sharrock, Ron Huggins, Dennis Trussell, E. W. Powell Chandler, A. Watkin-Jones, and two New Zealanders, C. R. I. Webb and D. Webb, both from Irish families, though unrelated, and Petty Officer Warne. His observers, led by Lieutenant (A) Paul House, RNVR, were Sub-Lieutenants, RNVR, Herbert Broadley, Harry Burns, Peter Couch, P. T. 'Pat' Calcutt, John Darby, Brian Jones, and J. McIlwraith, and Midshipman Frank Jackson. The telegraphist/air-gunners, led by Chief Petty Officer M. W. 'Mick' Dale, were Petty Officers David Todd, Hampton and Mears, Leading Naval Airmen Bill Amatt, 'Buzz' Brown, Basil Hall-Law, Laking, Joe Palmer, Johnny Puttock, Rawlins, Frank Smeeton, Spraklen, John Stone, Thompson, Charlie Wakefield and Chris Williams.

The Sea Hurricane component, led by ex-Walrus pilot Gough, comprised three New Zealanders, the experienced A. T. 'Jimmy' Green, Johnny Moore and Alister Martin; four RNVR subbies, Welshman Ken Corrin, Englishmen Peter Hellyer and D. R. Johnston, and Scot Bill McDonald.

They were very young. TAG Johnny Puttock.

Chief TAG. 825's young CPO Mick Dale.

There was almost as wide a variety of background among the air gunners as with the commissioned aircrew. Mick Dale, a young man to be a Chief, was a regular, the only one amongst them, but he had been a student at Brighton Art School before taking the direct entry into the Navy as a TAG. He had done his airborne W/T course at Worthy Down and Eastleigh, starting in May 1940, and had several times been flown by distinguished actors serving in the FAA, by Lieutenant Laurence Olivier, RNVR, at Worthy Down, and five times at Eastleigh by Lieutenant Ralph Richardson, RNVR, three times in a Proctor, once in a Skua and once in a Shark. Having completed his air gunnery course at Aldergrove in Northern Ireland, he had spent most of his time seaborne in Walruses.

He joined No. 825 Squadron at Thorney Island in January 1943, as a newly-made-up Temporary Acting Petty Officer. It was quite an ordeal for him. Not only was he in charge of other TAGs for the first time, but this particular outfit was already famous for the Channel affair, and, to make his ride even rougher, the TAGs made no secret of the fact that they were going to miss his predecessor, their beloved Ginger Sayer, who had flown with Percy Gick against the *Bismarck*, and that he looked like being a pretty poor substitute. The odious comparison gradually faded. He struck up a close friendship with Scot Dave Todd, whose father was an architect in Edinburgh and brother Ruthven a rising poet. Dave was a farmer and fisherman and his big, clumsy-looking hands could tie the most intricate trout flies. Hampton was very much a northerner, Joe Palmer a tough, outspoken Londoner, who once accosted Lieutenant-Commander Stovin-Bradford, RN, *Vindex*'s Air Staff Officer, with a friendly hug and a 'Wotcher, Stovin!' Johnny Puttock and John Stone were the youngest of the bunch. Stone, who had only joined the Squadron at Inskip, in particular seemed very green and bewildered by his lot.

On the afternoon of the following day, Sunday 19 December, *Vindex* was out again for deck landing trials. Peter Cumberland was made to do circuits and bumps, fortified by his young observer Frank Jackson, who insisted on flying with him for these practices, although it was not strictly necessary ...

At sea. HMS *Vindex* photographed from the rear cockpit of one of her 825 Squadron Swordfish.

'He had more confidence in my deck landings than I did. Anyway, we got away with it.' Five minutes after a landing with Cumberland at half-past two, Jackson took off in the same aircraft with Douglas Webb for some more of the same, all the time increasing the small number of deck landings in his flying log book. Gick and Stovin-Bradford seized the chance of getting airborne in a Swordfish to test the landing wires, the lift and the homing beacon, and put the handling party through their paces.

Next day flying exercises were terminated by bad weather. Bill McDonald, in poor visibility and with very little petrol left, crashed his Sea Hurricane on the flight deck. At 8 p.m. on 22 December night flying began in the area between Ailsa Craig, Turnberry Point and Pladda, and continued throughout the rest of the month, sometimes in co-operation with submarines. All the time No. 825 were making Fleet Air Arm history, as they were to be the first carrier-borne anti-submarine night flying unit.

On the 26th, Frank Jackson was making his first night deck landing, flying with pilot C. R. Webb, when the aircraft missed all the wires and crashed into the barrier. Johnny Moore also had a barrier crash in his Sea Hurricane. Four

In the circuit. Two 825 Squadron Swordfish circle *Vindex* preparatory to landing on.

A Swordfish with deck hook lowered approaches *Vindex*'s round-down. This is a Mark II aircraft. Radar aerials on the outer wing struts have been whited out by the wartime censor, but the outer bomb racks and inner depth-charge racks can be seen.

Swordfish were damaged in the deck park for'ard. A Barrier or Sharp End Club was formed in the ship and part of a broken metal Hurricane propeller was polished up and hung behind the bar in the wardroom, on which the names of pilots who had crashed into the barrier were inscribed. Some gained a bar to their name, some more than one, and few were ultimately spared a mention. There was also the Goldfish Club, for those who had saved their lives after crashing or ditching in the sea by use of their dinghy, a companion organisation to the Caterpiller Club for those who had taken to their parachutes.

On the 30th, young Ordinary Seaman S. P. Humphries was lost overboard. A lifebuoy was dropped and a whaler and motor cutter searched for him, but in vain. Dennis Trussell crashed his Swordfish returning from an evening flight and another Swordfish came to grief 24 hours later, with the ship heading into the Irish Sea for a more realistic extension of what was already an accelerated working-up.

Flying continued throughout the night, with the ship zigzagging, and into the next day. When darkness came down again Captain Bayliss had to order the 4-inch crew to close up and fire starshells to guide a lost aircraft home. They were still at sea just after midnight on Sunday 2 January and the ship had just secured from action stations when she picked up a radar contact with a small object, probably a submarine, about a mile off. There was some excitement in the ship, but the echo faded off the trace and she came to with the port anchor down in nine fathoms in Bangor Bay, Northern Ireland, at one hour's notice for steam.

By the early forenoon of the following day they were back in the Clyde for some daylight flying practice, with an anxious five minutes when the ship's engines briefly failed. Replenished with stores, shells and petrol, *Vindex* and her squadron put in some more exercising off Ailsa Craig.

Green hands in the Flight Deck Party were beginning to experience the hardships of their job. Lying on a wet flight deck holding chocks in the front and rear of an aircraft's wheels, exposed to the wind blowing down the deck and the slipstream of the machine in front, was miserable. When the Flight Deck Officer gave the Chocks Away signal (with flags by day, hand torch by night) you had to run, crouched low, crawl or slide to the side of the deck, watching out for the props of the other planes revving up, sometimes with the ship pitching and rolling. The worst position was on the last aircraft to go, as the slipstreams of all the planes ahead tore at you. Sometimes you had to cling to the chock or the wheels to stop being blown over the stern. Hands were rotated to give everyone a turn at the different jobs, with a different coloured helmet for each. There was the hookman, who disengaged the arrester wire from an aircraft's hook when it landed on. A lot depended on how fast he could move. There were the firemen who manned the various fire points in the catwalk. One of these wore the asbestos fire suit and carried an axe at the ready. The flight deck was a place for hard men with their wits about them, and the average age of *Vindex*'s ship's company

Telegraphist/air-gunners of 825 Squadron aboard *Vindex*. Back row: Leading Naval Airmen Short, Johnny Puttock, Chris Williams, Petty Officer Dave Todd, Chief Petty Officer Mick Dale, L/NAs Joe Palmer, Alf Bleasdale and Alun Jones. Kneeling: L/NAs Foster, Frank Smeeton, 'Buzz' Brown, Dave Dunlop and Alan Greedy.

was somewhere between 19 and 20. They had to grow up very quickly.

Staff Chief TAG Norman Lauchlan lived life at the rush. He had to be in the catwalk for every take-off, then rush into the Aircraft Direction Room to check the frequency for aircraft calling up the ship. After a landing he had to quizz the crew for any difficulties of communication. He was responsible for the correct functioning of the BABS radio homing beacon, with its transmitter on the gallery deck, and its aerial rotating on the mast, and was the ASO's right-hand man in the Air Staff Office. He also had to keep an eye on the efficiency and wellbeing of Mick Dale and his young TAGs, to whom he was 'Uncle' Norman.

It was a hard time for all on board, especially for the squadron observers, who had to learn how to handle their new ASV radar sets, and for the TAGs, with new radio transmitter/receivers to cope with. The Squadron was the first to have the new ASV Mark X, and it was still suffering from teething troubles. Scientists arrived on board from the Government labs at Malvern to sort them out.

One lovely day in the Clyde, Eddie Ward was flying with a boffin in place of his observer John Darby, with TAG Dave Todd at the radio. They were plodding peacefully to and fro when *Vindex*'s sister ship *Nairana* hove in sight. The latter was expecting the CO of her new squadron to make his first visit to the ship, sighted Ward's Stringbag, and jumped to the wrong conclusion. Ward was mystified to see her turn into wind and flash him the 'C' to land on. At first he ignored the signal, but when the carrier repeated it with her huge searchlight the situation became tricky.

At the time, though the TAG could reach *Vindex* on R/T, the only communication between him and his pilot was via the boffin and his observer's Gosport speaking tube, which the scientist did not know how to use. Thus cut off from his own captain's fatherly guidance, Eddie thought he had better not disobey another demi-god with four straight gold rings on his sleeve. He had one more try at putting things right by going low and flying along *Nairana*'s port side, hoping to get his message across somehow. As he flashed past the bridge he could see the ship's Commander (F) waving him in to land, which he proceeded to do.

Wings ran across the flight deck, climbed up the Stringbag's lofty flank, saw the strange face, and said, 'Who are you?' Ward told him, and he was not pleased.

TAG Todd had had his head in the cockpit as he tinkered with the radio, and his first knowledge of the landing was the bump.

Hastily he switched on. 'Aircraft has pancaked.'

Back came Ken Mason's rather acerbic voice from *Vindex*'s Air Direction Room. '*Where* have you pancaked?'

'Have pancaked at the wrong base.'

'Then return to the *right* one.'

'Taking off.'

As they flew back to *Vindex* the Captain of *Nairana* smugly made one of the

RN's famous Biblical signals to Captain Bayliss, who took the whole incident well, and simply said, 'Oh well, it gave them a little bit of fun.' In fact later, after Ward had landed to mass cheering and jeering from the Goofers, the Captain made a public presentation to his wandering pilot on the flight deck of a huge cardboard finger in a circle, the Most Honourable Decoration Of The Irremovable Finger.

A solid week of flying, day and night, in the Clyde and the Irish Sea, including dummy attacks on a submarine, one crash on deck in the blackness of the middle watch, and one Swordfish making an emergency landing with engine trouble, then it was back to Greenock, where a lighter removed the damaged aircraft, and the ship left for Larne, just north of Belfast, for a final, intensified, working-up session under the keen eyes of Flag Officer Carrier Training.

Just before midnight on 13 January a Swordfish was flown off the deck with the ship at anchor, working engines to keep her head to wind. Vindex then weighed for a short night exercise, anchored to give everyone a brief hour's sleep, and weighed again at 4.25 a.m. for a day of simulated anti-U-boat action. Planes were on and off the deck all forenoon. At 4.15 p.m. a simulated strike was flown, followed by a second wave half an hour later. After mock attacks on a submarine in the evening, three Swordfish crashed in succession, and a tired ship's company brought the carrier to in the Lough just before midnight.

After a day's practice operating with a convoy, Vindex left Larne for the Clyde. She was turned back by thick weather, but was in Greenock on 18 January for petrol, ammunition, victualling and repairs to her engines. She was back in Larne Lough by the following evening, one Sea Hurricane having pancaked on the flight deck on the way over.

At 10.30 a.m. next day Gordon Bennett landed Flag Officer, Carrier Training, aboard in a Swordfish. FOCT was none other than the formidable Vice-Admiral A. St G. Lumley Lyster. He knew Swordfish, and he had met the old 825 Squadron, having put them through their paces in Glorious in the Mediterranean pre-war, and an inspection by him was something to fear.

He was not pleased with what he saw in Vindex. There was a crash on deck in the afternoon. The ship weighed early next day for Greenock, and at 10 a.m. Bennet flew FOCT off again. Before he departed he said, 'When I return I shall expect not only an improvement, but a transformation!'

A chastened Vindex returned to Rothesay Bay, followed in by the American-built escort carriers HMS Pursuer, Hunter and Chaser. Pursuer was something special among RN escort carriers, a fighter carrier, with two squadrons of American-built Wildcats on board. The night after her arrival in Rothesay Bay her ship's company were rudely awakened when Vindex's puny anchors dragged, and her port quarter hit the other carrier's bow. In Vindex the batsman's platform, jutting out aft, was destroyed as well as 50 feet of the port walkway, and No. 6 Oerlikon gun platform was damaged. There was also a small underwater leak in a lower buoyancy compartment between stringers 61 and 73. Captain Graham of the Pursuer was not amused,

Weighed in the balance. Flag Officer Carrier Training, Vice-Admiral A. St G. Lumley Lyster is flown aboard *Vindex* for an inspection after trials. No. 825 Squadron's Senior Pilot, Lieutenant Gordon Bennett, is at the controls.

Swordfish trio. Left to right: Sub-Lieutenants Trussell and Burns and Lieutenant Varley. Trussell's Swordfish crashed into the sea on 25th February, 1944, with water-contaminated petrol, and his observer Sub-Lieutenant (A) Bert Broadley was killed. Harry Burns and Mike Varley, and their telegraphist/air-gunner Basil Hall-Law, were lost with their Swordfish on 19th March, 1944.

neither was Captain Bayliss, who was flown off to report the incident armed with the letter which he and Peter Isaacson had composed in trials, pointing out just such a likelihood. *Vindex* herself was back in the Clyde next day and remained there until 26 February, undergoing collision repairs, storing ship and sending men off on long leave preparatory to operations.

Vindex had now been allocated to Western Approaches Command for trade protection. 'To maintain', C-in-C Western Approaches decreed, 'a round-the-clock offensive against the U-boats and against bombing attacks while within range of Biscay airfields, we shall now, I consider, operate CVEs in pairs providing at the same time concentrated and increased air effort with economy in escorts ...'

By the end of January he had been allocated the British-built escort carriers *Activity*, refitted after her long stint as a training carrier, *Nairana* and *Vindex*, and the US-built 'Woolworth carriers' *Ameer*, *Atheling*, *Biter*, *Chaser*, *Fencer*, *Slinger* and *Striker*. On temporary loan were the Lease-Lend HMS *Tracker* and fighter carriers *Pursuer* and *Searcher*.

Vindex, which had been ahead of her rival *Nairana* in readiness for operations, because of the collision with *Pursuer* was now slipping behind. At

Take-off. HMS *Vindex* seen from one of her 825 Squadron Swordfish.

The return. Mark II Swordfish of 825 with deck hook down, preparatory to returning to *Vindex*.

1.15 p.m. on 13 February she left B2 Berth and entered drydock, pushed and pulled by tugs. Next morning the dock was pumped out, and an inspection of the underwater damage made.

While the clatter of rivetting reverberated round the dock, Boom McCoombe stalked the strangely lifeless ship, making sure that, with a reduced ship's company on board, she did not deteriorate through lack of attention. Walking out on the foc'sle one morning he shouted to a young Hostilities Only ordinary seaman, 'Cheese down those ropes' ends!' Shaken abrupty into life, the OD caught something about '... ropes ...', saw a rope made fast round some bollards, and hurriedly unwound it—thereby casting off a painter's stage and dropping the Scottish workman 40 feet on to the bottom of the dock.

Next morning Captain Bayliss received a letter from the man's solicitor threatening action in the courts. Bayliss sent for Peter Isaacson, who went to see Flag Officer, Aircraft Carriers, and he and the Admiral's staff put their heads together. Finally they found a loophole. Apparently it had been the foreman's responsibility to make sure that the workman be provided with a lifeline, which, as established by eye witnesses, had not been rigged. This got the Navy off the hook.

Repairs were completed by the end of 23 February. In the forenoon next day the dock was flooded and in the afternoon the carrier got under way out of the dock, assisted for'ard by the tug *Chieftain* and aft by the *Empire Frank*, and moved to C2 Berth, at two hours' notice for steam.

Two days later she weighed for flying exercises in the Clyde. At 11.35 a.m. Swordfish W crashed into the sea. At 11.50 Swordfish B, piloted by Dennis Trussell, a former engineering student from Enfield, who had left a reserved occupation to join the Navy, with Bert Broadley as his observer, also hit the hogwash.

Trussell was flying quite low when suddenly, without warning, the engine cut out and they went in. Under water, Trussell looked over the cockpit side

The approach. Pilot's eye view of the flight deck.

Safely down. A Swordfish, wings folded, is parked on the flight deck of *Vindex*.

towards the bottom of the fuselage and saw light. The aircraft had turned over and he was looking up at the surface. He had already swallowed a lot of water, and thought desperately 'Must get up to the light!' But he was caught by the R/T lead dangling from his helmet. The last thing he remembered was wrenching it clear.

He woke up in hospital, where he had been taken after rescue by HM Motor Launch *547*, which had also rescued the other crew. There was no one about, and he decided to take a little walk. He wandered into the next room, and saw Bert Broadley strapped to a table, face-down. He went over to him, and found that he was dead. Apart from a dislocated arm, he himself appeared to have nothing wrong with him. In fact he had also damaged his hip, which went black and blue, but this did not show at once. A little later Ian Taylor took him down to his old hospital, St Mary's, in London, and supervised treatment.

It was found that these two crashes, and probably several previous ones, had been caused by water in the petrol. This had got into the ship's petrol storage tanks. Some thought that it was produced by evaporation, others were certain that the water had been present in the petrol when it was taken on board. To his disgust Dennis Trussell found himself on a charge, according to the authority of a 1936 Admiralty Fleet Order which decreed that 'All pilots must be responsible for filtering petrol if the presence of water is suspected'. However, he considered himself to have carried out this duty, though technically after the event, when Ian Taylor gave him a test tube of silver nitrate and he checked the water in the drain tanks of several aircraft carburetters. The absurd charge was in any case dropped, but the source of the contamination remained for the time being undiscovered, which did not make for confidence in the machines. One of five Swordfish which scrambled next forenoon returned with engine trouble. The Squadron spent two days straining the petrol through chamois leathers to try to get rid of the water.

On 2 March *Vindex* weighed for Larne, which she reached at half-past two in the afternoon. Three staff officers came aboard for a conference, and that night *Striker*, with which *Vindex* was to be paired, joined her in the Lough.

Next day *Vindex* was in the Irish Sea, flying aircraft. A few minutes before one o'clock in the afternoon Acting Leading Air Mechanic (E) Samuel Aspinall was blown overboard by the propwash of an aircraft. The ship was stopped at once, the helm put hard-a-starboard to circle back, and the seaboat slipped. Five minutes after he had gone over, Aspinall was seen from the bridge. Three minutes later a heavy snowstorm set in, and in a few minutes he was lost sight of. The whaler's crew found the lifebuoy which had been streamed and a seaman's cap, but there was no trace of Aspinall, and after another half an hour's fruitless search the boat was hoisted and the hunt abandoned. The Swordfish flew that night, and in the following forenoon a memorial service was held for Ordinary Seaman Humphries, the young matelot lost overboard on 30 December, Sam Aspinall and Bert Broadley. Broadley, at 28, had been the old man of the Squadron. He left a widow and child. Then *Vindex* returned to the Clyde, flying off anti-submarine patrols on the way.

A Sea Hurricane is spotted on the lift ready for striking down into the hangar.

At Greenock 825's CO Zeke Cooper left the ship for a new appointment and 'Force On' Gough assumed temporary command, though leaving the practical working of the Swordfish to Gordon Bennett and Paul House. At nine o'clock on the morning of the 7th *Vindex*'s designated partner *Striker* was seen leaving harbour with the cruiser *Royalist*. Working as pairs, so as to provide effective round-the-clock air coverage of convoys, with each carrier working a watch-on, watch-off rota, or one ship specialising in daylight operations and one in night flying, *Activity* and *Nairana*, *Biter* and *Tracker*, were out working on the West Africa/Gibraltar convoy lanes, and *Pursuer*'s fighters were also helping to keep those waters clear of bombers and the new radio-controlled, deadly 'glider bombs'. A carrier was needed to cover the West Africa/Gibraltar Convoy OS70/KMS44, and *Striker* was the only experienced ship immediately available. *Vindex* would have to cope alone with the job which had been allocated to the pair.

Her task was to head a surface escort group to form a separate, independent 'hunter-killer' force to track down U-boats in the North Atlantic before they could get to the convoys, and *Vindex* herself would be the first specialist night anti-submarine carrier. US Navy escort carriers *Bogue*, *Card*, *Core* and *Santee* had each led such a group and had had great success against U-boats in 1943. But they had worked in the milder Central and South Atlantic and their efficient, far-ranging Avengers had operated only by day. *Vindex* would be working in the harsher North Atlantic, 'round-the-clock', by day and night, with only 12 Stringbags and six converted landplanes of Battle of Britain vintage.

C-in-C Western Approaches' War Diary noted: '*Vindex* and 6th EG to leave North Channel p.m. 9 March to operate in U-boat area especially those threatening trans-Atlantic convoys routed to south. 2nd EG to leave Londonderry 11 March to act as support group or striking force for *Vindex*. After 2nd EG have joined, corvettes of 6th EG will be required to return to N. Ireland for another operation. *Vindex* and escort to operate for approximately three weeks unless circumstances require otherwise.'

Vindex was now ahead of schedule. She weighed from B3 Berth at 11.45 a.m. on the 8th and steamed out into the Clyde, flying off three Swordfish. At 3.17 p.m. the officer of the watch logged Ailsa Crag abeam. At 7.45 p.m. the ship anchored in Larne Lough. At half-past two on the following afternoon the commanding officers of the ships of the Royal Canadian Navy's 6th Escort Group, the destroyer *Qu'Appelle*, frigates *Waskesieu* and *Outremont*, corvettes *Prescott* and *Edmunston*, reported on board the carrier for a conference, and at 6.15 p.m. the group weighed for sea, with Captain Bayliss as Senior Officer. Two new TAGs, Alf Bleasdale from Bolton and Mancunian Chris Williams, had joined *Vindex* from RNAS, Maydown, on Lough Foyle, where they had been on a MAC ship course with No. 836 Squadron.

Before they left harbour Captain Bayliss addressed the ship's company. 'We will be operating', he told them, 'in the areas where the largest concentrations of U-boats are known to be. The darker the night, and the worse the weather, the more chance we will have of catching them on the surface and destroying them.'

3

Round the Clock

THE NORTH ATLANTIC CHART on the bulkhead of *Vindex*'s Operations Room was thick with symbols. There were markers for every Allied ship, every convoy known to be at sea, every patch of ocean beneath which a U-boat or a wolf pack prowled, plotted from intercepted U-boat Enigma code broken by the cryptanalysts at the British Government Code and Cypher School at Bletchley Park in Buckinghamshire, or from HF/DF fixes obtained by escorts.

That evening ASO Stovin-Bradford and his assistant, Chiefy Norman Lauchlan, looked up as Captain Bayliss and Navigator Geoffrey Milner came in.

The Captain stepped up to the chart, studied it for a moment, then stubbed his finger on a spot in mid-Atlantic between Fastnet and Cape Race, where the little black swastika flags were thick.

'The main concentration of U-boats appears to be *there*. We are *here*. Take us across there, will you, Pilot?'

Vindex's hunting area was around 50° North, 28° West, a thousand miles out into the Atlantic. By sunrise on 10 March she was clear of Ireland, and nosing out into the grey ocean. The group went to dawn action stations and began zigzag.

They weaved their course across the ocean all day, breaking off zigzag only for the carrier to fly off Hurricane patrols, with the Swordfish being reserved for night operations.

The first of these went off into the darkness at 8.25 p.m., followed by another a quarter of an hour later. Forty minutes later the group got a contact off their starboard bow, and *Vindex* swung north to investigate, going to full speed ahead at 110 revolutions of her engines, and flying off another Swordfish.

The contact faded, the Stringbag was recalled. Half an hour later the carrier was turning into wind again and increasing to full revs to receive a Swordfish with engine trouble. An hour after this two more aircraft lumbered down the deck and climbed into the midnight blackness. Then the last Swordfish remaining airborne was safely batted down, briskly spotted on the lift and whisked below. At half-past one in the middle watch on the 11th the patrolling pair returned, and the carrier and her hunters zigzagged through the small hours, until the dawn patrol was sent off at four o'clock. For Paul House on his observer's wooden stool it was watch-and-watch, as he had only landed from his last patrol just before midnight. By quarter past six it was light enough for the Hurricanes to take a turn, and the tired dawn patrol of Stringbags returned.

The fuel-gulping fighters were back on board an hour later. Around midday two Swordfish were scrambled to investigate an empty Carley float which was floating forlornly on the sea, but there were no further signs of enemy activity, and *Vindex* ceased zigzag to top up the thirsty *Qu'Appelle*. The destroyer came up astern, and the black hose was being streamed down to her when an aircraft was sighted. The plane was a friendly Sunderland flying boat of RAF Coastal Command, and half an hour later oil began to flow from the carrier's capacious tanks into the escort.

It was a lengthy business, interrupted twice by aircraft alarms when *Vindex* cast off and went to action stations, and *Qu'Appelle* did not finish her drink until 7.30 p.m. The carrier had scarcely recovered the hose when she got an Asdic contact at 400 yards off the port bow, and almost at once heard underwater explosions in that direction. Captain Bayliss put the helm hard-a-port and rang for full speed. It was known that there were U-boats on station round their bow. A Sunderland had attacked one about 250 miles west of Rockall, and a second submarine had been bombed and apparently disabled some 350 miles west of Valentia Island, south-west Ireland, early that morning. A U-boat sighting report had been intercepted in the forenoon. At 8 p.m. Flying Stations was piped, and two Swordfish went off on anti-submarine search. As they were returning just after eleven o'clock, Swordfish NE 868, pilot Gordon Bennett, observer Peter Couch, TAG Joe Palmer, took off, followed by Peter Cumberland, Frank Jackson and John Stone in LS 428, to relieve them.

Both his own Chief TAG, Mick Dale, and 'Uncle' Norman Lauchlan were concerned about Cumberland's young tel/air-gunner. He and Johnny Puttock were the youngest of a young bunch, and Stone still seemed unsettled and bewildered. A few days previously his aircraft had had radio failure and could not communicate with the ship. Lauchlan had made Stone set up his radio in an aircraft in the hanger to find the fault. The Swordfish radio was a small set, with one 2-volt battery, one HT battery, and two small valves. To obtain voice R/T communication with the ship or between the crew of the aircraft a lever had to be moved to modulate the main transmitter signal. When Lauchlan examined the set he saw that Stone had not moved the lever. 'Oh dear,' he said to Dale, 'He doesn't know his stuff.' Dale said, 'I'll have to put him in the Rattle.' 'No,' Lauchlan said, 'You've got to live with him. I'll do it.'

It was a pleasant, moonlit night. Bennett had reached a position approximately 450 miles west-by-north of Valentia at about a quarter to twelve when he sighted the U-boat clearly, creaming along the surface. He dived to the attack and released his two 250lb Torpex-filled depth-charges. Couch, peering over the side, saw two white blobs straddle the submarine, the first close on the starboard quarter, the second alongside the port bow, but there was no explosion.

Bridge party, *Vindex*, March, 1944. Left to right: 'Wings' Percy Gick, 'Ops' Stovin-Bradford, Executive Lieutenant-Commander 'Boom' McCoombe, Lieutenant A.D.A. van Geffen, RNR (back to camera), Captain Bayliss (with pipe) and Navigator Lieutenant-Commander Geoffrey Milner, RNR.

A short way off, Frank Jackson got an echo from the U-boat on the trace of his ASV, and guided Cumberland towards her, breaking off frequently to hang over the side and look for her ahead. At last they saw her, sitting on the surface, and promptly attacked. Then up came the cannon shells. It was this crew's first experience of ack-ack. To Jackson they seemed to be passing miles away from them. Cumberland thought, 'What are those pretty lights?' The pretty lights came closer … 'They're shooting at me!' He kept on and dropped his DCs.

Suddenly there was a loud bang and a blow in the port side of the cockpit aft. Jackson, who had been leaning over to port, felt a sharp pain in the back as if someone had punched him in the kidneys. His knees gave way and he crumpled to the cockpit floor. Both men heard Stone call out 'I think I've been hit, sir!' Then he was silent.

Cumberland circled round the sub. He did not quite know what to look for, but was fairly certain he had not seen any flash of an exploding depth-charge. He did not know how badly Stone was hurt, and decided to break off the attack and return to the ship. He called up the Air Direction Room* and told them he was coming back early, with his TAG wounded, dropped a marker flare, and headed for *Vindex*.

They were not far away from the carrier, and landed on again about 1.30 a.m. The medics rushed out to attend to Stone and Cumberland and Jackson reported to Commander (F) and the ASO in the Ops Room.* Norman Lauchlan nudged Stovin-Bradford and pointed to Frank Jackson's parachute harness, which was in tatters. He was packed off to the Sick Bay, and Charlie Kilpatrick found a scar on his back about the size of a shilling, where the observer had been nicked by a piece of metal. Kilpatrick probed around, picked out some slivers of aluminium, and put a dressing on.

The Sick Bay tiffies who had rushed to help Stone could not get him out before the aircraft handling party folded the aircraft's wings and pushed it aft on to the lift. Down in the hangar Ian Taylor found the after cockpit soaked in blood, and Stone slumped over the set, which was still switched on. It was difficult to get at him properly with the wings folded, and Taylor could not move him. Then Dennis Trussell, on hangar duties since his injuries in his crash, managed, being thin, to get up into the cockpit and, forgetting that he was recovering from a dislocated shoulder, dragged the inert young TAG out. Peter Cumberland, who had made his report with difficulty, having almost lost his voice, went along to the Sick Bay to enquire after Stone. He asked, 'Is he badly hurt?' Taylor said, 'I'm afraid he is.' 'How badly?' 'I'm afraid he's dead.' Jackson worked out that the cannon shell must have penetrated the fabric skin of the fuselage, passed right under his arm, exploded, and scattered pieces of metal, with poor Stone getting the worst of it.

There was an immediate inquest on the depth-charge failures. Homing on

---

* The Aircraft Direction Room and the Operations Room were located at two opposite corners where a passageway joined the gallery deck.

March, 1944 Left to right: Swordfish pilot Lieutenant Ron Huggins, Air Gunnery Officer. Lieutenant John Baker, Officer of the Watch Sub-Lieutenant D.E. Cooper, Air Direction Officer Ken Mason.

The docs. Medical staff of HMS *Vindex*. Seated (left to right): Surgeon Lieutenant I.G. Taylor, RNVR, Surgeon Lieutenant-Commander C.A. Kilpatrick, RNVR, Surgeon Lieutenant F.O.J. Shaw, RNVR. Extreme left, back row, Petty Officer Sick Berth Attendant Gormley (Hostilities Only). Extreme right PO SBA Austin, a regular.

Rescue. Doctor Ian Taylor's seaboat recovers Sea Hurricane pilot Al Martin from the sea in February, 1944. Tragically, Martin was drowned in a similar accident on May 5th.

Cumberland's flare, a third Swordfish, LS430, had made another attack with two Torpex. As the aircraft passed over the U-boat the observer saw sparks fly off the submarine's hull, but there was no explosion.

The Swordfish of Sharrock, Jones and Amatt took off at 2.45 a.m. with orders to contact the *Qu'Appelle*, which had reported a U-boat contact. Jones soon picked up the destroyer on his ASV radar, then on R/T. The ship was streaking about here and there in a very odd way. It was obvious to Jones that he could not keep up a continuous radar watch for U-boats as well as maintain a record of the Swordfish's position relative to *Vindex*, so he called up *Qu'Appelle* and asked her if she would be kind enough to give him a course to steer for the carrier when the search was over.

'Sure, sure,' said the Canadian voice. Jones then gave his undivided attention to the U-boat search for the next two hours, relying on the destroyer for navigation.

About 4.30 a.m., after what seemed like a grand tour of the Atlantic by night, *Qu'Appelle* informed them that she had lost all trace of the U-boat, and was giving up the search. Jones asked her for a course to steer for *Vindex*, as promised, only to be told, 'Sorry, we don't know where the hell we are. Say, if you have to ditch, we have some sausages cooking. You're welcome to be our guests.' Sharrock climbed to 3,000 feet and Jones picked up *Vindex* and her escorts on his ASV screen, 30 miles away. They were able to refuse Canadian hospitality and in fact pass the carrier's position to *Qu'Appelle*, who seemed unconcerned about being lost.

With other aircraft searching the area, frigates *Waskesieu* and *Outremont* and the *Qu'Appelle* went hunting. *Outremont* picked up a U-boat contact and made an attack with DCs. *Edmunston* investigated an oil patch just after seven o'clock, then left for Moville with the other corvette, *Prescott*, as the 2nd Escort Group was now in the offing. Sea Hurricanes flew searches and patrols throughout the morning of the 12th. Single aircraft, both Hurricanes and Swordfish, were scrambled to follow up contacts during the afternoon. One armed Swordfish accidentally fired an RP along the deck, narrowly missing the bridge. During a three-and-a-half-hour patrol in the evening, Bennett, Couch and Palmer picked up three submarine contacts on the ASV. One disappeared off the trace when they had closed to three miles, another at a mile and a half. The sloops of the 2nd Escort Group,* which had left Lough Foyle at 11.21 p.m. on the 11th, followed up their lead and made a very determined search.

At nine o'clock next morning, Monday 13 March, *Vindex* sighted the ships of EG2, 15 miles off her starboard bow. At three o'clock in the afternoon the body of John Stone, sewn up in canvas, was buried at sea. The other youngster, Johnny Puttock, took his place in Peter Cumberland's crew and made his first flight in a Swordfish from a carrier when they took off in the dark shortly after midnight on the 14th, one of a patrol of three. One aircraft of the three contracted engine trouble, fired off a flare to show its position and landed on just before two o'clock. The remaining two machines stayed on patrol until half-past three, when they were relieved by two more aircraft, and there was another change just after six in the morning. At ten minutes to eight C. R. Webb crashed his Swordfish into the barrier, though no-one was hurt.

At 10.40 a.m. the five sloops of EG2 were in sight of the carrier on the horizon to port, but they altered course and made off in a westerly direction. At 11.27 *Waskesieu*, maintaining an EG6 presence, dropped two DCs over a contact, and marked the position with a flare float.

At 11.54 *Vindex* was once more refuelling *Qu'Appelle* astern when McCoombe's voice boomed out of the Asdic cabinet.

'Torpedo one-nine-o degrees!'

Captain Bayliss, who never seemed to leave the bridge, called immediately 'Hard-a-starboard, emergency full speed ahead!'

With the destroyer still gulping oil, *Vindex* swung over. The torpedo noises passed astern of her, and Mr Archer, the ship's Warrant Torpedo Gunner, who was just coming on deck aft, reported a torpedo wake passing the carrier's side.

By the afternoon the threat of U-boat attack on *Vindex* seemed to have receded, at least temporarily, and EG2 closed the carrier again. *Vindex*'s aircraft carried on with their dogged patrols.

---

*HMS *Starling* (Captain Walker, SO EG2), *Whimbrel*, *Wild Goose*, *Magpie* and *Wren*.

Frigate HMCS *Waskesieu* of the 6th Escort Group.

Below Canadian escort: destroyer HMCS *Qu'Appelle* of the 6th Escort Group about to be refuelled by *Vindex*. Both these ships were part of the escort for *Vindex*'s first operation, 19th–28th March, 1944.

Swordfish pilot. Sub-Lieutenant (A) Norman Sharrock, RNVR, from Bromley, Kent.

Norman Sharrock, with his regular observer Brian Jones and TAG Chris Williams temporarily replacing Bill Arnatt, who had gone sick, was first off the deck of three relieving Swordfish which began taking off into the night sky.

Sharrock, an alumnus of Bromley, Kent, County Grammar School, had, as a King's Scout, sung songs round the camp fire with Princess Juliana and Prince Bernhard at the World Jamboree in Holland in 1937, and his first-ever flight had been a 7s 6d, 20-minute joyride over London in a DeHavilland Dragon Rapide from Croydon airport during his summer holidays in 1938. He left school a few weeks after war broke out, and took an electrical testing job with J. Stone's of Deptford. This was a reserved occupation, but Sharrock, with his keenness to fly, also wanted to join the Navy, spurred on by the example of his father, who had served in the Merchant Navy under sail, taken his Extra-Master's ticket, and as an RNVR navigator in World War I had been in one of the minesweepers which had swept ahead of the Grand Fleet before the battle of Jutland.

Norman joined the Y-Scheme for entry into the Fleet Air Arm as a pilot. After months of correspondence, medicals and an Admiralty Board, he went to HMS *St Vincent* at Gosport in 1941 on the 27th Pilots' Course. He got his wings at RAF, Netheravon, on 20 January 1942, on a Miles Master III aircraft, with 159 hours in his flying log book. He graduated to Swordfish and Albacores, and trained for operational flying in No. 776 Squadron at RNAS, Macrihanish, under Lieutenant-Commander Edgar Bibby, RNVR, who had won the DSC for his work with the famous No. 830 Swordfish Squadron which had fought, and was still fighting, Rommel's convoys to Africa. At Macra Sharrock crewed up with former chartered accountant Brian Jones as his observer, and Leading Naval Airman Bill Amatt as his TAG, before joining 825 Squadron at Thorney Island, thence to *Furious*, *Pretoria Castle* and *Vindex*.

It was dark on this night of 14 March, with no moon. Sharrock gave his engine a good warm-up, but as he took off it belched massive sparks and lost all power. Jones thought *water in the petrol*, switched on the R/T and asked for an emergency landing. With four 250lb depth-charges weighing the Stringbag down, it flew straight into the sea. Jones' request was answered just as the water started lapping over into the cockpit.

As the aircraft hit the water Chris Williams struck his head on one of the flame-float canisters mounted on the gun ring in place of the Lewis, which made him dizzy for a moment or two. The ship missed them, and the aircraft floated for about two minutes, just time enough for the M-type dinghy to erect itself out of the top of the upper wing, much to the relief of Sharrock, who was Squadron Air Safety Officer.

They climbed across from the cockpits to the dinghy almost without getting wet. After about half an hour they heard something which sounded like the rumbling of a ship's engines. Williams had some 2-star distress candles attached to his Mae West, and they fired their first-ever flare up into the night. Suddenly, to their huge relief, the blackness above the waves was stabbed by a ship's navigation lights, which stayed lit for some ten seconds. The airmen fired another flare. The dark outline of HMCS *Outremont* appeared, and a boat seemed to spring from her side. The three men were swiftly hauled aboard and as smoothly transferred to the frigate, which had slowed but did not stop.

Chris Williams was rushed down to the Sick Bay and strapped to a 12-inch operating table to stop him rolling with the ship's motion, while a surgeon put a few stitches in the gash in his forehead. Brian Jones reported to the Captain of *Outremont*, a very cool and unusually experienced middle-aged ex-Canadian Merchant Navy captain, who apologised for taking so long to pick them up. He himself had marked the position of the crashed Swordfish as soon as it had gone down and had immediately turned to the rescue, but his SOE in *Waskesieu* had first ordered him back on station, then countermanded the order. Captain Bayliss had taken *Vindex* straight on ahead for fear of a U-boat attack on the precious carrier if she slowed or stopped.

The three visitors, all dressed in flying clothes and wearing no badges of rank, were hustled towards *Outremont*'s wardroom. Chris Williams, a leading hand, whispered to Jones, 'What shall I do?' Jones whispered back, 'Norman and I won't say anything, if you don't. You've been invited in. Why worry?' He pushed the TAG ahead of him into the wardroom, and all enjoyed Canadian hospitality together.

The remaining Swordfish of the patrol were taken aboard. A red light was sighted away on the starboard bow, and half an hour later the white phosphorescence of starshell bloomed in the sky where the hunting sloops of Walker's group were at work. Just after one o'clock in the middle watch on the following morning three flares were seen in succession off *Vindex*'s port quarter, as she steamed towards the action at 14 knots, protected by the faithful *Outremont* and *Waskesieu*.

Swordfish patrols were changed again between half-past one and two o'clock. In the darkness and cold at 1.50, Bennett, Couch and Palmer's LS380 was patrolling near the ships of 2nd Escort Group when Couch picked up a likely U-boat contact on his ASV screen, just ahead of the searching sloops. Ten minutes later another echo appeared. It was too dark for the Swordfish crew to see anything below on the water, but they dropped sea markers and flares with great accuracy over the contact points to guide EG2.

Walker had also picked up echoes on his radar, and the hunt began. The sloops followed the scent for nearly three hours. Then *Wild Goose* got a strong echo, and *Magpie* picked up the same one. In what was intended to be the preliminary move in a 'creeping' attack, with one ship steaming quietly in towards the target while another tracked it and relayed its position, Walker's own *Starling* destroyed the U-boat with depth-charges. Quantities of tell-tale wreckage came to the surface to confirm the kill, of which *Vindex* was

'The sea was lively . . .' – North Atlantic, March, 1944.

Secret weapon on the flight deck of *Vindex*, March, 1944. Left to right: Sub-Lieutenants, RNVR, Jock Morrison, Brian Jones, Johnny Moore, Cooper, Ken Corrin and Norman Sharrock.

Clearing snow from *Vindex*'s flight deck, March, 1944. Al Martin, who in better weather flew a Sea Hurricane, is piloting the tractor.

Swordfish crew. Left to right, Sub-Lieutenant (A) Frank Jackson, RNVR, (observer), Leading Naval Airman Johnny Puttock (telegraphist/air-gunner), Sub-Lieutenant (A) Peter Cumberland (pilot).

Observer Frank Jackson showing his pilot Peter Cumberland the shrapnel holes in his parachute harness after the fight with the U-boat on 11th March, 1944.

credited with half.

U-boats were too close to *Vindex* for comfort. *Waskesieu* got a contact to port at half-past three, and Captain Bayliss took immediate avoiding action to starboard. The normal morning patrols began at four, and at 9.40 a.m. *Vindex* began oiling the ever-thirsty *Qu'Appelle*. Two hours later, with the destroyer still plugged in, Asdic got a contact to starboard. Bayliss ordered 'Stand by to slip the oiler'. *Vindex* stopped pumping, but the contact was lost and the process was resumed.

Outremont got a scent and dropped DCs on it just after 1 p.m., then lost touch again. *Vindex* stopped pumping at four o'clock, and ten minutes later ran into rain clouds, a sign of the worsening weather, with visibility about one mile. In a few minutes the skies were clear again, and *Qu'Appelle* was cast off, topped up with 280 tons of diesel oil. But the weather deteriorated again, and flying had to be curtailed during the rest of the day and through the early hours of the 16th, until Paul House's Swordfish took off on the dawn patrol at 4.25 a.m.

At 8.47 *Vindex* was steering due east, and reduced speed from twelve to eight knots so that *Waskesieu* could close for refuelling. At 9.30 steadying line and pipe line were made fast on board and 20 minutes later pumping started. She had barely begun to suck in oil when she got an Asdic contact, urgently requested *Vindex* to stop pumping, and cast off. *Qu'Appelle* got a contact at 11.26 and dropped DCs. At noon *Vindex* picked up a ping passing down her wake. Ken Mason, who was on deck, saw the torpedo pass down the ship's side. She dropped a smoke float, and told *Qu'Appelle*, ceased pumping oil to *Waskesieu*, slipped the frigate, and turned into wind to fly off aircraft.

Waskesieu dropped a DC at 1.15 p.m., but the area around the carrier seemed clear enough by four in the afternoon for her to commence fuelling *Outremont*. The ships of EG2 came in sight and Bayliss had to tell Walker that he now had insufficient oil in his tanks to look after any ships other than the frigates of EG2. As it was, he intended to detach *Qu'Appelle* to return to base without further refuelling unless there was a convenient convoy with tankers available. 'Unable therefore to fuel EG2 without seriously prejudicing my available sea time,' he signalled to C-in-C Western Approaches. He stopped pumping to *Outremont* at six o'clock and took in the oil hose when *Waskesieu* reported dropping depth-charges on a contact. As night drew on, other escorts joined in a hunt, and the carrier altered course to leave the area and give them a clear field.

There was very little flying, for a change, on the 17th. By now there was an undercurrent of discontent and frustration among the tired aircrews. Initial keenness had been blunted somewhat by the disappointment of the malfunctioning depth-charges, and the possibility of ditching or crashing as a result of water in the petrol was a constant worry. The strain of round-the-clock flying by just eight full aircrews was beginning to tell, and the frequent torpedo scares made everybody jumpy.

What made all this hard to bear for the aviators was the difficulty of getting sustenance before a night flight. They were supposed to exist on the three regular meals served in the wardroom: breakfast, lunch and dinner. A crew taking off at midnight needed a meal before they faced the bitter cold and darkness, the stresses of anti-submarine searches and the anxieties of navigation over the trackless ocean. On the 17th Paul House, as Senior Observer, found himself the spokesman for a group of discontented airmen at the ante-room bar. Commander (F) was given to understand that if they were not properly fed they would not fly. Gick was nonplussed, but Captain Bayliss came down to the wardroom and spoke to them quietly of the vital need to continue operating against the U-boats, so the 'mutiny' subsided. An improvement was made in the victualling of aircrews.

Flying went forward through the small hours of the 18th, and in the afternoon a programme of testing to find the fault in the useless DCs was carried out. There was the inevitable buzz circulating, this time suggesting that the DCs had been filled with sawdust by way of sabotage. Swordfish dropped 17 DCs in all, and all but two failed to explode. The fault was eventually traced to the safety mechanism, the whole of which had been made into an electrical system, one washer having been inserted at the factory in the wrong sequence. These new RDX charges had not been test-dropped before and on the first two nights of operations it had not been clearly understood

Emergency. While HMCS *Waskesieu* of the 6th Escort Group was refuelling from *Vindex* on 16th March, 1944, an asdic contact was reported. The frigate immediately cast off the pipe line, and a torpedo passed down *Vindex's* side.

that they were not exploding. But for this carelessness in assembly, *Vindex's* score of half a U-boat might well have been three or four.

At 6.50 p.m. *Vindex* stopped engines while Norman Sharrock and his crew, still queasy after four days of violent small-ship motion, were transferred back from *Outremont*. Chris Williams returned minus his flying kit, including wool-lined leather jacket, which had been stolen while hanging up to dry in the Canadian frigate's engine room. Water in the petrol was thought to have been the cause of their ditching. Then the Stringbag patrols began again, with the carrier making various courses and speeds to avoid suspected contacts. The ship ran into a belt of fog at 3.30 on the following afternoon, Sunday 19 March, with visibility about a mile, but scrambled a striking force when a contact was picked up at five miles. The contact faded, the aircraft returned. Night patrols began at 8.15 p.m.

Fatigue, weather and mechanical failures were not all that the aircrews of 825 had to contend with. On two nights their radio frequency of 4340 kilocycles was completely swamped by stock prices delivered in a fast, butch female American voice from Miami, 3,000 miles away, and had to be changed to 6,550 kc/s. Some unidentified German also interfered with normal R/T communication.

At 10.50 p.m. the Swordfish of ingoing and outgoing patrols were exchanged. At 10.55 the Swordfish of Mike Varley, Harry Burns and Basil Hall-Law crashed into the sea with fuel failure four cables off *Vindex's* starboard beam. They managed to drop a flame float before hitting the sea, and *Vindex* immediately flew off a Swordfish to find them, but two minutes after it had taken off the ship ran into thick fog. The aircraft had to be recalled. *Waskesieu* and *Outremont* went looking for the Stringbag's dinghy in the wild black waste of sea.

At three o'clock in the morning the fog began to clear, and at 6.30 Bennett, Couch and Palmer went off in Swordfish K to search for Varley's crew, together with two other Stringbags. They found nothing. Peter Couch had been a particular friend of observer Harry Burns since their days in *Furious* together. It was, he wrote in his flying log book, the 'most miserable flight of my life'. Gordon Bennett, flying one of the other search aircraft, also recorded: 'A very depressing flight in, out and down under rain squalls constantly'. He and Burns had been the last of Winkle Esmonde's men. At 9.20 a.m. *Waskesieu* reported finding an empty dinghy and a piece of wreckage from the crashed aircraft, but there was no sign of the crew. 'Search abandoned, crew presumed lost,' was entered in the ship's log.

Flying continued. There was a heavy rain squall in the afternoon, but *Waskesieu* was refuelled again. An outbreak of radio and compass failures was cutting short the sorties of some of the Sea Hurricanes. Moving these fixed-wing machines around the small hangar and getting them up on deck for ranging with only one lift was often a nightmare. Sometimes six or seven machines had to be extracted from the hangar and parked on deck to get at the aircraft needed for operation.

At eleven o'clock on the morning of the 21st, *Qu'Appelle*, which had refuelled from a tanker in Convoy ONS31, rejoined, bringing Captain Bayliss some official correspondence. The weather began to worsen steadily until, at 6.25 p.m. on the 22nd, all *Vindex*'s aircraft were struck down into the hangar, and the ship, pitching and rolling in savage seas, was battened down. At half-past eight Captain Bayliss was forced to reduce speed. Just before midnight the port and starboard gyros and the steering gear failed, and *Vindex* began steering by main engines. The Lower Power Room for'ard was reported flooded, and the sea was washing through messdecks and flats.

The steering gear was quickly repaired, but it was a good two hours before the messdecks were habitable again. By then the emergency circuits for power and lighting were being threatened by flooding of the after switchboard, but at six o'clock in the morning Captain Bayliss was able to increase speed again to ten knots.

When Norman Sharrock's Swordfish was ranged at 9 a.m., Brian Jones and Chris Williams in the rear cockpit, the weather was dull and rough, with a heavy sea running. *Vindex*'s steel deck was very slippery with spray, and the handling party were hanging on like heroes to the aircraft, which juddered and slithered about as the ship rolled, and pitched some 40 feet.

In weather like this it was difficult for Commander (F) to pick the right time to give a pilot the green light. The ideal point was when the ship was riding up out of a trough. This time the sea outsmarted him. Sharrock got the green at the top of a crest, and by the time the Stringbag reached the end of the flight deck *Vindex* was pointing down into the next trough, and Sharrock flew slap into it. Williams had not fastened the 'dog lead' to his parachute harness, and was catapulted out of the cockpit.

Bayliss' swift 'Stop starboard, hard-a-starboard!' saved them from being run down by the ship, which swung so quickly she seemed about to roll over.

The aircraft sank immediately. Jones surfaced from about 20 feet down and was caught in the ship's bow wave. Sharrock struggled free under water and was thrown on his back by the bow wave. He inflated his individual K-type dinghy.

Chris Williams, struggling for the surface, heard a deep booming noise and thought the depth-charges on the aircraft must be exploding. Suddenly he broke surface and found himself up against the side of the ship. The booming was the sea pounding her hull. A voice from above sang out, 'Watch for the screws!' Williams struck out away from the ship. He had an empty feeling in his stomach when he turned and looked back and found himself alone in the sea, with the carrier's stern disappearing over the next wave crest.

He wallowed about for a few minutes, then a wave lifted him high and he spotted their M-type dinghy about 50 yards away. He swam over to it and found that it had torn loose from the aircraft mooring line, leaving a one-inch hole and the dinghy only half inflated. He found the correct size screw stopper, screwed it into the hole, and was about to start pumping the dinghy up when he heard his name being called. It was Brian Jones, a poor swimmer, who was unable to inflate his Mae West and was having trouble staying afloat.

Williams swam over to him and towed him back to the dinghy. He shouted, 'Hang on to it while I pump it up!' But Jones, who was in a bad way, shook his head and made the TAG push him up on to the dinghy, which, only half full of air, folded up like a sandwich. However, with the observer spread across the one side of the dinghy, and Williams in the water hanging on to the other side, they managed to keep it fairly stable. After a short time Sharrock paddled up in his one-man dinghy, and his help further eased the situation.

About ten or fifteen minutes went by, and one of the ships of EG6 came in sight. To their frustration and fury, she appeared to ignore them. Her rails lined with gum-chewing matelots, she steamed on, making no attempt at rescue. The airmen shouted feebly at her in Navy language. But eventually over the horizon came the *Waskesieu*. When the frigate came up with them and stopped, taking care not to overrun them, Chris Williams, at some risk to himself, swam off towards her to collect a line and bring it back to Jones and Sharrock, but when he caught the heaving line thrown to him and turned round to swim back with it he was peremptorily hauled on board. The Canadians then collected the other two men. Jones saw a scrambling net dangling from the ship's side, and a couple of beefy Canadian matelots leaned right over the side, grabbed the canvas handles of his Mae West, and almost threw him inboard off the crest of a wave, taking the full weight of his waterlogged body as the sea crest abated. Then he passed out.

Two newcomers, the Royal Canadian Navy frigates *Cape Breton* and *Grou*, had now joined the *Vindex* group, and in the afternoon the former exercised her short-range weapons, with a nervous Stringbag from the carrier providing a target. *Cape Breton* and *Waskesieu* flexed their pom-pom and Oerlikon muscles shortly afterwards, using snowflake and HE bursts to aim at. At quarter to eleven at night flying started again.

At 1.25 in the middle watch on the early morning of the next day, 24 March, New Zealander Douglas Webb brought his Swordfish, observer McIlwraith, TAG Mears, back off patrol. The ship was pitching badly. Webb cut his engine, missed all the wires and sailed on. The heavy cable of the barrier sliced off his undercarriage, the Stringbag pancaked heavily on the for'ard end of the flight deck and came to a grinding halt eight feet from the round-down, with two unused depth-charges still on her racks. Everyone on flight deck and bridge, and in the Goofers, held their breath.

Petrol leaking from the carburetter was ignited, and the Swordfish started to burn. Webb and McIlwraith tore off their harness, jumped out of the cockpit and ran aft down the flight deck. Mears leaped out and was pulled up sharply by his 'G-string' or 'anti-cavorting' chain, which still tied him firmly to the cockpit. He scrambled right back into the plane, unhooked the harness and tried again. McIlwraith suddenly turned and he too ran back to the wreck of the Stringbag, climbed up into the rear cockpit and disappeared. He had been so thoroughly indoctrinated with the sacredness of Government

Write-off. Sub-Lieutenant Douglas Webb's Swordfish after crashing and burning out on Vindex's flight deck, 24th March, 1944. Norman Sharrock's Swordfish crew saw the fire from Waskesieu, which had rescued them from the sea.

property, that he was looking for his observer's dividers, worth approximately four and sixpence.

He found them and got out again just as Mansfield and his flight deck party came up with the hose which had been rigged. One DC was visible and they played the hose on that. The other could not be seen in the flames and wreckage.

At 1.45 the darkness was shattered by an explosion from the smouldering wreck. A neat circular hole eight feet by four was blown in the flight deck and a smaller hole in the deck immediately below that. On the next deck down Ordinary Seaman A. B. Hampton was asleep on the padded cushions of the forward recreation space, where the next watch of the aircraft handling party used to sleep in case extra help was needed in a hurry. A sliver of metal from the DC went straight into his stomach and killed the young matelot instantly.

By 1.55 the fire had been brought under control. At 2.30 the Swordfish which Huggins had been doggedly flying round and round the ship was brought in. Huggins, his observer Pat Calcutt and his TAG Hampton went to the Ready Room. Hampton, who had been very upset by the sight of the crash, said to his pilot, 'Lieutenant Huggins. I shall never be able to thank you enough for that lovely landing you just made.'

By 7 a.m. it was judged safe for the flight deck party to start clearing away the wrecked Stringbag. The engine and some other valuable fittings were salvaged, and the remainder was given the deep six over the side. By 11.15 a.m. temporary repairs had been made to the flight deck, and Vindex was able to carry on flying off aircraft and resume her course.

Flying went on throughout the rest of the day, but after a patrol had landed at 10 p.m. the weather had become too rough for any further

The return of the prodigals.

HMCS *Waskesieu*'s whaler returns Sharrock's crashed Swordfish crew to *Vindex*, 26th March, 1944.

Waskesieu's boat alongside *Vindex*, with Norman Sharrock and Brian Jones in the sternsheets.

operations and the aircraft were battened down in the hangar for the night.

The next plane did not take off until seven o'clock next morning. At 2.30 that afternoon the colours were half-masted and the canvas-wrapped body of young Ordinary Seaman Hampton was committed to the ocean.

In *Waskesieu*, Sharrock's Swordfish crew had been awakened to see Webb's aircraft burning aboard *Vindex*. Heavy seas, which ripped out the frigate's forward-firing anti-submarine mortar, also prevented them from being returned to the carrier for four days. In the afternoon of the 26th, the day after Hampton's funeral, the waters were just calm enough for them to be collected. Even then the whaler was smashed against the ship's side and lost two oars. For the second time Chris Williams had his flying kit stolen in the rescue ship.

By three o'clock in the afternoon the wind was freshening from the south-east and the swell increasing in length, making the motion on the ship very lively. Four aircraft took off just after four o'clock. Two returned 15 minutes later, and the second of the pair crashed into the barrier. The other two were taken back aboard just before nine. A Stringbag took off at ten past ten, another at quarter to eleven. A Swordfish orbiting somewhere round the carrier at half-past two the following morning had to drop a flare to see where

Sharrock's crew back aboard *Vindex*.
Left to right: Brian Jones (observer)
Norman Sharrock (pilot), Chris
Williams (TAG).

it was. The patrols continued, with returning Swordfish now under orders to jettison their unused DCs before landing on, after the lesson of Doug Webb's crash.

It had been originally intended that *Vindex* should keep the seas among the U-boats for three weeks. But after this pioneer effort, amounting to 14 days and nights of round-the-clock operations under the strains of insufficient food and sleep, equipment failure and bad weather, the Squadron, though they had done everything asked of them with outstanding determination and grit, had had enough. They had lost three old and experienced friends, and their aircraft were seriously depleted. Four Swordfish had gone to the bottom and there were several others in the hangar with major damage. Eddie Ward, one of the best pilots in the Squadron, taking off in the dark in bad weather, had hit the bridge island and torn off four feet from both his starboard wing tips. It was only his flying skill which had enabled him, after ditching his DCs and flares, to land on again.

The Sea Hurricanes had had a bad time, too. After one of their three night sorties a fighter had returned to *Vindex* to find her stern pitching 25 feet. The pilot took seven wave-offs before making a good landing. They had two barrier crashes, one by the experienced and popular Jimmy Green.

In the wardroom the aircrews sang,

> ... The boys in the Goofers all think I am green,
> But I draw my commission from Supermarine ...
> Cracking show! I'm alive!
> But I still have to render my A.25 ...

The only concrete achievement had been half a U-boat. Now the weather was playing up again and fog threatened. At 5.46 p.m. on 27 March the last landing of the operation was made and *Vindex* altered course for home.

As she steered for the North Channel intermittent fog patches blew across her bows from the north-east, cutting visibility to one mile. The murk persisted as the carrier sighted Rathlin Island at 9.40 a.m. on the 28th, when she altered course for the Clyde. She groped her way in thick fog towards the swept channel, passing the ghostly shapes of ships. At noon, with visibility improving to half a mile, she entered the swept channel, passed the Boom Gate at 3.20 p.m., and at four o'clock came to rest in B5 Berth with six shackles on her starboard anchor.

In their round-the-clock fortnight the Swordfish of 825 had notched up 235 hours and 100 deck landings, with 40 hours and 22 deck landings by day. The Sea Hurricanes had put in 46 daylight hours of flying on 36 sorties and had flown one and a half hours at night on three sorties. The efforts of the aircrews had been, C-in-C Western Approaches acknowledged, 'an outstanding achievement under conditions of considerable adversity which augurs well for the future of night air A/S operations. The utmost resolution on the part of all concerned was required to achieve the results. The conduct of this

Barrier. A Sea Hurricane has missed all the arrester wires and hit the crash barrier. The pilot is being extricated.

operation reflects the greatest credit on the Commanding Officer, Captain H. T. T. Bayliss RN, the air staff of the ship's company of HMS *Vindex*, and on the skill and determination of No. 825 Squadron, whose efforts deserve a greater reward.'

With aircrews sometimes flying three times a night, fatigue was a great problem. Gick and the doctors used to vie with each other in picking out any crew member who had had enough. If a pilot did something on landing a bit more eccentric than his normal personal style and repeated it two or three times, Wings got worried. One of the MOs would always sit in the Ops Room when a crew returned, chatting and listening for signs of strain.

Gick himself, with all his abundant energy, found his programme tiring too. Throughout all flying he had to brief each crew, be on the bridge when they took off and when they landed, and debrief them. But he had a cabin opposite the Ops Room, and he soon found that the great art was to do everything he could lying flat on his back there. The crews came in for briefing, then they went on deck and manned their aircraft, and when everything was ready for flying off, Gick was told, flung himself into his one-piece 'Goon suit', and on his way up to the bridge thumped on Bayliss' cabin door, who invariably called out, 'Turn into wind.'

By the time the ship had the wind blowing down the deck, the Captain was on the bridge. The outgoing patrol flew off, the returning one landed on, and as the last aircraft got into the wires, Captain and Commander (F) rushed straight back to their bunks, and Gick debriefed the crews from there. It was the only way to conserve enough energy to cope. Wings had a rope rigged from FlyCo down to the flight deck, and would do a fast slide down it to deal with an emergency, in his personal rig of the day of white submarine sweater and bright red woolly nightcap with a long tassel, which made him look, thought armourer John Guise, 'a bit like Scrooge without his candlestick'.

4

'Contact firm, classified submarine'

THE SHIP NEEDED REPLENISHMENT, the ship's company, and especially the aircrews, rest and refreshment, before *Vindex*'s next round-the-clock engagement, Operation CW, which was to be carried out in much the same area of the North Atlantic as before, just slightly further north, around 53° north, 28° west.

They had to take their turn in the queue, as all the anchorages in the Clyde were full and there was brisk naval traffic all the time. The lighter *Marc Miller* appeared with oil on the forenoon of 1 April, the NAAFI boat with fags and nutty next day, the ammo lighter on the 4th. The hands on part of ship took time off to lean on brooms and squeegees and watch the ships go by. There were escort carriers *Biter* and *Ravager*, and the new Yankee-built CVE HMS *Khedive* with fighters filling her flight deck, their own narrow sister *Campania*, the homely *Pretoria Castle*, the old *Argus*, the battlewagon *Anson*. On the afternoon of the 8th a party of ATS girls came to tea in the wardroom, which was all right for some ...

It seemed to Percy Gick that his Sea Hurricanes ought to have rocket projectiles, so that if a U-boat was damaged by a Swordfish he could flash a fighter out to finish her off. When they had finished flying and were on their way back to Greenock, he had had a Hurricane wing brought up on the flight deck, made fast a Swordfish RP rack to it and fired four rockets. Then an aircraft was fitted with two rockets under each wing. Gick dictated a letter, which the Captain signed, describing their successful preliminary trial and extolling the advantages of an RP-fitted U-boat-busting fighter, and requested that Boscombe Down should carry out official airborne trials with *Vindex*'s modified Hurricane within the next two days, so that they could have the aircraft back on board and equip the others before they sailed again. He rushed down to the Admiralty, managed to get his letter of authorisation signed by all the relevant heads of departments and a couple of Sea Lords, and got it to Boscombe Down just as Blitz Gough arrived there in their special Sea Hurricane.

This pleasantly crazy and frequently outrageous ex-Etonian was stronger on flying than diplomacy and had a run-in with an awkward RAF wing commander, but Wings got his clearing letter signed by an air commodore, agreeing that it was safe to use the installation. Three days later *Vindex*'s Hurricanes had been fitted with RPs, five of them retaining their four cannon

Sub-Lieutenant (A) Eric Johnson, RNVR, (left) was pilot to Sub-Lieutenant (A) Malcolm Piercy, RNVR's observer (right), with Leading Naval Airman Alun Jones as their TAG, in a new Swordfish crew which joined *Vindex* in April, 1944.

as well. The other fighter had two of its cannon removed to make way for two marine markers for the rapid investigation of HF/DF U-boat bearings.

Commander (F) usually flew ashore ahead of the ship with the report of the operation just completed for C-in-C Western Approaches, Sir Max Horton, and he and Bayliss often had dinner with Sir Max. One evening Gick complained that they needed radio altimeters, which were in stores in London but unavailable to them. Sir Max promptly threw them out halfway through their dinner to catch the night train to London, where a signal of authorisation from Liverpool was waiting for them, they loaded the altimeters into a lorry and landed with them back on *Vindex* at night while she was anchored off Greenock.

On the evening of 10 April Surgeon-Lieutenant John Shaw joined the Medical Department in *Vindex*. He had trained at the Middlesex Hospital, and in August 1943 he and five other Naval Medical Officers were posted to HMS *Daedalus* to do the new Aviation Medicine Course, for the training of medics who would be mainly responsible for the care and wellbeing of aircrews. The course was designed to give them an idea of the physiology of flying. They were encouraged to fly, mainly in Barracudas, to experience anoxia and the effects of gravity when going into a steep dive or turn, when the pilot was liable to black out. After the course he was posted to the air station HMS

Another new crew for the second sortie: (left to right) Sub-Lieutenant (A) M.G. 'Drip' Oakley, RNVR (observer), L/NA Alan Greedy (TAG) and Sub-Lieutenant (A) Bob Shaw (pilot).

Jackdaw at Crail, in Fife, which trained torpedo pilots. Here he flew in various aircraft, mostly Barracudas and Avengers, and after a few months was posted to *Vindex*.

He found the medical supplies and equipment in the ship's Sick Bay reasonably adequate, though there was no penicillin, which by this time was the essential antibiotic. Attached to the Sick Bay was a ward with a dozen swinging cots, as well as an operating theatre, though he wondered how he would manage to keep his feet to do any surgery at sea.

The air squadron was still without a CO, but early in the forenoon of 12 April Lieutenant-Commander F. G. B. Sheffield, RNVR, came aboard to take command. To take over from Zeke Cooper was a difficult task, but the short, balding, lively Freddie Sheffield, a former Oxford don and latterly Walrus pilot, who had to have special blocks fitted to his rudder pedals, soon settled in and became very popular. Observer John Vallely, a Scottish VR lieutenant, followed him 24 hours later, to take over from the tired Paul House, who had seen enough action for a while, though he himself was not pleased when he got a transfer to the observer school at Arbroath as an instructor.

...and new weapons. Sea Hurricane aboard *Vindex*, with new rocket projectiles fitted under the wings. Gun armament of four 20-millimetre cannon can be seen in the wings.

On the 14th *Vindex* was surrounded by supply boats. No sooner had oiler *Juliana* finished pumping on her port side when the *Thermal* took over, while to starboard the petrol lighter *Guidesman* plugged in and the stores lighter *C617* took over from the *C8*.

While all this was going on, five new Swordfish crews joined the Squadron: Lieutenant J. A. Higginson and his observer Sub-Lieutenant A. G. Winfield, Subbies E. R. A. Johnson and M. F. Piercy, R. E. Jordan and Gareth Jenkins, R. J. Shaw and M. G. Oakley, Kiwi pilot H. Hames and observer J. Paterson.

Young Eric Johnson, who had been a clerk in a gravel company, was a natural pilot, and had rated a 'Much above average' assessment after deck landing training aboard HMS *Ravager*. He and his observer, Londoner Malcolm Piercy, with TAG Alun Jones from Nottingham, worked well together as a crew. With Jordan's and Shaw's crews they had been sent, after *Ravager*, to join No. 836 Squadron at Maydown in Northern Ireland to form the little air group for one of the hybrid Merchant Aircraft Carriers, known as MAC ships, but had been switched suddenly to the General Service *Vindex*. Swordfish observers J. P. M. MacDonald and Alf Murrant also joined the Squadron. 'Force On' Gough had departed for a new appointment. There was a new Sea Hurricane pilot, W. A. Johns, and Jimmy Green had taken over the leadership of the fighter contingent.

They finally got rid of the *Guidesman* at half-past seven on 15 April and the hands could be put to cleaning and storing ship. The *C617* cast off at ten o'clock, the cable party was mustered on the foc'sle at noon, Special Sea Dutymen closed up 20 minutes later, and *Vindex* was under way by one o'clock. Afternoon and evening were spent in the Clyde exercising with Hurricanes, Swordfish and three visiting Fulmars, then the ship anchored in her familiar T Berth in Rothesay Bay, at two hours' notice for steam, the Fulmars still aboard. She weighed at nine o'clock next morning for a 4-inch practice shoot and more flying with the Fulmars, as well as deck landing workouts for her new Swordfish crews. The Stringbag TAGs had now lost their Lewis guns, which they had never fired in anger. These were replaced by cameras, not the light type promised, but the old large unwieldy F24 variety.

Flying practice continued in the Clyde. On 17 April Kiwi Hurricane pilot Johnny Moore volunteered to fly a Swordfish taking Denis Trussell and New Zealand pilot Hames to Machrihanish. Moore had had some experience in Stringbags, but his take-off was frightening—to everyone in the aircraft and on the flight deck. The aircraft started off down the deck, but Moore had forgotten that the airscrews of Hurricane and Swordfish turned, and thus exerted torque, in opposite directions. To counteract the torque, therefore, he applied starboard rudder instead of port. The Swordfish veered sharply to starboard, and none of the pilot's frantic movements on rudder bar or joystick could stop it. The starboard wing hit the bridge, smashing the glass screens. Moore retained the memory of Captain Bayliss' startled face. Percy Gick picked up a large piece of glass which had missed him by an inch and dropped it fastidiously over the side. On the 21st the Stringbag of Ron Huggins, Pat

Calcutt and TAG Hampton ditched with suspected petrol pollution. When rescued, the tall, thin Huggins, dripping wet, said thoughtfully, 'Never a dull moment.'

On Monday 24 April, Commander McCoombe, who had done so much to bring the carrier to a state of efficiency, left the ship, handing over to Commander J. K. Whittaker, RNVR. *Vindex* began night deck landing training for the new crews, and one Stringbag went into the barrier. For take-off Percy Gick had introduced a new ploy which helped to keep down the accident rate even in the most trying weather. When the Squadron had joined the ship there was a tendency among pilots to haul their aircraft off the deck as soon as possible. This involved a risk of dropping a wing amongst guns or other objects projecting above flight deck level. It was most dangerous when the ship was out of wind, as immediately the wheels left the deck the aircraft started to drift. Now pilots were taught to keep their wheels hard down on the deck until they reached the forward round-down. Using this technique pilots had frequently flown off at night with the ship 20 degrees out of wind and still swinging, without noticing any adverse effect.

He had much the same answer to the difficulty of landing in filthy weather, and would tell his pilots, 'The moment you're committed to a landing, stuff the pole hard forward. At least if you miss the wires you'll enter the barrier like a gentleman—not amongst your friends ahead of you.'

In a Swordfish, in fact, a barrier aboard *Vindex* was not usually a great disaster. At the far end of the hangar was rigged an assembly box with mainplanes on either side, a complete tailplane assembly just above, an undercarriage below, and in front an engine unit with propeller requiring only four bolts to fix it to the front of a fuselage. Their best turn-round was an aircraft which made a very ungentlemanly arrival, wrote off its starboard mainplane on a pom-pom at the after end of the bridge island, its port mainplane in the barrier, buried its engine in the island, and damaged its after fuselage. This aircraft, or what was left of it, with the same number painted somewhere on the fuselage, took off again 13 hours later. Unfortunately someone had left a slack plug in the bottom of the engine sump, and just 13 minutes afterwards the oil ran out and the plane ditched. It was timed that it also took 13 minutes for a destroyer to rescue the crew from the water. It was lucky/unlucky 13.

With no catapult, getting a Swordfish off the deck with a worthwile warload was a problem. One answer was the Robinson Patent Disengaging Gear sited on the very curve of the round-down aft, with the aircraft attached to it by a single strop. The pilot opened up to full revs, the strop was released, and he went off with a head start equivalent to about a knot and a half of wind speed.

In the evening of the 24th the ship anchored while the Canteen Manager took on more stores, then she pulled up the hook and was off down the Clyde and round the Mull of Kintyre heading for Ireland. Swordfish did circuits and bumps until half-past two in the morning, a four-plane patrol was flown off in the forenoon, and *Vindex* came to in eight fathoms off Moville early in the afternoon. At half-past eight the commanders of the ships of the 9th Escort Group, with which *Vindex* was to operate this time, came on board for a conference, and the carrier weighed at 8.45 p.m. for operations in the Atlantic against U-boats, followed shortly afterwards by her close escort, the RCN frigates *Matane* and *Stormont* of the 9th EG.

An hour later two Swordfish fitted with the new ASV Mark XI were flown off but the proximity of land made radar conditions almost impossible, and they were recalled. One aircraft returned without difficulty, but the Stringbag of Higginson and Winfield got into severe navigational difficulties in cloud, during which they tried to jettison their depth-charges upside-down, and eventually found their way to RAF, Ballykelly, in Northern Ireland, then on to RNAS, Maydown, next day, finally catching up with the ship on the 29th.

Vindex, meanwhile, had left Tory Island to port and begun zigzag. The RCN frigate *Swansea* joined her escort at 6 a.m. on the 27th, and Hurricane patrols were flown throughout the forenoon.

One of these sighted the three frigates HMS *Bickerton*, *Aylmer* and *Bligh*, forming the First Division of the 5th Escort Group, commanded by Commander Donald MacIntyre in *Bickerton*. The 5th EG had been acting in support of the escort of Convoy ONS233. It was a fairly new team, and this assignment, uncomplicated by U-boat attack but made interesting for the first three days by the usual Atlantic gales, served as a good shakedown cruise. 'A large proportion of the ships' companies,' MacIntyre wrote, 'had hardly been to sea before, except to bring their ships back from building in the States, where they had lived on the fat of the land and had grown soft. The first days were therefore more of a "throw-up" than a "shake-down" for them.'

The convoy appeared to be unthreatened and on 26 April MacIntyre had been ordered to join the *Vindex* group, which 'gave us hopes of livelier employment ...'

He was, however, worried about the fuel state of his thirsty steam frigates and as soon as he came up with *Vindex* he signalled her requesting a topping-up. Bayliss' close escort were diesel ships with a capacity and consumption commensurate with his own, but to give MacIntyre the amount he wanted would drain off 20 per cent of his total capacity, and he could not forecast how long he might have to keep the sea with the 5th. He was also concerned about the length of time he would have to steam on a steady course at slow speed while refuelling without being able to take avoiding action except in a clear emergency, by which time it would probably be too late. On the first operation he had had to withdraw his entire group to screen *Vindex* while refuelling, and had lost many hours of valuable hunting time. He could cope with his close-escort diesel boats, but he told MacIntyre he could only have 75 per cent of what he was asking for, at least until a clearer picture of the tactical situation had formed.

On this understanding *Vindex* veered her oil pipeline to *Bickerton* and began pumping. SOE slipped, and *Bligh* came up for her drink, followed by

Postman. An American-built frigate manned by the Royal Navy delivers mail to *Vindex* in the North Atlantic, April, 1944.

Aylmer. MacIntyre then made off, and *Vindex* was free to resume patrols, only to find that there was not enough wind. It was not until the end of the middle watch that a Stringbag was able to get off with a depth-charge, and in the morning the Hurricanes took over. Johnny Moore intercepted a bogey which turned out to be a Coastal Command Halifax not showing IFF.

At midday MacIntyre's Second Division, ex-American turbo-electric destroyer-escorts, classified in the RN as frigates, HMS *Keats, Goodson* and *Kempthorne,* came thirstily up for a turn at the teat. The first two got their quota, but it grew dark and the third little frigate got none that day. Overlapping patrols of two Swordfish at a time flew through the dark hours, pushing out to 50 miles ahead of the carrier, and one of the first two back crashed on deck. Jordan and Jenkins, one of the new replacement crews, took off on their first operational patrol at 3 a.m., after Roy Jordan had made his fifth consecutive practice night landing. Two Hurricanes scrambled at the beginning of the morning watch; four fighters went off just before noon. *Aylmer* and *Kempthorne* joined, the latter for the sustenance she had missed the day before. While she was happily glugging away, a solitary Swordfish appeared amongst the scrambling Hawkers. It was Higginson's prodigal Stringbag from Maydown. He had to wait for the frigate to cast off and two Hurris to take off before the carrier's new batsman, J. A. G. 'Jagger' Mills, could bring him in.

Swordfish were swapped for Hurricanes at eight bells in the second dog watch, and just after midnight Bob Shaw's Swordfish J made a forced landing in the sea with petrol trouble, 15 miles from *Vindex*.

Shaw and his TAG got into the K-type dinghy, but observer Oakley had a struggle to reach it. Exhausted and practically unconscious, he only saved himself from drowning by keeping his helmet on and fastening the chin strap to the top of the dinghy, thus keeping his head above water. Meanwhile the others were firing red rockets, and in *Vindex*'s Air Direction Room Keith Brading, who had both Stringbags of the patrol on his screen, guided Swordfish A from 32 miles away to the exact location of the dinghy, which A's observer picked up on his ASV when they were two miles off. This crew fired flares, and *Aylmer* was able to make straight for the castaways and take them aboard. Pilot and TAG were transferred to *Vindex* in the carrier's whaler in the forenoon, but Oakley had suffered from his immersion and was kept on board the frigate. He had been in the water for 45 minutes, but after the first ten minutes he remembered nothing until coming to in *Aylmer*'s Sick Bay.

Signals were received from the Admiralty at midday. Shortly afterwards the three ships of the 9th EG left for a new area and the Second Division of the 5th closed to form *Vindex*'s screen, while the First Division steamed ahead, spread out at visibility distance from the carrier, to form a striking force. Bayliss then shaped course for the area of the U-boat weather reporter, known as Uncle Willie. Very little flying was possible en route, owing to bad weather, poor visibility and a temporary failure of the ship's type 281 radar, though at 2.15 p.m. on the 30th Johnny Moore's Hurricane was scrambled to intercept a bogey picked up some 80 miles away. He made a swift interception of yet another Coastal Command Halifax not showing IFF, a failure all too common among RAF maritime aircraft.

Vindex and her screen reached Uncle Willie's patch at about 8 a.m. on 2 May. All MacIntyre's HF/DF teams were inexperienced, but at 8.41 Bligh got a bearing on an enemy making weather-type signals, received in *Vindex* immediately after the dawn patrol had landed on. Three more Swordfish fitted with ASV Mark XI were flown off immediately and made a very thorough saturation search of the area throughout the forenoon, but without success. By that time it had become clear that *Bligh*'s operator had read off the reciprocal of the correct position, although *Bligh* hotly denied it. Swordfish searched until midnight, when the weather became too bad for further flying. MacIntyre's green operators failed to pinpoint Uncle Willie's evening weather report. The U-boat knew that the hunters had HF/DF, and constantly varied the frequency on which he broadcast, which made the job of intercepting that much more difficult.

The weather was too rough for Hurricanes on the 3rd, but Swordfish nosed around the area of a fix reported by the Admiralty after Enigma interception. By now it had become possible, from the accumulation of HF/DF reports, to narrow down the area of the German met man's likely reappearance, and from

My next trick . . . Senior Pilot of 825 Squadron, Lieutenant Gordon Bennett, approaches *Vindex* to pioneer the landing of aircraft while the carrier is refuelling an escort vessel, 5th May, 1944

now on saturation sweeps were made from shortly before the next report was due, every 12 hours. The bad news was that a gremlin had got into *Vindex*'s YE beacon, and the Hurricanes were deprived of any means of homing if they had R/T failure. MacIntyre's First Division again came in to refuel, *Bickerton* and *Bligh* on the 4th, *Aylmer* on the 5th.

While the frigate was still plugged in astern, *Vindex* flew off and landed on two Swordfish to prove that this was possible while refuelling, and at 3.30 p.m. stopped engines and lowered her seaboat to reclaim 'Drip' Oakley, who had been aboard the frigate for five days since his ducking on 30 April.

At 4.50 three Hurricanes, flown by the fighter leader Jimmy Green and the two New Zealanders Alister Martin and Johnny Moore, who had left New Zealand together and trained at the same air station, took off on a routine U-boat search. When he was about 70 miles from the ship Ali Martin called up *Vindex* and reported that a loss of Glycol coolant was causing his engine to overheat. He turned back for the ship, led by Jimmy Green, with the latter keeping up a steady stream of instructions for nursing the failing engine, and Moore telling him to 'hang on, Al'. About six o'clock when Martin's Hurricane was about 14 miles from the carrier, the engine seized altogether, and he called up the ship to say that he would have to bale out. He left the aircraft at 3,000 feet and dropped into a sea with a temperature of about 30° below zero.

Green and Johnny Moore circled, marking the spot for *Vindex*'s radar, and kept Martin in view until relieved by Jordan and Jenkins in the standby rescue Swordfish at 6.25. Jenkins had three spare dinghy packs in the rear cockpit to drop as near as possible to the swimmer. They were semi-inflated so that he could get into one without too much effort.

There was a heavy swell running and to drop a dinghy in the right position was virtually impossible. Jordan manoeuvred the Swordfish as close as he could and shouted 'Now!' Jenkins let go, but unknown to him the dinghy lead attachment had wound round his intercom leads and the compass rose bowl. The dinghy flapped in the slipstream, and Jenkins was being slowly throttled, until he managed to untangle himself. One of the dinghies did drop quite close to Martin, but he had been in the water a long time and was too weak to reach it. Jordan and Jenkins orbited the spot, helplessly watching him struggle in vain to reach the dinghy. At a few minutes after seven he was picked up unconscious by Lieutenant-Commander Frank Allen's ex-US frigate HMS *Goodson* of MacIntyre's Second Division.

Goodson did not carry a medical officer, and *Vindex* at once sent Ian Taylor across to the frigate in the seaboat. It was the second time in three days that Taylor had been called out to the New Zealander after a crash in the sea. On the earlier occasion Martin had ditched his Hurricane and got clear from 20 feet below the surface. Ron Huggins had wanted to dive off the carrier to rescue him. In a strong wind and moderate sea, with an unpractised boat's crew, Taylor had tried to get upwind of Martin, with the carrier trying to give him a lee. There was no long line in the whaler, so Taylor had thrown an oar to the swimmer. Martin had gripped it, they floated down on him, grabbed an oar and pulled him in.

When Taylor reached *Goodson* this time he found Martin still unconscious, in spite of the efforts of the frigate's sick berth attendant to revive him. Taylor then started artificial respiration. For what seemed like hours he went on, pumping, pumping ... The whaler made a second trip from *Vindex* with oxygen and carbon dioxide cylinders, but all efforts failed. Martin's heart had stopped, and he never regained consciousness. At nine o'clock *Goodson* signalled *Vindex* that he was dead. An hour later the whaler brought a weary and despondent Ian Taylor back to the carrier.

By this time the *querencia* of the weather reporter had been narrowed down to a strip about 20 miles wide, and half an hour after the seaboat had been hoisted, the last detail of the day, three Swordfish, went up to carry on Operation Swamp and saturate this patch.

Aircraft X, pilot Ron Huggins, observer Pat Calcutt, TAG Frank Smeeton, had been flying for about 40 minutes when Calcutt picked up a contact on his Mark XI ASV, some 90 miles from *Vindex*.

Calcutt, who was now Senior Observer of the Squadron, held the target, which he definitely considered to be a U-boat. Visibility was down to one mile. Calcutt tried a flare, but cloud had forced the Swordfish down to 350 feet, and it went into the sea without igniting. They made a second run on the target, but the blip disappeared at three-quarters of a mile. He marked the spot, Smeeton signalled the position to 5th EG, and the Swordfish had to turn back and head for *Vindex*, as its fuel load, restricted in order to lift two depth-charges off the deck, was running low. For the same reason Huggins requested permission to dump the DCs before returning to the ship, and let them go when the aircraft was about 15 miles from *Vindex*.

He had barely dropped them when he sighted a fully-surfaced U-boat directly beneath them. Cursing his luck he did what he could to hang on to the enemy to buy time for other attackers to reach the scene. By continually crossing and recrossing the submarine, low enough to make the Stringbag too tempting a target for the U-boat's gunners, he held her on the surface for 15 minutes, time for him to mark the spot with a smoke float, and for *Vindex*'s radar to fix it.

The other two Swordfish aloft were vectored to the scene and at 10.40 p.m. another Stringbag took off from *Vindex* to assist. The light was leaving the sky as this aircraft approached the area, and a heavy mist began to roll up quite quickly. When they got to the fixed position they could just see Huggins' smoke float from 50 feet. Several Swordfish were now circling round in the fog. In *Vindex*'s Air Direction Room the R/T speaker crackled. 'For God's sake step us up!' The FDO obliged. Chris Williams' aircraft, the last to find the fix, was at the bottom of the pile.

By the time they got the signal to return to the ship they were flying blind in fog and darkness. In his previous accidents Chris Williams had had no time to be afraid, but this time he had his first experience of real fear. With their radar they located *Vindex* easily enough, but they could not see her and by this time their petrol was running dangerously low.

The ship could hear them droning overhead and tried to help by beaming a searchlight straight upwards, but this only blinded them as they flew into it. Then *Vindex* dropped a string of flame floats astern to give them a flarepath, but the fog hid them from the groping Stringbag.

By now the three airmen could hear the note of panic in each other's voice. To make things worse, the radio altimeter, which normally read from 50 feet downwards, had broken down. The pilot thought he was at 50 feet, until his wheels skimmed the wave crests. In the rear seat Williams felt utterly helpless. Aimlessly he tried to stand up to look about him, but his rubber-soled boots slipped on the wet metal cockpit floor.

The pilot took the Swordfish higher, hoping to find a gap in the fog, and miraculously they burst into a clear patch with, right below them, the carrier, every light on her blazing. Down went the nose of the Stringbag and it was soon bouncing along the flight deck like a rubber duck. As they came to a stop, the engine coughed, spluttered and stopped, the last droplet of petrol used up. Chris Williams climbed out and kissed the deck. His oppo Alf Bleasdale rushed up and said 'Christ, you look as white as a sheet!'

Visibility now closed down to within 400 yards, with cloud at sea level, and all aircraft were recalled. At half-past three towards the end of the middle watch Freddie Sheffield, with John Vallely as observer and Chiefy Mick Dale as his TAG, took off in Swordfish V and made contact with Lieutenant-Commander Keene's *Keats*, which was hunting through the fog in the marked position of the U-boat's disappearance. He began a square search in weather conditions which Dale periodically reported to *Vindex* as 'Cloud base zero, visibility nil'.

Keats got a radar contact just after four o'clock and closed it, firing starshell. The contact immediately disappeared, and shortly afterwards the frigate's Asdic got a ping and she began an attack, but the wily Uncle Willy had released an SBT Submarine Bubble Target, and *Keats* was depth-charging her own original DC disturbance in the water.

The U-boat herself was safe at 200 metres. An hour later John Vallely, a virtuoso on ASV, picked up 5th EG and directed them, through Dale's radio, using radar to keep track of all the ships involved, to *Keats*. *Vindex*'s Air Direction Room received a mangled message from *Keats* reporting that she was engaging a U-boat and Sheffield's aircraft was vectored across to make a Cobra search for the enemy.

Keats was still banging away when, at 5.18, MacIntyre in *Bickerton*, still about two and a half miles from *Keats*, heard his Asdic operator Bill Ridley report 'Contact firm, classified submarine' over the loud-speaker on the bridge. Twenty minutes later, with the U-boat last heard about 700 yards on her starboard bow moving deep at about two or three knots, *Bickerton* began directing *Bligh* in a creeping attack, passing her ranges and bearings of the submarine and course to steer. Masked by her own propeller noises, the U-boat's hydrophones could not now hear the frigate approaching slowly from dead astern.

At 5.51 *Bligh* ceased transmitting on Asdics and began a listening watch, reducing speed to five and a half knots. At 5.58 she was in station ahead of *Bickerton*.

It was not easy to steer the courses ordered by *Bickerton*. The sea was rough and with *Bligh*'s slow speed made her sluggish to answer full rudder. Every so often Lieutenant-Commander 'Jackie' Cooper asked his engine room for short bursts of revs to take her to ten knots to point her on the desired heading.

Right on six o'clock MacIntyre's very familiar voice, hoarse with excitement, was heard over the inter-ship radio to order 'Stand by to plaster!'

One minute passed. 'One hundred yards to go!'

Another long minute. 'Sixty yards to go!'

Thirty seconds ... Fire!'

Bligh commenced firing a 26-charge pattern, with settings for 500 and 856 feet. Twenty-two charges were fired, then excessive vibration on the quaterdeck made reloading of the throwers virtually impossible. One charge jumped off the loading rails on to the deck, and all the hinged flaps on the thrower rails were severely buckled. Some charges detonated prematurely in the water. The sixteenth charge went off at very shallow depth. Soot belched out of *Bligh*'s funnel and her stern whipped with the shock of the explosion close under her stern. A column of water thrown 100 feet high collapsed and swamped the quarterdeck.

At five minutes past six, as the last charge was exploding, the 750-ton *U765* broke surface half a mile dead astern of *Bickerton* and *Bligh* in the centre of the DC pattern and wallowed, engines stopped, in the heaving sea. MacIntyre could see 'the twisted, buckled plating of the U-boat's conning tower ... evidence that at least one depth-charge had found its mark.' The three frigates immediately opened up a very accurate fire upon the enemy.

Sheffield, Vallely and Dale in Swordfish V saw the U-boat come up about one mile on their port beam. Sheffield opened up to full throttle and turned towards her. At a range of 100 yards he dived to attack through mingled fire from the escorts and a weak defensive fire from the U-boat's ack-ack which nevertheless damaged his centre section and starboard mainplane.

Coming down at 120 knots on the submarine's port bow, he released his DCs at 75 feet. Dale saw them straddle the conning tower, 40 feet apart, one exploding under the conning tower, one close to the U-boat's starboard quarter, just abaft the conning tower. Some 30–45 seconds later the submarine broke in two, bow and stern each rising to 45 degrees, the position some 700 miles west-by-south of Valentia, and the two halves sank, leaving a dozen survivors in the sea. Two of them waved at the Swordfish as Sheffield flew low over them. *Bickerton* came up and rescued eight men.

Swordfish V landed aboard *Vindex* at 6.43. As the flight deck crew released the deck hook from the wire, Stovin-Bradford rushed across to the aircraft, climbed up the fuselage and asked Dale for his camera. A man from the ship's

Celebration. Wardroom party after *Vindex*'s first U-boat victory, 6th May, 1944.

photographic section stood by waiting to rush his pictures of the action below for developing. When Dale told him that he had forgotten all about pictures in the excitement of the action his face was a study in anguish and Dale himself felt very bad about it.

The identity of the U-boat was discovered from some of the prisoners, who also revealed that she had been one of five weather reporters, one of which was detailed for duty in turn. *U765* had been on the point of being relieved when she was attacked and her Captain, *Korvettenkapitän* Werner Wendt, thought that the earlier boat contacted by Huggins' Swordfish X had been her relief. In a signal sending Bayliss 'Warmest congratulations,' C-in-C Western Approaches confirmed 'Information from U/B Captain is considered correct'. MacIntyre was so elated at his group's share in the kill that he signalled to his frigates that they could now call themselves The Fighting Fifth—'a flamboyant gesture very much out of character for me'.

Immediately after this success a gale hit the group and blasted the ships for 48 hours. This appeared to stir up water resting in the bottom of the ship's petrol storage tanks, and after the next refuelling several pints of water were found in aircrafts' tanks. The precautionary measures which had to be taken, including the careful filtering of the petrol with the special filter developed by the Air Engineer Officer Lieutenant Molyneux and Senior Engineer Dan Shields, seriously handicapped flying for the rest of the operation, on top of the savage weather.

Despite rising weather, however, wind gusting at 45 knots and heavy hail showers, the Swordfish of 825 flew throughout the night of 6/7 May in pursuit of the second U-boat. '*Vindex*,' recorded Donald MacIntyre, 'had ideas of her own as to what was suitable weather for flying and used to keep her aircraft up in the most fearful conditions . . .' It was only when seas were breaking over the forward end of the flight deck and the carrier's stern was rising and falling 50 or 60 feet that flying was suspended, after three Swordfish had landed on with some difficulty at a quarter past six in the morning. At 9.45 a heavy sea hit and damaged P1 pom-pom sponson. An hour later the bridge watch-keepers, who felt marooned on their island, with seas breaking all round them, saw the melancholy sight of an empty raft on the starboard bow, and later a waterlogged ship's boat away to port. At nine o'clock in the evening the ship was still lurching heavily, with a roll of about 25 degrees, and three oil pipes were carried away, and next morning two fishes were found entangled in the wire barrier on the flight deck.

It was not until midday that day that MacIntyre and the Fighting Fifth were able to renew their search for the elusive second weather-reporting U-boat. The weather was now clear enough for flying, and when Bayliss received a report from Convoy ONF235 that it was in contact with one, possibly two, U-boats, with no new information on Uncle Willie's nephew, he decided to send Swordfish to protect the convoy. But the westerly gale had held up the latter as well, and it was now some considerable distance astern of its anticipated position, beyond Swordfish range, so Bayliss headed *Vindex* in that direction to close the distance.

At 4 p.m. MacIntyre in *Bickerton* reported an HF/DF bearing of a U-boat transmitting weather signals. By this time *Vindex* was 90 miles to the south-west of him. Bayliss, doubtful of the reliability of 5th EG's still green operators, thought that they might be reading off the reciprocal again, but gave them the benefit of the doubt, flew off a search of two Swordfish to a depth of 120 miles to cover this possible U-boat position, and altered course himself towards it.

The ships of the 5th EG were in the middle of the Gulf Stream, 'in waters teeming with shoals of fish and porpoises'. *Bickerton*'s Asdics were saturated with echoes all round the ship and her inexperienced operators could not distinguish shoals from submarines. 'Sometimes we were helped', MacIntyre found, 'by seeing the fish break surface in panic as they fled before some pursuer, or porpoises would be seen on the bearing, hurrying along with their graceful, arching motion.'

At last, when the Swordfish from *Vindex* were some 35 miles from the ships of the 5th EG, Lieutenant-Commander Campbell in *Aylmer* reported that he thought he had a submarine on Asdic. Bayliss at once ordered his aircraft to carry out Cobra patrols. The Stringbag of Eric Johnson, Malcolm Piercy and Alun Jones was airborne for three hours and 20 minutes on one of these stints.

Campbell attacked his contact but lost it, MacIntyre closed with *Bickerton* and *Bligh*, picked it up again and set up another creeping attack, guiding *Bligh* until she was once again astern of the enemy and slowly overtaking her.

The sea was still rough, and once again Cooper found it difficult to keep *Bligh* on a steady course at slow speed. MacIntyre, in his eagerness to get a kill and to anticipate detection by the quarry, gave in to temptation and allowed Cooper to increase speed. The increased turbulence from *Bligh*'s screws immediately cut off *Bickerton*'s Asdic beam and was picked up by the U-boat's hydrophones, so that the submarine was able to make the vital alteration of course as *Bligh*'s depth-charges were sinking down through the water towards her, and when they exploded she was just clear of their 30-foot lethal range. Bubbles which rose as the U-boat vented her ballast tanks to go deeper gave MacIntyre cause to hope against hope that the submarine had after all been holed, and he was bitterly disappointed when at dawn next day Huff-Duff picked up the usual U-boat weather report.

Vindex had had trouble during the night from interference on the Fleet Air Arm R/T frequency, caused by another carrier using an exercise call sign, which was so bad at Strength 5 that all three Swordfish airborne were out of R/T touch for three-quarters of an hour when they were over 70 miles from the ship. Then a worse calamity occurred.

Young Peter Humphreys, engine room subbie turned Flight Deck Engineer, was always tired. He had spent the previous forenoon, as usual, inspecting all the flight deck gear, particularly the arrester equipment. The wires themselves and the shackles and sheaves at the end of them had to be closely checked for wear and replaced if too dangerously frayed—it took half an hour to fit a new wire. To inspect the big hydraulic rams, and the system of pulleys which led the wires to them, which controlled the expansion and contraction of the wires, meant crawling along narrow spaces immediately underneath the flight deck, and there were the controls on the catwalk to inspect, the levers for raising and lowering wires and barrier, the foot pedal for returning the stretched wires to their pre-engaged positions athwart the flight deck.

Also under Peter's charge was the all-important aircraft lift situated aft in the flight deck. The movement of the huge slab of the lift platform itself was controlled by a 220-volt electric motor in a compartment below the bottom of the lift well, assisted by a counterweight to balance the weight of the lift platform and any aircraft on it, located inside a sealed casing, which had no inspection doors, on one side of the well. By the morning of 9 May, with all the intensive use of this single lift for the round-the-clock movement of Swordfish and heavy Hurricanes in and out of the hangar, the wires on which the counterweight was hung had become stretched. There came the fatal moment, at 9.45 that morning, when the counterweight reached the bottom of the lift well before the platform had reached flight deck level. The switch which normally tripped when both weight and lift reached the extreme of their travel, cutting off the motor, did not trip. All the wires of the motor windings burned out trying to push the lift platform up the last important foot or so, and the lift was stuck—with the morning patrols to fly off.

The lift could be operated by hand cranking, but it took a whole hour to move it either up or down. Chief Engineer Weir and the Senior, Dan Shields, were called. Hector Weir could not help remembering that just before they had sailed, he had lectured to an audience of Sea Cadets on the operation of an escort carrier, and the first question afterwards, by a young scout had been, 'Sir, with only one lift, what would you do if it broke down?'

A messenger was sent for the Flight Deck Engineer. Humphreys, after his inspection schedule in the forenoon, repairs in the afternoon, and the whole night on the catwalk supervising his stokers in the operation of the arrester controls, had done what he had now got into the fixed habit of doing and got his head down in a bunk in the Ready Room. The bosun's mates knew his routine and knew where to find him for a shake three or four minutes before any flying was due. But he normally slept in a middle bunk. This time, finding the middle one occupied, he climbed up into the top bunk. The messenger could not find him in his usual sack, and he was left to sleep on. When eventually he awoke and strolled sleepily to the wardroom for some breakfast, someone said, 'My God, they've been piping for you all over the ship. We thought you'd fallen overboard. The lift's broken down. Percy's having kittens.'

When he rushed down to the lift well he found that his seniors had already started emergency procedures to get the lift moving again under power. The lift motor was beyond the resources of the ship to repair, and the only alternative means of power was the after capstan motor. Supervised by Hector Weir, work had started to move the motor from its bed on the quarterdeck, take it through the torpedo workshop and down into the lift motor space, for connection to the lift mechanism.

This was an awesome chore, with the ship pitching and rolling, and in the midst of operations. Very slowly the capstan motor was manhandled forward. This was a seaman's job, and was organised by Percy Gick. The engineers were responsible for the cutting of holes in bulkheads by oxy-acetylene torch, for securing it to the bottom of the lift well.

Meanwhile, flying had to go on. Using the agonisingly slow manual procedure, an aircraft which had crashed on deck was lowered into the hangar, replacement machines were inched up, and thereafter the ship was operated much like a tanker MAC ship, which had no hangar, with all aircraft being maintained on the flight deck. The capstan motor was lowered into place below the lift well, the engineers welded it to the deck, connected it to the driving drum of the lift motor, and Commander (F) could range his aircraft properly again. This process was never entirely satisfactory with only one lift, which meant that much pre-operational planning for the use of individual aircraft had to be done, and even then, with a super-efficient garage manager like Press-On Percy, sometimes half a dozen aircraft had to be pulled out on deck before the right one for take-off could be ranged.

The repair took 24 hours. While it was under way Gordon Bennett, Peter Couch and Joe Palmer landed on in Swordfish LS416 with the lift down and *Keats* being refuelled astern. Following the previous experience of take-off and landing while *Aylmer* was oiling on 5 May, the frigate kept well out on *Vindex*'s quarter, as for foul weather refuelling, and there was no trouble.

With *Keats*, the most in need of replenishment, topped up, Bayliss was not too worried when foul weather did return again, with a Force 7 wind and a heavy sea and swell. He decided to postpone refuelling the other two ships of the close escort, which had enough fuel for a further ten days, but he could not spare any more for the three steam frigates of MacIntyre's 1st Division, *Bickerton*, *Bligh* and *Aylmer*, which had reached the prudent limit of their endurance, and at noon on 10 May he sent them home. He himself remained in the hunting area with the 2nd Division, *Keats*, *Goodson* and *Kempthorne*, and at one o'clock in the afternoon he was also in company with the sloops *Starling*, *Wild Goose* and *Wren* of Walker's 2nd EG. Together they continued the search.

Patrols went on throughout the night of the 10th/11th, with a very heavy swell building up all the time. At half-past three in the middle watch on the 11th Doug Webb's Swordfish M, observer Jimmy McIlwraith, TAG Al Mears, came in to land on. Norman Lachlan was as usual on the gallery deck and saw what happened next. 'The ship was heaving all over the ocean, bucking, yawing, it was a hell of a night. He got to the deck just as she took a terrific heave up ...' The starboard wing hit the deck, and the Stringbag skidded along trailing its wing, which snagged a wire. The aircraft slewed round to starboard and plunged over the side of the ship immediately abaft the bridge superstructure.

Aerial view of *Vindex* from astern. The aircraft lift is half-way between flight-deck and hangar, and was stuck in this position when Gordon Bennett landed his Swordfish aboard ship on 8th May, 1944. *Vindex*'s twin 4-inch quick-firing high-angle gun can be seen right aft.

Bayliss swiftly ordered 'Hard-a-starboard! Stop starboard!' The ship swung. 'Slow ahead together.' Frank Allen's *Goodson*, stationed five cables on *Vindex*'s quarter for just this purpose, also closed the spot. She reached the position of the crash first and spent two hours searching the ugly sea for survivors. Her whaler's crew sighted two men holding on to a rubber dinghy, but none inside it. The men were too weak to hold on. The whaler had men over the side with lines, but only managed to secure one, McIlwraith, in time. At half-past six the search for survivors was abandoned, and *Goodson* rejoined *Vindex*. A quarter of an hour later she reported that McIlwraith was dead. 'We did our best ...' signalled Allen. Neither Webb nor Mears was ever found. It was the TAG's second crash, and he carried a sharp knife in his flying boot, as he was always worried that he might be trapped in the cockpit under water.

Colours were half-masted at ten o'clock for the crew of Swordfish M. Shortly afterwards flying was suspended, as the ship was rolling too badly. Searches resumed at night were fruitless, and at nine o'clock on the morning of the 12th *Vindex* shaped course to clear the area and return to base. She reached the Clyde on the morning of Monday 15 May, after an uneventful passage.

As soon as 'Stop engines' had been ordered, Hector Weir turned his full attention to the urgent problem of the petrol contamination, which had not been solved by filtering. Night after night he had spent lying awake counting the aircraft landing on the flight deck above, wondering if any of the Squadron's young men, any one of whom could have been his son, had ditched in the cold, savage sea with a dead engine, blaming himself for the continuing unreliability of the fuel.

Round and round went his thoughts. The water could not be in the petrol when it was piped into the ship ... Something was happening *inside the storage tanks* ... The answer came to him slowly, but he became more and more convinced that he was right. The petrol was pumped from the storage tanks to the aircraft refuelling points in the hangar by compressed air ... When air is compressed it gets *warm* ... The six interconnected storage tanks were surrounded by *cold* water, as a safety precaution ... When the warm compressed air got inside the tank it was rapidly cooled, and condensed into *moisture* ... It was this water which was adulterating the petrol ...

So the compressed air method had to go. The alternative he came up with was daringly simple ... Dispense with the surrounding water. Fill the whole petrol system, tanks and pipes, with sea water, by ballast pump, driving out all air. Take aboard the petrol from the refuelling lighter, at the same time opening the outlet valve to the sea so that the sea water was forced out as the fuel came in. The light high-octane aviation gas would not mix with the salt water, and the result would be a tank completely full of uncontaminated fuel. When it was required to refuel aircraft, sea water was once again pumped into the system at one end. The sea water, because of its greater density, displaced the aviation spirit, driving it back through the system and up to the refuelling points. Having convinced Bayliss, he was given permission by the Admiralty to convert *Vindex*'s petrol system to the new arrangement. Luckily the ship now had a few weeks in which the work could be done.

Percy Gick also put this time to good use. To maintain round-the-clock flying, they had to get the crews out of the air, turn them round, and get them up again. Adjoining the crew room he had built a special air-conditioned, noise-proofed compartment containing a number of comfortable bunks in tiers, numbered and with reading lights at the head. As each crew came aboard they were debriefed, fed, allowed to wash, then installed in the bunks. The identity of the crewmen and the number of their bunks were then put on the availability board. After a certain number of hours a tally was put on the board indicating the amount of rest they had had, and thus their availability. It was a rough life for the crews, and as far as possible Bayliss and Gick, both flying sailors themselves, would try and release them after about four or five days for what Wings called a 'carefully controlled piss-up' in the wardroom.

The Irish connection. Bumboats alongside *Vindex* at Moville, Northern Ireland.

5

My A25

VINDEX sailed from Moville at 8.30 p.m. on Saturday 1 July with frigates HMS *Awe*, *Goodall* and *Bullen* and HMC minesweeper-escort *St Thomas* on another quest for U-boats. On 6 June Allied armies had landed in France, and the Battle of the Atlantic had taken second place in importance to the Second Front, with naval activity centred on the waters between England and the artificial Mulberry Harbour in Normandy. The heavy demand for escorts there had also resulted in the temporary suspension of convoys to Russia.

There was no flying on *Vindex*'s first night at sea. At 7.30 next morning a Swordfish flew Commander (Ops) Stovin-Bradford to Hatston in the Orkneys for a conference on the tactical situation, and returned through ominously thick weather at 9.45 p.m.

The murky visibility which the ships encountered as they steamed north towards Iceland did, however, seem to be the ideal conditions in which to try out the Squadron's brand-new Swordfish Mark IIIs, delivered from Abbotsinch on 21 June. These aircraft were all fitted with the new ASV radar Mark XI. This set had a rotating scanner housed in a big bulge under the nose of the aircraft, replacing the wing-mounted aerials of the old Mark II Stringbags, and the new machines looked pregnant. The observer now had a PPI (Plan Position Indicator) screen in the cockpit, with a revolving scan, in place of the old vertical scale. The positions of ships and land masses all round the operator were revealed as the scanner beam passed over them.

The new machines were also equipped with RATOG (Rocket Assisted Take-off Gear). The rocket tubes, five inches in diameter and 41 inches long, each weighing 66 pounds, were mounted on the aircraft in two clusters below the fuselage, one on either side, each cluster comprising from one to four tubes according to the all-up weight of the aircraft. The idea was to fire the cordite charge towards the end of a take-off run, thus reducing the amount of deck required and/or allowing a heavier warload to be lifted, even with light wind over the deck. In good conditions, four depth-charges could now be carried.

Take-off using RATOG was begun normally, with special emphasis on keeping the aircraft straight, as it was not easy to straighten up when the rockets were firing. When the optimum point was reached, the firing button on the throttle was pressed, hopefully setting off all the rockets simultaneously. The extra boost continued for about four seconds until all the cordite had been burned. The rockets and carriers were then jettisoned.

Getting aboard: Mark III Swordfish, with radar scanner visible under the nose, photographed from another Swordfish, about to break off to rejoin *Vindex*.

There *were* a few snags in using RATOG. It was better to fire late than early, or else the cordite could be used up before take-off speed was reached. Due to the vertical component of the rockets' thrust the aircraft could actually get airborne before normal flying speed had been reached, and when the cordite gave out, the plane sank dramatically, so the pilots were told not to be too anxious to press the button. It was also unwise to use RATOG to give extra climb, because when the sparks stopped flying the pilot could find himself in a stall.

When a RATOG cluster was fired at night it produced a 'Brock's Benefit' pyrotechnic display which could be seen for miles, giving away the carrier's position. A pilot, in a natural desire to see what the man ahead of him was doing, could be dazzled by the latter's fireworks, and it was prudent to keep one's head down.

The Swordfish pilots' front guns had been removed when RPs had been fitted, and it was an obvious convenience to use the joystick button to operate RATOG, the throttle button being connected, through selectors, to the weapons.

To make up for all the extra weight in the Mark III the TAGs were dispensed with. This meant that the observer had to look after the radio as well as radar and navigation, and be ready to man the Lewis gun, though these were hardly ever used and were often not carried. The 'O' still had to use a chartboard clamped to the for'ard bulkhead, though navigation was mostly

Swordfish peels off to make its approach.

The approach. The batsman guides the aircraft down. Note the other aircraft parked for'ard.

Down. The batsman has given the pilot the signal to cut his engine and he has hooked a wire and touched down.

done by ASV. A more comfortable bucket seat replaced the old collapsible stool, with straps to hold the observer in, rather than the 'G-string' or 'anti-cavorting chain' attaching the parachute to the cockpit floor. By the end of July all the TAGs of 825 Squadron had said their farewells to the *Tindecks*.

New RNVR Swordfish pilots Griffiths and Peter Brookes, and RNR Lieutenant D. A. Hook, who had formerly been a Second Mate with the New Zealand Shipping Company, had joined 825, and observers Currie, Drysdale, Eldridge, Michie and Wilkinson, to make up 14 crews in all.

An addition to the ship's staff who knew all about navigating a Stringbag in fog over the ocean was Stovin-Bradford's new understudy in the Ops Room, Lieutenant-Commander J. H. Palmer, RNVR, a very warm, friendly and sympathetic man who soon became generally popular. He knew when he was appointed to *Vindex* on 5 June that he was going to a ship with a great go-getting reputation, and found when he joined her on the 6th that she had a very efficient organisation. He found Captain Bayliss slightly intimidating at first. It was difficult to get used to a four-ringed RN Captain after dear old Captain Riddell of the MAC ship *Empire MacAlpine*, who hardly ever wore uniform. However, a party for some Wrens on the 7th helped him settle in.

Jim Palmer had been in HMS *Biter* on her maiden voyage across from the USA to Britain in June 1942. He had shared the general anxiety when this early escort carrier's suspect engines had broken down as she accompanied a fast convoy, the nail-biting moments when a Swordfish armed with a depth-charge crashed into the bridge island, and the Amatol-filled DC had had to be carefully extricated from the wreckage and lowered over the side.

In September 1943 he had been in one of the three crews which had flown their Swordfish aboard the *Empire MacAlpine*, the first MAC ship to see

The flight deck party rush to spot the Swordfish on the lift.

The aircraft, wings folded, is struck below.

Below in the hangar of HMS *Vindex*.

service, when she had accompanied the 66 merchantmen and 17 escorts of the combined convoys ONS18 and ON22 across the Atlantic through wolf packs armed with the new acoustic torpedoes.

Thick fog had closed in, and flying conditions were too bad until the afternoon of 1 September, by which time the U-boats had already made their attacks. The fog lifted briefly, and Sub-Lieutenant Singleton, with Jim Palmer as observer, took off from *Empire MacAlpine* for a patrol astern of the convoys. Ten minutes later the ships were enveloped in thick fog again. The Swordfish returned through the murk, blind except for Palmer's ASV and the MAC ship's own Mark 251 radar. So skilful were both operators, and so unusually free from error were their sets, that the aircraft passed directly over the ship and with the help of an Aldis lamp in the ship and a batsman using illuminated bats the Stringbag was brought safely down after only one wave-off.

Jim was an outdoors man. He loved walking and cycling in the countryside and was an expert at messing about in boats of all kinds. He enjoyed pulling an oar in the whaler race between the *Vindex* executive officers and her fighter pilots on 20 June, even though the young Hurricane jockeys won.

Vindex's Executive Officers also changed again and Commander Archbold joined the ship. He did not like cats and had them all drafted ashore from *Vindex*. But the rat colony on board soon got out of hand, and a fresh cat party had to be press-ganged into service.

Vindex's new Mark IIIs began their searches at 9.15 a.m. on 2 July and flew on throughout the day and night, then rain and mist and low visibility grounded them on the morning of the 3rd and kept them there for 24 hours.

The anti-submarine destroyer HMS *Bulldog** joined the group and assumed Senior Officer Escort.

Flying resumed at 10.50 a.m. on 4 July with a search by two Swordfish. One of these, Cumberland's and Jackson's NR885, soon developed ASV trouble, returned to the ship and was replaced by another Swordfish. This was the first of many failures by the new sets which beset the Swordfish for the first seven days of the operation. In that period 20 out of 69 sorties failed because of faulty ASV, and crews dripped and compared the new equipment with the old Mark X used on the first cruise, when in 95 sorties only eight had had ASV failures.

The cabling of the new installations in the aircraft was bad, and many of the components, notably the High Frequency unit and the scanner, were faulty. The whole assembly of the set was bad for positioning, especially the leads, which were exceptionally badly made. Loose, broken or twisted sockets were responsible for nine of the faults discovered in the air, and possibly others. Brand-new clips were of such poor wire that they would not hold, and leads would come adrift in the air for no apparent reason. Grub screws on some of the sockets were not threaded sufficiently to grip the inner conductors, or the conductors were too short or too badly broken for the screw to make proper contact. Four times this caused a complete breakdown of the set in the air. In three aircraft the Indicator Unit mounting tray collapsed because a little thing like the stop pin in the elevating gear was too short. The transmitter valves had been used before on operations and were beginning to fail. There were many more defects, and with a demand on this operation for 12 aircraft to work round the clock without even a breathing space of a non-flying period during the day, the ASV repair/maintenance facility on board the carrier was swamped.

When a set *was* serviceable its ranges were good. A mountain on Lewis was picked up 67 miles away, and *Vindex* registered on the screen at 60 miles on two sorties, and often at between 40 and 50 miles. Sea returns at five to eight miles rose to 12 miles as serviceability gradually improved and the operators became more used to the new gear. In fact some embarrassingly accurate runs were made. One aircraft on a calm night homed on a blip which proved five times to be a double patch of oil. Another picked up a blip at 15 miles and homed on a dead flame marker in the water. Other aircraft ranged on the same tiny object at ten and eight miles.

Fog closed in again in the afternoon of 4 July. Two aircraft still in the air made brilliant landings through the vile murk with the help of R/T control from *Vindex*'s bridge, flame floats, Very cartridges and searchlights from the ship, as well as their own ASV and the YE homing beacon. Then flying was once again abandoned. The corvette *Pevensey Castle* joined at tea time, and the escorts then divided into two groups, destroyer *Bulldog*, frigate *Goodall*

* Converted from her old Fleet destroyer form, with a Hedgehog launcher replacing her forward 4.7-inch gun, and extra depth-charge throwers substituted for the aftermost 4.7-inch.

and *Pevensey Castle* acting as screen for *Vindex*, with frigates *Awe*, *Bullen* and *St Thomas* being detached to operate as a hunting group some 30 miles ahead.

The weather cleared after lunch on the 5th, with the mist and drizzle of previous days evaporating, and the 12 Stringbags kept watch-and-watch in the air.

About 9 p.m. the trawlers *Noreen Mary*, *W. H. Podd*, *Starbank* and *Colleague* were fishing approximately 19 miles west of Cape Wrath when one of the crew of the *Starbank* reported to the bridge that two torpedoes had just missed the ship. 'He's blind as a bat,' the Master said, 'he saw two big fish.' Two minutes later a U-boat with the number *U11* on her conning tower surfaced and began to attack the *Noreen Mary* with machine-gun and shell fire. Her Skipper called up the *Starbank*, which immediately slipped her trawl, steamed away from the attack and appealed for help on her R/T.

It was not until 20 minutes later that the lighthouse keeper at the Fair Isle Light reported that he was receiving faint and jumbled messages from an unknown vessel suggesting that a U-boat had surfaced ten miles west of Cape Wrath and was attacking ships.

The RAF's 18th Group could not help as all their bases were fog-bound, but anti-submarine trawlers at Aultbea and Stornoway and the big Fleet destroyers *Milne*, *Marne* and *Verulam* in Scapa Flow raised steam. At 10 p.m. the lighthouse keeper at Cape Wrath reported that he had been hearing gunfire to the south-west for about half an hour. *Vindex*, which was some 80 miles to the north-west of this position, 70 miles north of Scapa Flow, immediately scrambled Peter Hellyer and Johnny Moore in two Sea Hurricanes which happened to be on deck at the time. After 40 minutes' flying the two fighters reached the search area and patrolled for half an hour with no sign of a submarine. They then realised that their fuel was too low to return to *Vindex*, and headed for land, though they were also out of R/T touch with the carrier and could not let *Vindex* know their movements. They made a landfall but with darkness coming down had no idea where they were. The only possible place to land was a football pitch, with two big posts at each end. Pete Hellyer tucked his Hurricane under Moore's port wing. They made two passes at the field, and on the third both landed with wheels up, about 20 feet apart, unhurt, and found they were near Thurso, Caithness, on the northern edge of Scotland just west of the Pentland Firth. A Swordfish collected them and returned them to the ship two days later.

All these frantic efforts were too late to save the little *Noreen Mary*, which sank at ten o'clock with well over 100 shell holes in her. Some of her crew got away in a small boat but the U-boat machine-gunned them and only two badly injured men were left alive from a crew of ten.

Meanwhile more Swordfish striking forces were aloft, and Lend-Lease frigates HMS *Manners* from Londonderry and *Burges* from Larne joined *Vindex*, while HMC minesweeper-escort *Huntsville* led the anti-submarine trawlers *Lady Madeleine* and *Vizalma* from Stornaway, and the *Lady Beryl*,

York City, Brontes, Dauy, Cape Mariato, Southern Shore, Spurs and *Wolves* from Aultbea on Loch Ewe to prevent the retreat of the murderous U-boat between Cape Wrath and North Rona. Six Navy Hellcat fighters and one Flying Fortress took off from Stornoway to sweep the area of the *Noreen Mary* sinking looking for survivors and any further signs of U-boat activity. Just after midnight one of *Vindex*'s Swordfish got a good ASV contact seven miles northeast of the Butt of Lewis. The blip went off the screen, but aircraft patrolled the Cape Wrath–Butt of Lewis–North Rona triangle throughout the night.

The seemingly tireless *Vindex* aircrews continued with square searches in the same area well into the 6th. At 5 a.m. *Lady Madeleine* found the two badly wounded survivors of the *Noreen Mary*. Searches by overlapping flights of three Swordfish continued throughout the night of the 6th/7th, but all this maximum effort by the aircrews of 825 went unrewarded by anything other than continued disasters.

Firing circuits were being tested in a Swordfish at the after end of the flight deck prior to take-off. With the leads to the rocket projectiles on the underwing racks hanging down, the normal procedure was to insert a small bulb in the fuselage socket for the air mechanic in the cockpit to test the circuit. By mistake a tired armourer plugged in the rocket lead instead of the bulb. The man in the cockpit pressed the firing switch, the rocket fired. The blast killed the armourer, and the RP shot up the flight deck and badly damaged a Hurricane in the deck park for'ard, though miraculously no-one else was hurt.

Doggedly 825, motto *Nihil obstat*, let nothing prevent the round-the-clock patrols. Though the fog grounded Coastal Command, the Swordfish kept the air.

A force of three aircraft was ranged at 9.45 p.m., but one had water in the petrol and could not get off. This did cause some anxiety, as everyone had been confident that the trouble which had so plagued the Squadron in initial working-up and during the first Atlantic operation, the curse which had killed Bert Broadley, Mike Varley, Harry Burns and Basil Hall-Law, had been layed by the conversion of the after storage tanks to the patent *Vindex* displacement system.

The fault was quickly traced to human error under the pressure of operations. Petrol had been on transfer from the for'ard to the after tanks when the order was received to fuel aircraft in a hurry, which was actually nothing new aboard this ship. Down below in the refuelling control room a junior engineer was in charge of the petrol system. In the confined space he was half drunk on the petrol fumes, a sickly gas which could kill if inhaled long enough, and this young man had been on duty, because of a shortage of engine room staff, for more than 60 hours. He hastened to turn the valves back, but omitted to alter one very vital one, with the result that salt water was sucked directly into the system. This seriously impeded operations for 36 hours, until the contaminating water had finally been pumped clear, along with 500 gallons of precious petrol, but no disciplinary action was taken against the exhausted young officer.

A second aircraft of this strike had to return shortly after take-off with its ASV unserviceable, but the experienced observer of the third aircraft, Swordfish F, got a very good contact just before midnight about 40 miles south-west of the ship. He remained over the spot until relieved, and finally landed on with enough petrol left for about 15 minutes' flying. A flame float dropped by his relief, which should have burned for two hours, sizzled out after a quarter of an hour. Bayliss kept two Swordfish continuously over the spot, in spite of the suggestions from his surface vessels, two of which had reached the place, with the other two sweeping towards it, that the contact was a mine, a Merchant Navy raft or a whale.

Next day, 8 July, Bayliss recorded 'Still hunting, albeit on a somewhat catchy scent, hounds were finally lifted and laid on to a fresh fox.' Acting on a signal from C-in-C Western Approaches that the U-boat would pass to the north of Rockall, Bayliss ordered his four frigates *Goodall*, *Bullen*, *Burges* and *Manners* to establish a 60-mile patrol line on longitude 14° West, with its southern end close to Rockall, but a coding error put the ships many miles to the eastwards when the submarine actually rounded Rockall.

Bayliss was now worried about his fuel state. On his previous two operations he had only used 50 percent of the petrol in his tanks. He considered this an adequate working margin, and had brought only that much with him this time. But this had been seriously reduced by the unusual amount of flying and wastage, and he calculated that at the previous night's rate of consumption he had enough for only three more days of operations. The weather helped him save a little more, as it made flying impossible, with visibility only a few yards, from 3.30 p.m. until eight o'clock in the evening. A Swordfish got a good contact on the morning of the 9th. The hunting frigates were ordered to close and he compromised with his dwindling petrol stocks by restricting his permanent patrols to two Swordfish apiece. That way he thought he could just about squeeze four more days of flying. Then the weather cleared, and when reinforcements of Coastal Command Sunderlands and Liberators arrived to join the hunt, he was able to ration his patrols still further.

Another good contact was found and lost. It seemed clear that the U-boats had very good radar warning them of the approach of the hunters, and from the length of time they were remaining submerged they must be using the new schnorkel tube, which enabled them to ventilate and charge engines below the surface. Bayliss found himself wishing for the equally new sono-buoys, but reflected that a Swordfish carrying them would be seriously reduced in either offensive load or search area, and aircraft would have to fly in pairs, one with sono-buoys only. Now all his surface hunters were getting short of fuel as well, but he kept them on the trail. Then a savage gale and thick fog threw them all off the scent.

On the 10th he shifted to the north-east and refuelled *Goodall* and *Bullen* as he went. He was just wondering what else could go wrong to add further gall to this thankless mission, when the refuelling hose parted close to the carrier after only 30 tons had been delivered to *Bullen*. His seamen tried to recover the hose from the frigate, but *Vindex*'s thick wire messenger parted after taking the weight of the hose. *Bullen* then tried to get the hose aboard but got it wrapped round her starboard propeller. Three lengths of hose were eventually recovered and transferred to *Vindex*, and C-in-C Western Approaches ordered *Bullen* and *Goodall* back to Liverpool.

This left *Vindex* with *Manners*, *Pevensey Castle* and *St Thomas*. When a Coastal Command aircraft reported having attacked a U-boat 21 miles west-sou'-west of him, Bayliss sent *Manners* off to the spot. Then *Manners'* Asdic broke down. Retaining her for some sort of protection, he packed off *Pevensey Castle* and *St Thomas* in her place, and sent up more patrols.

The Swordfish had now been flying continuously, except for a break of five hours on 10 July, for 60 hours, and the crews were very tired. When at 6 p.m. *Vindex* was joined by HMS *Striker*, the Yankee-built CVE was very welcome. Now, at last, right at the end of another hard-pressed solo performance, *Vindex* had a partner. Now a proper arrangement could be made, whereby *Striker* took over all daylight flying, while *Vindex* was responsible for the dark hours.

Searches were flown throughout the night of the 11th/12th and begun again on the evening of the 12th. Johnson, Piercy and Jones, Jordan, Jenkins and Agger crewed the first two Swordfish up from *Vindex*. Johnson steered north-east, then north, along the coastline, Jordan headed east, then north. Taff Jenkins picked up a surface contact on his radar screen at about five miles range, near the area of attack on the fishing boat. The blip disappeared off the screen at two miles. They homed on to the position, dropped flame floats, and orbited the spot until a corvette came along to search. About midnight visibility closed down to 300 yards.

The patrol was recalled. Three Swordfish made it down safely, but the fourth crashed on deck.

The fifth was running out of petrol. *Vindex* could not pick out the aircraft on her radar, but she registered on the Swordfish's ASV screen, and eventually the carrier received a signal from the aircraft 'Am crossing the end of your flarepath'. Then there was silence. Somewhere up there in the murk, near but yet so far, the pilot was trying to go round again and get on to the proper line of approach for a landing, with the last few pints of petrol in his tank.

One of the escort vessels reported 'Aircraft passing low overhead'. Time passed and it became obvious that the Swordfish had used up its fuel and had ditched in the sea, time and place unknown.

Foreboding and frustration prevailed on the bridge of *Vindex*. Then Geoffrey Milner had a sudden feeling of absolute certainty that the missing crew could and would be found. He rushed down to the Ops Room, where the radar PPI was located and also the ARL (Admiralty Research) Table, on which a drive from the ship's gyro and log produced an illuminated automatic plot of the ship's position.

The ARL Table had been marked to show the ship's position when the messages from the lost aircraft and the sighting escort had been received. Milner asked and was quickly told how long the flares astern of the ship would have lasted, and with this information and the carrier's speed was able to estimate how far astern of the first mark the aircraft had then been. The escort which had sent the second message could be plotted by her known position in the escort screen relative to *Vindex* at the time, and by joining the two aircraft positions its probable course and speed could be deduced.

Of course, the basic data were imprecise. The duration of flare illumination varied, escorts had been known to get out of position ... There was also the snag that the ARL plot worked on a scale of 10 miles to the inch, too coarse for Milner's purpose. He had intended to alter this scale to 1 mile : 1 inch, but quickly realised that to alter all the previous positions accordingly would take too long and might compound error, so he stuck to the large scale.

All he could offer was a probable course and speed of the Swordfish at the time of the last message, nothing more, but he still felt supremely confident of success. A few minutes later another escort signalled that one of her hands had just reported that 'some time ago' he had heard a loud splash from the sea close by. Milner could not plot the position of the escort at the time of the splash because of her seaman's imprecise report, but by transferring the present position of the escort from the PPI to the ARL Table and back-plotting her course line it could be assumed that where this line cut the aircraft's probable course, as previously estimated, should be the position of the ditching—if the aircraft had not altered course.

Their rearmost escorts had not yet advanced very far from this position. On the PPI the nearest was HMS *Manners*, and Bayliss detached the frigate. Watching her on the PPI and continuously transferring her position to the ARL Table, Milner was able to pass her the necessary course alterations for his splash position.

When *Manners* arrived there, *Vindex* signalled her 'Aircrew should be close on your port beam'. Immediately, almost crossing this signal, the frigate replied 'We can hear shouting to port', and was soon picking up the Swordfish crew from the water. There was rejoicing in *Vindex*, and Captain Bayliss told Jordan and Jenkins that the corvette which had homed on their flame float had sunk the U-boat.

Vindex parted company with *Striker* and returned to the Clyde escorted by the minesweeper-escort HMCS *Arnprior* and the corvette *Launceston Castle*, which had brought *Striker* to the rendezvous, and anchored off Greenock at 10 a.m. on 14 July. The sociable Jim Palmer was one of those who was glad to get off the ship for a short time. He visited friends aboard the escort carriers *Activity* and *Biter*.

It had been fourteen days of fog, fatigue and technical failure, the sort of episode that was as much a part of war as the big battles. The serviceability of the new ASV sets had improved in the latter part of the operation, with only nine failures in 84 sorties between 7 and 13 July, but it was too late to affect the success of the operation.

Kilpatrick, the Senior Medical Officer, reported that the flying crews were '... fatigued but, despite the fact that flying had been more intense than on any previous occasion, the condition is more a true physical fatigue than the mental strain which has characterised the former operations ... the aircraft were operating at close range ... for at least a part of the operation there was land within possible range, and the sea was calm, making rescue, if necessary, much easier; all comforting thoughts to the flying crews and tending to increase morale. Also, there were more contacts, which lent more interest, and, lastly, there was very little dark, though this was to a large extent counteracted by the low cloud and fog ...'

Nevertheless, this operation had been carried out at greater pressure than either previous one, from the time the first U-boat was reported off Cape Wrath at ten o'clock on the night of 5 July until the welcome respite provided by *Striker*'s arrival at six o'clock on the 11th. Some 360 hours had been flown in this period, and towards the end of it exhaustion up to and sometimes beyond the efficiency threshold of the aircrews was reached, 'and I know,' reported Captain Bayliss, 'that, latterly, I myself was feeling considerable fatigue.' If he had, he had never shown it. As far as the ship's company could see, he never left the bridge, never slept, sitting up there on the special wooden chair he had run up for him by the ship's chief chippy.

The exhaustion of ground crews working in the hangar had produced an increase in minor injuries, and the maintenance of the faulty ASV sets and the RATOG installations had caused increasing strain among air electrical and armament ratings. The MOs had to deal with many cases of 'industrial fatigue'. Visiting the hangar, especially at night, they saw 'the same picture of men physically exhausted and dulled with lack of sleep, doing their routine jobs woodenly, almost automatically, though willingly'. Bayliss thought that more reliefs were vital, even if this meant swelling the numbers in the already overcrowded accommodation spaces in this small ship with the complement made unduly large for her size by all the Squadron personnel. And if only one carrier was to be used for the sort of operation which they had been working, another, back-up, squadron would have to be provided on top of this. A second carrier, as in the all too brief few hours of co-operation effort with *Striker*, was the best answer.

Meanwhile, there was a run ashore. Jim Palmer was able to go aboard his old *Empire MacAlpine* on 18 July and pay his respects to Captain Riddell, whom he would always remember with affection. Ten days later he was on board the MAC ship again to help the Master celebrate his birthday. For some there was leave, beautiful leave. *Vindex* normally lay two cables up-river from Gourock, and liberty boats ran to Princes Pier for the bars and dance halls of Glasgow. The usual rendezvous for officers was Rogano's Bar and Restaurant. Ratings often used the Central Hotel.

Warrior. *Vindex* shows the marks of sea time as she lies at anchor, Swordfish and Sea Hurricanes on deck. On this occasion her puny merchantile anchor appears to be holding.

Aircraft were used for leave whenever Nelson turned a blind eye. Bayliss lived in County Carlow in Eire, and discovered that MO John Shaw's wife was staying with relatives in Wexford, the adjoining county. Whenever he went on leave the Captain always arranged for Shaw to fly with him in a Swordfish from the ship to Sydenham airport in Belfast, from where they used to catch a train to Amiens Street Station in Dublin. At the end of leave a Stringbag would pick them up at Belfast and land them back on the ship.

Four days leave for each watch were given after one trip, and many of the ship's company had used up the four free rail passes granted per year. Navigator Geoffrey Milner had spent his, but Guns John Baker, who had a fiancée in the Midlands, said to him, 'I'll ask the Skipper for a Swordfish, and I'll fly us down to *Dryad* at Bournemouth.' Bayliss agreed, and they arranged to take off for Abbotsinch next morning on the first leg of the flight south. In

the wardroom that night John Baker said innocently to the Swordfish pilot sitting next to him, 'Look, I'm a Walrus man. How do you fly a Stringbag?' Milner, on the other side of him, felt himself turn pale, and almost cried off there and then.

But Baker took off without incident next forenoon, with Milner and Lieutenant Willett, the Mate of the Upper Deck, in the rear cockpit. Milner found the air navigation easy, and all went smoothly until they reached the Solway Firth, when there was suddenly a loud hush as the engine cut out and the propeller stopped revolving. The two passengers wanted to use their parachutes, but Baker told them to put their trust in him and the Almighty, and fiddled with the controls as the aircraft began to lose height. The engine started, then stopped again, and Baker pointed downwards.

In his excitement the other passenger pulled the ring which released his parachute in the cockpit. Baker made a good emergency landing in a farmer's field, but the aircraft, with the white parachute streaming behind it, hit a hummock and was a write-off. Milner was temporarily knocked out, but the farmer appeared with a bowl of water and a bottle of whisky. They were taken to the farmhouse, where the farmer's forbidding-looking wife telephoned the police. While they waited, the farmer tried to repair Milner's trousers, which had been torn in the crash, with his wife looking on reprovingly. The police arrived with the local Home Guard, there was more whisky, Baker got the bus for Dumfries, clutching his parachute, and the others managed to get travel warrants, arriving on leave one day late.

Baker, who did not fly on operations, seized every other opportunity to get airborne. He flew the Captain from Abbotsinch to Aldergrove in Northern Ireland, and was supposed to fly back there in two days to pick him up, but bad weather held him up, and Bayliss had to catch the ferry from Larne to Stranraer like a tourist.

The use of a Squadron aircraft for these trips was of course strictly unofficial and irregular, but later in the summer Percy Gick and Air Engineer Officer Molyneux, who had been collecting parts of written-off Swordfish for some time, finally managed to get them all assembled as a complete Stringbag. This aircraft was on nobody's charge, and pilots not on operations could fly it with impunity. It became the Captain's personal aircraft and was used to fly him to Maydown on leave.

Chief Steward Charlie Arkell was an important ingredient in the running of a happy ship like *Vindex*. With his curly red hair and baby face he looked bland and innocent, but as a former Cunard man he had many connections in the right places and knew how to use them to procure creature comforts for his ship, especially the aircrews. Early in the ship's commission while they were anchored off Northern Ireland, he asked Captain Bayliss 'Is it possible, sir, to fly off an aeroplane while the ship is lying here at anchor?' Bayliss said, 'Well, yes,' thinking how much the Chief Steward looked like an admiral in the Swiss Navy, with his three big MN gold stripes, worn because neither RN nor RNR had the equivalent of a Chief Steward. 'Well, sir, if you could possibly fly me off, say, two days before we sail, and just stop off in Ireland on the way up to Scapa ... I have contacts in the Republic, and I think I could lay my hands on some extra rations ...'

Charlie Arkell did not get his Stringbag delivery, but he did pull strings. The carrier anchored in Loch Foyle, and out came a drifter, gunwhales piled high with six thousand dozen eggs and a ton of butter. It became normal for bumboats to come out from the Donegal side of the Loch to peddle eggs, nylons and other goodies to the ship's company, who would lower buckets over the side. After one of these brisk trading sessions, many men seemed to have got quite tiddly. The ship's police were baffled, and it was some time before a close inspection of the goods coming out from the Republic revealed that the eggs, sold at half a crown each, had been filled with poteen. When the Captain was told, he said ruefully, 'Nobody ever offered me any.'

The Chief Steward also asked the Captain if he could 'Have some work done in the Ready Room.' 'What sort of work?' asked Bayliss suspiciously. 'Well, I want to set up a hotplate,' said Arkell, 'so the lads who are flying can have bacon and eggs right through the night.' 'That's all right,' said the Captain, 'provided you leave me enough power to operate the lift.'

To provide eggs more economically, John Baker bought what the Irish swore to him was a good egg-laying hen. The bird was christened Emily and put in a crate by the 4-inch, which was scrupulously avoided by the Captain on his rounds. But Guns' face was red when the hen turned out to be a cockerel, which grew too big to be looked after, and Baker had to take it home by train in a carrier bag. He did not find the pun very funny.

The Captain liked a drink, and after one Atlantic trip he invited some of his young airmen who had distinguished themselves to his cabin for a jar. He offered them gin, whisky 'or some of my brew?' Most of them chose the latter. 'That's very nice, sir,' said Peter Cumberland. 'What's in it?' 'Oh, just about everything,' Bayliss said. He appreciated an invitation to the wardroom, and was always welcome there. One evening it had been solemnly decided that the dress of the day should include bow ties but no collars. Then Ian Taylor remembered with horror that the Captain had been invited for drinks. Diffidently he went to the Captain's cabin and explained that collars would be *de rigeur*. 'I understand,' said the Captain gravely, and duly appeared later with a black tie round his bare neck. Another evening he was sitting in the wardroom talking to Percy Gick, when the latter criticised the current drill for dropping a torpedo from 60 feet. 'In *my* day,' said Commander (F), 'we went down to *twenty* feet before we released.' 'In *my* day,' said the Captain, 'we landed on the water to drop it.'

The wardroom was often the scene of letting off steam, and there were some strenuous games, usually led by Ian Taylor, who was not all that long out of medical school, involving the destruction of the furniture. There was a very close rapport between *Vindex*'s young doctors and aircrew. Ian Taylor was always ready with his rescue whaler's crew to pull to the help of a ditched airman, and they were on one occasion able to return his medical favours when he allowed some of them to stitch up his scalp after he had split it open on a bulkhead. John Shaw once ate a chrysanthemum soaked in rum at a TAG's party. The Maori *haka* war dance, as performed by the All Blacks rugby team, was often repeated in *Vindex* by her New Zealand pilots, at gin time and in harbour or on visits to other carriers.

There was a piano in the wardroom, which was played on social occasions by Freddie Stovin-Bradford or Air Radio Officer Jock Morrison. With the addition of Chief MO Charlie Kilpatrick on his trombone, Gordon Bennett on trumpet, Norman Sharrock on flagiolet, Ellis's bassoon and Chief Steward Charlie Arkell's fiddle, the Gindex Orchestra was formed. And there were the usual songs, Old Man Riley's Daughter, The Ball Of Kirriemuir, Cats On The Rooftops, and, of course ...

> I fly for enjoyment, I fly just for fun.
> And I'm awfully anxious to shoot down a Hun,
> But as for deck landings at night in the dark,

As I told Wings this morning, stuff that for a lark!

Cracking show! I'm alive!
But I still have to render my A25 . . .

Vindex sailed again from Greenock at 7.45 a.m. on 4 August for two days of flying exercises in the Clyde exercise area, but she was off Ardrossan at one o'clock next morning when Bayliss was ordered by signal to hunt a U-boat. Vindex met the corvette Morpeth Castle and the minesweeper-escort sloop Petrolia ten miles south of Barra Head at 11.30 a.m. on the 5th, but it turned out that these two ships were not yet worked up. Morpeth Castle's HF/DF was not calibrated, and she had gremlins in her radar, Asdics and radio. The frigates Bazely, Burges, Thirlmere, Tillsonburg and Windermere were added to Vindex's ad hoc Force 31 hunting group. Air searches began at 7.15 a.m. on 6 August with three Swordfish. By the time the Swordfish returned to the ship at 9.45 thick fog had come down, with visibility 150 yards and cloud base at 200 feet.

These aircraft were brought aboard safely by a combination of flame floats, searchlights and a new experimental method of controlled landing in thick weather.

Tired of the agony of watching pilots groping for the flight deck in nil visibility, Geoffrey Milner had remarked to Percy Gick, 'Why don't we use an ASV set in the ship to bring them in?' Wings, always ready to try anything which might improve the performance of his aircraft, passed on the idea to the ship's Air Radio Officer, Temporary Sub-Lieutenant (A) John Mackenzie Morrison, RNVR, who modified a Mark XI unit and set it up outboard on the starboard side aft.

The basis of the unit was an inverted scanner which could rotate continuously in a horizontal plane. A tubular feeder and all control leads were taken down to the other part of the installation in the ASV workshop immediately below.

The success of the system depended on a much modified Indicator Unit Type 97. Aircraft orbiting the ship anywhere within eight miles were picked up by this set and could be tracked in to 100 yards from the round-down, and bearing accuracy could be maintained to within a few degrees. Presentation was on a small PPI as used in an aircraft, but instead of a centre spot being the start of range markings, a 2-inch circle represented the zero. An aircraft was controlled from the blip on this screen, right up to the approach path until it disappeared inside 100 yards. If an aircraft had to go round again, the blip reappeared soon after it had passed the bows of the ship, and the aircraft was under control virtually throughout, whereas an aircraft's set was ineffective for the last few hundred yards of an approach.

Eddie Ward was the first pilot of 825 to be brought safely down by the Morrison Method.

His Stringbag was brought back to within five miles of the ship by Keith

Brading in the Air Direction Room and handed over to Jock Morrison, as Control Officer, who passed the pilot the ship's course, and Ward began his run-in from about three miles astern, while Control were given their holding positions on each beam.

The pilot was ordered 'Over to Control', and from then on flew in the correct attitude for landing, at 75 feet on his radio altimeter, steering the ship's course, with the Control Officer following him on his own special PPI and ordering any necessary change of course . . .

'Charlie, Port Ten.'

'Port Ten.'

'Charlie, Steady.'

'Steady.'

In this way the pilot was talked down to within some 100 or 150 yards of the ship. The batsman, wearing headset and throat microphone, called a larynguaphone, had been listening to all these orders, and on sighting the aircraft shouted 'Bats!' The pilot immediately kicked on right rudder and looked over his port side for the special illuminated bats. A last 'Skid port' and 'Come down' from Bats, and the Stringbag was dropping to the deck, her undercart struts straining, her hook snagging a wire and pulling it out like a startled boa constrictor.

Ward was one of the best pilots in the Squadron, but with practice any pilot was able to make the Morrison Blind Approach System work for him, and it was adopted in *Vindex* for all bad weather landings in lieu of the Type 257 radar of the BABS system. Any type of aircraft fitted with R/T only, and preferably a radio altimeter, could be controlled in this way.

Flying was suspended after these landings, with the fog too thick to operate aircraft. Two Hurricanes scrambled to intercept a bogey had to be brought back and landed on again, with the cloud base under 100 feet. The under-rehearsed *Morpeth Castle* got a contact but lost it again, and the only thing sighted by *Vindex*'s Swordfish during a brief thinning of the fog was an empty raft.

6

Voyage to Vaenga

THE SEA LANES TO NORTH RUSSIA were haunted by ghosts, the ghosts of the cruiser *Edinburgh*, sunk with her Russian gold,* of HMS *Trinidad*, destroyers HMS *Matabele*, *Punjabi*, *Somali*, *Achates*, *Hardy*, *Mahratta* and the Russian *Sokrushiteiny*, minesweepers *Gossamer*, *Niger*, *Leda*, *Bramble*, the little armed whaling catcher *Shera*, the submarine *P551*, the CAM ship *Empire Lawrence*, the aircraft and the scores of merchantmen savaged by submarines and by air strikes from Norway, with the German heavies, *Scharnhorst*, *Lutzow* and the mighty *Tirpitz* an ever-present menace, lurking in Alten Fjord off the flanks of the convoys.

Blackest spectre of all was the memory of PQ17, scattered and sent to its virtual destruction by an armchair decision taken under the green domes of the Admiralty, a thousand miles from the scene of action. PQ17 haunted anyone and everyone who had ever been on a Russian convoy or had lost a friend or a brother in that butchery.

PQ18, the follow-up, with the carrier air power which PQ17 should have had, changed things. HMS *Avenger*, aptly named, had truly avenged, with her Sea Hurricanes fighting off the massed Heinkels and 88s, but even this hard-fought action had left ten merchantmen dead on the bottom of the Arctic Ocean.

Three Stringbags of 825 Squadron had been the unwelcome guests in *Avenger* for that operation, and Gordon Bennett, the sole remaining Squadron member who had been there, remembered those cheerless days and nights with Colthurst when *Vindex* was sent north early in August to go with Convoy JW59 to Russia on Operation Victual. *Scharnhorst* was gone now, sunk by the guns of HMS *Duke of York*, and *Lutzow* was refitting in Germany. *Tirpitz* was still there, twice immobilised by Midget submarines and by Naval Barracuda bombers, but now repaired, and the Luftwaffe bombers were still in Norway, the U-boats patrolling off North Cape.

Vindex, with her consort *Striker*, would be only the latest in a succession of escort carriers which had accompanied Russian convoys in recent months. *Dasher* should have gone next after *Avenger*, but someone lit a fag in a passageway foul with petrol vapour and she blew up. *Chaser*, American-built,

*Sent by the USSR to pay for American military supplies and recovered from the wreck in 1981 by a British salvage team.

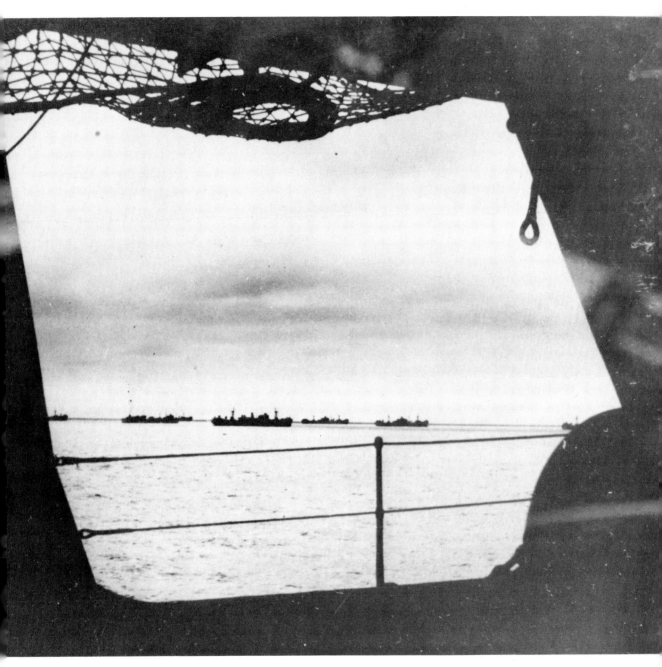

Merchant ships of Convoy JW59 to Russia seen from *Vindex*.

was actually the next to go, 'arcticised' with steam heating at all gun mountings, flying stations and catapult machinery, but that was not until February 1944, 17 months after PQ18. The heavy-rolling *Tracker* and the un-arcticised British-built *Activity*, released from her training stint in the Clyde, had been to Kola and helped the surface escorts to give the U-boats and the Luftwaffe anti-shipping units a beating. *Activity* had no sooner reached Scapa from that operation than she was turned round and, minus all her experienced aircrews but with some borrowed from *Chaser*, had gone back again, this time with *Fencer*, with her seasoned 842 Squadron but no experience of the Russian run, to bring back convoy RA59 and the empty freighters which had been accumulating in north Russian ports. One of *Activity*'s green Swordfish pilots pulled his deck hook out, ditched and was picked up by *Vindex*'s old friend the frigate HMCS *Waskesieu*, and another smashed his undercarriage, but the convoy got through. On the return trip *Fencer* carried the Soviet Admiral Levchenko and his staff, who were coming to Britain to take over the battleship *Royal Sovereign* and eight old destroyers. Another 2,300 of his men were in other ships of the convoy. The aircrews flew through snowstorms. *Fencer*'s Swordfish, aided by Wildcats, sank three U-boats with RPs and depth-charges. The convoy lost one merchantman.

The Navy seemed to be in control of convoys to Russia. But you never knew what the Germans would do. Vice-Admiral Sir Frederick Dalrymple-Hamilton was given a strong force for Operation Victual, the passage of convoy JW59, the first of a new series of convoys to Russia after the gap caused by the absorption of all available escort vessels in Second Front operations. With his flagship (the cruiser *Jamaica*), the 'arcticised' *Vindex* and *Striker* would form the Heavy Escort, and he was also allocated five ships of the 3rd Destroyer Flotilla (the big Fleet boats *Milne*, *Musketeer*, *Marne*, *Meteor* and *Nubian*) and the eleven-strong 20th Escort Group, under Commander A. H. Thorold, RN.

The merchantmen for North Russia assembled in Loch Ewe, western Scotland. There were 28 freighters, 14 of them loaded with explosives; two tankers; two escort oilers, from which the always thirsty destroyers and the frigates, sloops and corvettes could be topped up en route; a rescue ship and a special crane ship. Also in the body of the convoy were to go 12 MTBs for Russia. Commanding the convoy was Commodore Hector Creswell, RNR, in the SS *Samtredy*.

On Sunday 13 August up in Scapa crews from *Vindex* came first and second in the whaler races. On Monday there was an escort conference in the Loch Ewe anchorage aboard the *Jamaica*, minus the commanding officers of the destroyers *Keppel* and *Whitehall* and the sloop *Kite*, which had not yet arrived.

By 8 a.m. on the 15th all the ships of the 20th Escort Group had assembled in the Loch, comprising *Keppel* and *Whitehall*; Thorold's flagship *Cygnet*; two other sloops, *Peacock* and *Mermaid*; the frigate *Loch Dunvegan*; and the corvettes *Bluebell*, *Oxlip*, *Honeysuckle* and *Camellia*. Other escort vessels were scheduled to join the force later on in the voyage. At 10.30 a.m. the usual

Merchantmen of Convoy JW59 under the after twin 4-inch guns of *Vindex*.

Convoy Conference was held, with Vice-Admiral Dalrymple-Hamilton presiding over the Masters and COs of all the ships, and afterwards *Jamaica* pulled up her hook and left at the rush for Scapa Flow. At 3 p.m. the 20th EG were steaming through the gate, followed by the first freighter. The last ship went through at five o'clock.

At 9.30 p.m. Dalrymple-Hamilton in *Jamaica* joined his two carriers and the destroyers of the 3rd Flotilla in Scapa Flow. CS10 was an old Russian convoy hand. He had commanded the escort for the *Tracker/Activity* operation, Convoy JW58, when the old fighting *Keppel* had sunk U360 in a Hedgehog attack. He had exercised command from the cruiser *Diadem* for this and the return convoy RA58.

When Rear-Admiral Roderick McGrigor brought back RA59 in April he flew his flag in the same ship but borrowed an experienced fighter direction officer from *Activity* to be better able to keep in touch with carrier operations, direct general policy and co-ordinate the efforts of surface and air escorts. *Jamaica* had no air staff, so for JW59 Dalrymple-Hamilton borrowed Lieutenant-Commander Desmond Vincent-Jones, RN, who was FAA Liaison Officer on C-in-C Western Approaches Max Horton's staff at Liverpool, as his Air Staff Officer. Vincent-Jones was a veteran Fleet Air Arm observer who had served in *Illustrious* and *Formidable* when those famous Fleet carriers had suffered the worst that the Luftwaffe could do to them in the Mediterranean. He also knew the Admiral's two Staff Officers, Commander David Heber-Percy and Flag Lieutenant Michael Chichester.

Then Dalrymple-Hamilton went one better. At 8 a.m. on Wednesday 16 August, after persuasion by his staff, he transferred his flag from *Jamaica* to *Vindex*, thus handing Captain Hughes-Hallett back his day cabin, but giving Captain Bayliss a problem in the already overcrowded escort carrier.

It was clear that communication between the two carriers could become a problem. 'You know my Captain hates flying planes,' *Striker*'s Air Staff Officer Malcolm Graves confided to Vincent-Jones. Captain Carne's was a very Pusser ship, in contrast to the relaxed establishment run by Temple Bayliss, with whom Vincent-Jones had served in the cruiser *Norfolk* before the war. Graves and Vincent-Jones, with Freddie Stovin-Bradford's cheerful connivance, fixed up a private line through which the Admiral's directives could be translated into action without any misunderstanding and with the best use of air power. There was a difference in aircraft operating techniques between the two carriers. Whereas *Vindex*'s 825 Squadron was allowed to land by turning in sharply on to the deck, *Striker*'s Swordfish and Wildcats of 824 had to make the officially approved, straight-and-level approach from well astern. This affected the speed of operations.

By this time the convoy had passed the Orkneys on its way north and was in the process of manoeuvring into its formation for the passage to Murmansk. When the great mêlée had at last settled down there were ten columns of ships abreast. At this stage there were only two ships in Column 4, the Norwegian escort oiler *Herbrand* following the freighter *Kufi J. La Farge*; one ship, the

Convoy JW59. HMS *Striker* from the stern of *Vindex*.

freighter *Port Glenora*, in Column 5; one, the Commodore's *Samtredy*, in Column 6; and two ships, the SS *David B. Johnson* leading the other escort oiler *Luculu* in Column 7. Behind the *Fort Glenora* and the *Samtredy* were two stations left empty for HMS *Jamaica* and USSR *Arkhangelsk*, the former HMS *Royal Sovereign*, now known in the RN as the *Royal Rouble*, which was due to join up together with eight old ex-US Navy four-piper destroyers latterly in RN service which had been handed over to the Russian Navy. Behind the four abbreviated centre columns was a 'box', four ship stations deep, in which the two escort carriers would take station, steam and manoeuvre. Stationed at the rear of Column 8 so that she could easily drop out of the convoy if the need arose, was the rescue ship *Rathlin*. Stuck away in the last but one station in Column 2 was the crane ship *Empire Buttress*. This was a position which did not acknowledge her importance. This little ship was a heavy-lifter. The port facilities at Murmansk, adequate to unload ordinary peacetime cargo, had never been able to cope with the huge quantities of very heavy war material which had flowed into the port through the convoy pipeline. The heaviest crane could only lift eleven tons, and thus could not handle tanks. *Empire Buttress* was as good as gold-plated.

At 11 a.m. *Vindex*, flying the flag of CS10, sailed from Scapa Flow to catch up with the convoy, in company with *Striker* and *Jamaica*, with the temporary protection of the destroyers HMS *Volage*, *Verulam*, *Virago*, *Whirlwind*, *Wrangler* and *Scourge* and HMCS *Algonquin*, which would screen the Heavy Escort as far as its rendezvous with the Convoy. CS10 also picked up a modified selection of ships from the 3rd Destroyer Flotilla, comprising HMS *Milne*, *Marne*, *Musketeer*, *Meteor* and *Caprice*. At 3 p.m. both carriers carried out a combined flying exercise, which was completed by eight o'clock, and no more flying was considered necessary that day, with Catalinas from Shetland overhead.

Just after 6 a.m. next morning a Swordfish took off from *Vindex* to look for the convoy. Gordon Bennett also flew a spare tailplane over to *Striker*. While it was being unloaded he was aware of 824 Squadron pilots glowering at him for doing a split-circuit and getting away with it unreprimanded. 'The poor lads,' he noted, 'had to do an approach similar to that of an elementary flying school, whereas *Vindex* allowed us to do anything we could get away with. I believe we could catch a wire within 45 seconds of receiving the green light at 1,000 feet, so *Vindex* could just skid into the wind and back again.'

With a carrier operating inside the convoy in a box two and a half miles wide, speed of landing on was essential. Time into the wind to receive aircraft could be as little as six minutes. The aircraft would probably also be low on fuel after a long patrol, and a wave-off could mean waiting while the carrier turned to avoid collision and retraced her course for another attempt. With the time of survival in the icy water so limited, even a shaky landing was preferable to a ditching with empty tanks.

Landing in the dark or in bad visibility was made easier when Chief PO Charlie Waldram, who was in charge of the electrical Air Staff in *Vindex*, put

Convoy JW59. Swordfish leaving *Vindex*, with Striker to port.

Armourer Norman Pickup (left) and Charlie Waldram, in charge of *Vindex*'s Electrical Air Staff, added several important innovations to the operation of aircraft, including the repositioning of the switches in the Swordfish cockpit for ease of operation.

together a pair of illuminated bats for the DLCO to bring down tired pilots groping for the deck. He started with two sections of $\frac{3}{4}$-inch electrical conduit, fitted a 12-volt bulb in a socket in each end, and added one of two Benjamin-type 4-inch, 45-degree reflectors of the kind that he had used in Civvy Street, and which he found in the lighting system in the heads. The wires from the bulb socket were led through the hollow tubular handles to an aircraft dimmer switch mounted on a small harness on the batsman's chest, and to two 6-volt batteries at his feet. With the dimmer switch he could control the amount of light transmitted. Percy Gick landed a Swordfish to test the new bats, and pronounced them 'Bloody marvellous!'

Waldram and armourer Norman Pickup fitted an illuminated target disc on the windscreen of each Swordfish to help the pilot aim the aircraft in the dark. Another valuable modification they made was a repositioning of the switches in the Swordfish pilot's cockpit. All the switches had been fitted originally down the starboard side of the cockpit, which made them very awkward to operate, especially when wearing the usual thick gloves. One pilot thumbed the wrong switch accidentally and dropped a flare, just missing one of the flight deck crew. The air staff altered the wiring and rebuilt all the switch assemblies across the front of the cockpit. It meant relocating a maze of wires, and the staff airframe riggers had to drill holes in the airframe.

The first machine to incorporate this modification was ready after 48 hours non-stop work. The first time this machine flew again it was ditched, so Waldram and Co had to start from scratch with another aircraft. Lieutenant Molyneaux, the Air Electrical Officer, sent details of the process to the Admiralty, a Fleet Order was issued, and new Swordfish, as well as all those on active service, were fitted with the modification.

The searching Swordfish sighted the convoy 30 miles ahead of the Heavy Escort, which made rendezvous with it at 9.30 a.m. some 240 miles west-by-south of Trondheim, Norway. CS10's ships took up their allotted stations with the convoy, *Jamaica* behind the Commodore's ship, the two carriers behind her in the box. The warships adjusted to the slower speed of the convoy, while the destroyer screen which had brought them to the rendezvous returned to the Faeroes. The station alongside *Jamaica*, where the USSR *Arkhangelsk* should have been, was empty. She and her destroyers were having difficulty making the rendezvous.

With the destroyers of the 3rd Flotilla and *Bluebell* and *Honeysuckle* forming the close screen round the convoy, *Loch Dunvegan*, *Camellia*, *Cygnet*, *Whitehall*, *Oxlip* and *Charlock* were deployed as the Outer Asdic Screen, *Peacock* and *Mermaid* pushed out ahead as the Port Bow Striking Force, *Keppel* and *Kite* forming their equivalent to starboard.

The main body of the convoy and its escorts now steered a course almost due north which would leave Jan Mayen Island some 200 miles on their port beam and Alten Fjord, where the *Tirpitz* lay, 400 miles to starboard. After Jan Mayen had been passed abeam they would be beyond the range of the RAF Coastal Command Catalinas.

There were some veterans of anti-U-boat warfare among the convoy escorts. The corvette *Bluebell*, for example, was a survivor of some of the early convoy battles in the North Atlantic. The destroyer flotilla leader *Keppel*, launched in 1920, modified as a short-range convoy escort but retaining her full torpedo armament, was no stranger to Russian convoys, and had been the flagship of Captain Jackie Broom, commander of the close escort with PQ17. *Vindex* could hardly be called a veteran, though her aircrews felt as if they

Vindex by moonlight, from one of her Swordfish.

had been flying Stringbags over the ocean forever. HMS *Whitehall* had started life as one of the classic W-class destroyers, launched in 1919, with the distinctive tall for'ard funnel and short stumpy after one. For her anti-submarine role in this war she had been hacked about. A Hedgehog multiple mortar had replaced her A-gun on the foc'sle, her for'ard funnel had gone, and so had her torpedo tubes, replaced by big depth-charge reload racks on deck for the continuous use of her four DC throwers and the chute right aft. With strict W/T silence in force she had also been selected to act as 'postman' between CS10 in *Vindex* and the escort striking forces. She made her eighth round trip at 4 p.m. and burned 15 tons of fuel doing it.

Aboard the carrier, Sub-Lieutenant (E) Paddy Boal became Flight Deck Engineer, and Peter Humphreys switched to the orthodox role of Junior Watchkeeping Officer in the engine room. Down there it was less tiring but more frightening. He was out of the limelight of the flight deck drama, air-locked into this big steel box filled with thundering machinery, unable to see, but free to imagine what might be threatening them in the sea around. Peter would give himself a scare by touching the thin hull plating, the sea only three-eighths of an inch away. With the ship as a target he had his finger on the bullseye. Mounted and clipped in place above the engine room control platform were some heavy pieces of engine spares, including a cylinder lever weighing well over a ton, and he tried to develop a reflex action that would make him automatically jump out of the way should it break loose in the event of a big explosion. When depth-charging was going on around the ship, down here it was like being inside a big base drum during a Souza march. They just had to hope that the bangs were theirs and not the enemy's.

The watchkeeping engineers developed strong leg muscles tramping up and down ladders and round the four tiers of inspection platforms which surrounded the huge pounding Doxfords. The top platform carried the oil-purifying machinery and a workshop, the next one down ran right round both main engines at upper piston level, the third tier encircled them at camshaft level. On the bottom catwalk, between the two engines, was the control position. Outboard of the main engines were diesel generators, auxiliary boilers, evaporating plant, air compressors, lubricating pumps, water pumps and bilge pumps. For'ard were the heat exchangers and the lubricating oil coolers. Abaft the main engines, at second platform level and running almost the whole width of the engine room, was the main switchboard, manned by electrical artificers.

A Junior's watch could seem endless ... Drag yourself out of your warm bunk, climb into your overalls, stumble down ladders and along dim passageways, down through the double doors and the airlock (necessary, as the engine room was under slight pressure from the air supply fans) into the pit. Then the routine began ... Check engine room auxiliaries, especially the diesel generating sets, report to the Watchkeeping Engineer Officer ... Forward generator room, after generator room, check that the leading stokers of the oncoming watch were closed up, and everything in order. Back to the engine room. Change over from one daily service fuel tank to the other. Pump up fuel oil gravity tank. Purify oil from the gravity tank to the daily service tank used during the previous watch, ready for the succeeding watch. Supervise the cleaning of the centrifugal purifiers ... Check the compressed air. Charge up if necessary. Check the bilges for oil and pump out if necessary—but only in darkness, when the U-boats won't find it, and you ... Check auxiliary boiler water level gauges. Check and blow down the evaporator to rid the coils of scale. Check the salinity of the fresh water being produced ... Every so often visit the external generator compartments. Every hour check main engines, diesel generator, fuel storage deep tanks, double bottom tanks, fresh water tanks, log pressures, temperatures, levels ...

... Once every watch climb down the ladders through the vertical escape shafts to the propeller shaft tunnels to check oil levels and temperatures of the shaft bearings. If you were on the ladder in heavy weather you got a queasy feeling of weightlessness when the ship rolled. Plodding crouched-down along the tunnel, with the shaft revolving alongside you, was eerie and not for claustrophobics. If there was anything wrong down there, the shafts were connected by telephone to the engine room, and thence to the bridge.

From the bridges of the ships of JW59 fog was making visibility poor. Commodore Creswell was in a fog himself as to the exact destinations of the ships in his charge. There had been no Ministry of War Transport representative at the Convoy Conference to give him any definite information on what situation to expect when he reached Russia, and he had no idea that the main part of the convoy was intended for Murmansk and the remainder for Archangel and other ports on the White Sea. In fact he had quite the opposite impression. When he had asked before sailing whether it would be possible to arrange the ships according to their destinations he was told that no destinations were known, and that all the information he needed would be sent to him by signal from Russia. As far as he knew he was simply heading for a rendezvous eastward of Kola Inlet, which led to Murmansk. He was not particularly worried that he had been given no instructions about the *Rathlin*, as in previous convoys rescue ships had had separate orders and counted as part of the escort.

With Coastal Command Catalinas from Iceland and Shetland still giving escort to the convoy all through the 17th, *Striker* flew Swordfish anti-submarine patrols. Both carriers had been briefed to listen out for the German 'Zenit' weather reconnaissance aircraft which flew at regular intervals every day out from Trondheim to Jan Mayen and back to gather meteorological data. *Vindex* vectored two Hurricanes to what looked as if it might be this aircraft, only to intercept the inevitable Catalina not showing IFF.

There were bad fog patches, and all the carrier patrols had to land aboard *Vindex* at 5 p.m., with *Striker* completely hidden. 'Aircrews in *Vindex*,' reported *Flight Deck*, a restricted magazine published by the Director of Naval Air Warfare and Flying Training, 'are reputed to have perfected a new method of homing. On several occasions, when a pea-soup fog prevailed and none of the widely advertised navigational aids were available, the ship made smoke (black by day, white by night), the aircraft flew along the smoke path with their starboard wings ten feet inside and six feet above it and just waited until they arrived on deck.' In a later edition, however, the magazine alleged that 'the idea of homing on a smoke trail had its ironical origin in the fact that *Striker* has a habit of letting off clouds of black smoke whenever she tries to pile on the knots for landing on.' Rather more seriously it was acknowledged that 'The *Vindex* system is actually the streaming of flame floats from the port side and the use of the Morrison Blind Approach System.'

The convoy also began to encounter headwinds, which reduced the speed of advance, a problem aggravated by the poor performance of the little *Empire Buttress*, the crane ship, struggling along over on *Vindex*'s port quarter. A coal burner, and about a third the size of any of the other ships in the convoy, she had done a speed trial in the Mersey lasting several hours and had achieved ten knots. The Master, who was new to the ship, had signed a certificate in all good faith to the effect that his ship could maintain that speed in a moderate sea with wind Force 4, but here she was often slowing to six knots, making good considerably less, and was very nearly left behind in the Faeroes. But she put all available hands in the stokehold, including the Naval DEMS gunners, and did her best to improve.

Single aircraft from *Vindex* carried out Viper patrols on 18 August, while behind them at midday a powerful force consisting of Admiral Sir Henry Moore, C-in-C Home Fleet, in the *Duke of York*, with the Fleet carriers *Indefatigable*, *Formidable* and *Furious*, the escort carriers *Trumpeter* and *Nabob*, the cruisers *Devonshire*, *Berwick* and *Kent*, six destroyers and five frigates, left Scapa on Operation Goodwood, another attack on the *Tirpitz*, which lay on short notice for steam in Alten Fjord on the flank of JW59.

At 7.20 a.m. on the 19th the operator on *Vindex*'s Type 281 radar set picked up what was almost certainly the Trondheim Zenit, and two Hurricanes left the deck to intercept it. But it never came within their visual range, and as R/T silence was in force they were recalled. Two more Hurricanes, plus Wildcats from *Striker*, were scrambled at 9 a.m. to catch him on his return trip, but he was not sighted.

Now it was decided to divide the duty of Controlling CVE into 12-hour periods, with *Striker*'s aircraft flying the 'daylight' patrols, and *Vindex*'s Swordfish, with their ASV Mark XI radar, the 'night' flights, changing at 10 a.m. and 10 p.m. daily. In reality, with the convoy steering to pass Bear Island to the north, as far away from the Luftwaffe in Norway as possible, the further north they steamed the longer grew the day, until the sun just kissed the horizon and rose again, even though it was two months past Midsummer Day.

Just before 9 a.m. on the 20th, when the convoy was to the east of Jan Mayen Island and right on the point of no return for the Coastal Command Catalinas, Hurricanes and Wildcats were scrambled again after what was thought to be a Trondheim Zenit, fixed by HF/DF bearings, but again the aircraft remained out of range. The Admiral was hoping that the plane had not sighted and

Flight deck hockey aboard *Vindex*.

reported the wandering *Arkhangelsk* and her brood, which were known to be in the area and were expected to rendezvous with the convoy during the day. He thought that Admiral Levchenko might have got ahead of him, after the slowing down of the convoy by a headsea and a heavy swell. Three Swordfish flown off at 11.10 a.m. failed to find the *Royal Rouble*, but at 5.54 p.m. her high spotting top was sighted from Norman Sharrock's Swordfish as she struggled along 48 miles to the south-west. The seas and headwinds had retarded the ponderous battlewagon and the old flush-decked American-built destroyers even more than the convoy. The Swordfish signalled them the convoy's position, course and speed, and Levchenko finally joined up at 10.15 p.m. Dalrymple-Hamilton could not rely on the old Russian-manned four-pipers as active escorts, and added them to the convoy, four down each flank.*

The German aircraft fixed by HF/DF had been a Ju 88 of the 5th Air Fleet, and his transmissions had been reporting his sighting of the main body of

* These eight ships were the: *Deiatelnyi* ('Active', ex-HMS *Churchill*, ex-USS *Herndon*); *Derskyi* ('Saucy', ex-HMS *Chelsea*, ex-USS *Crowninshield*); *Doblestnyi* ('Glorious', ex-HMS *Georgetown*, ex-USS *Maddox*); *Dostoinyi* ('Worthy', ex-HMS *St Albans*, ex-USS *Thomas*); *Jarkyi* ('Fiery', ex-HMS *Brighton*, ex-USS *Cowell*); *Jgoochy* ('Scorcher', ex-HMS *Leamington*, ex-USS *Twiggs*); *Jivoochy* ('Lively', ex-HMS *Richmond*, ex-USS *Fairfax*); *Zhostkyi* ('Hardy', ex-HMS *Roxborough*, ex-USS *Foote*). A ninth four-piper, *Druzani* (ex-HMS *Lincoln*, ex-USS *Yarnall*), was sailed to Russia later, with JW60, to provide spare parts for the other eight.

Flight deck party, HMS *Vindex*, dressed for Russian convoys.

JW59. On previous Russian convoys with air support it had been the policy to restrict air patrols to defensive sweeps round the convoy, to avoid giving away its position prematurely, and strict W/T and R/T silence had been preserved. For JW59, however, it was decided to stage full anti-submarine air searches to a depth of 80 miles, and early on 20 August these were begun. R/T was also to be used in appropriate circumstances, and in *Vindex* Chris Williams, Alf Bleasdale and one other TAG had been retained for this voyage to work it in the operations room.

Secret Ultra information from decoded U-boat signal traffic had indicated the likely positions of enemy submarines athwart the convoy's path, and at a few minutes before six o'clock *Milne* and *Whitehall* got the first HF/DF U-boat bearings, fine on their starboard bows, 38 miles from the convoy. The convoy had joined contact with the five U-boats of the Trutz Group. A pack of that name had been so roughly handled by the Avenger TBFs of the US Navy escort carriers *Bogue* and *Card* in the North Atlantic in 1943 that *Grossadmiral* Dönitz, *Befehlshaber der U-boote*, had disbanded it once. A flight of Hurricanes scrambled and searched in vain, and at night *Vindex*'s Swordfish took over, two aircraft probing ahead, one in the area of a contact astern. As the existence and position of the convoy was now presumed known, the ban on R/T silence was relaxed so that the aircraft and ships could talk to each other.

At 10.45 p.m. *Keppel* got a contact on her starboard quarter. *Kite* joined her, and a *Vindex* Stringbag watched the destroyer and the sloop blasting away with DCs and Hedgehogs. They hunted through the night, anti-Gnat Foxers streamed. At 4 a.m. on the 21st the convoy altered from the northerly course which it had been holding since 9.30 a.m. on the 17th, when the Heavy Escort had joined up, on to a heading of 050° in the direction of Spitzbergen, from which it would alter again later to round Bear Island and run down to Kola Inlet. The noble efforts of the reinforced black gang in the *Empire Buttress'* stokehold had enabled the ships to increase speed again from seven to nine and a half knots.

At 6.44 a.m. HMS *Kite*, after a long and fruitless hunt, had slowed to six knots, and was clearing her Foxers, which had become twisted round one another, when she was hit on the starboard side aft by two torpedoes from *Kapitänleutnant* Pietsch's *U344*, the Trutz contact keeper. The ship heeled over to starboard at once. Men on deck and a lookout on *Keppel*'s bridge saw the conning tower as Peitsch surfaced briefly to assess his attack. *Kite*'s stern broke off, floated clear for a few seconds, then sank. Her bow floated for about a minute, then sank at a steep angle.

At 7.30, with *Mermaid* and *Peacock* on an 'Observant' patrol round the scene, *Keppel* stopped to pick up survivors. There were some 30 men alive in the sea when she started, but there was a carpet of very thick, choking oil on the water, and some of the men had no life jackets. Some had very few clothes on. The destroyer hauled 14 men with great difficulty from the clinging evil muck which made it all the harder for any of them to do anything to help themselves, wounded, exhausted or shocked as they all were. If a man wore a capok jacket or a cork lifebelt he could be heaved up with a grapnel. Of the 14 rescued, five died on board *Keppel* within a few minutes. A *Vindex* Swordfish also orbited the area while *Keppel* finished searching, and remained until other escorts had come up, then flew off on its normal anti-submarine patrol.

Between 8 and 10 p.m. HF/DF picked up an almost continuous stream of U-boat transmissions, all in the ground wave. The pack was closing in. *Vindex*'s plot showed three U-boats in the area between her port and starboard quarters, following at ranges of between 40 and 60 miles, with another approaching from the east.

While *Striker*'s Stringbags searched, *Vindex*'s Hurricanes scrambled three times to follow up fixes. The U-boats behind the convoy were still opening their big mouths, and Huff-Duff fixed them on bearings of 160°, 200° and 225°, closing all the time. *Vindex* sent off Swordfish down these bearings, four at a time, throughout the night. A bogey was picked up nine miles away from the ships at 10.30 p.m. Two Wildcats scrambled in a hurry but returned empty-handed. At 2 a.m. on the 22nd the convoy altered course due east to round

Bear Island. At 2.40 another bogey registered at 30 miles, and *Vindex* scrambled another Hurricane pair. They opened their throttles but the range began to open and he left them behind. Half an hour later another blip came on the screen 20 miles to the east. As two Wildcats scrambled and climbed, the *Vindex* Hurricanes were recalled to avoid confusing the radar operators.

An aircrew's greatest fear in the middle of an ocean was to return to where they thought the carrier was—to find she was not there. This now happened to Norman Sharrock and observer Alf Murrant, who had had one scare already when only one RATOG rocket had fired on take-off. They asked *Vindex* for a homing, but a loose or broken aerial lead produced a very weak R/T signal, and they could not read the ship's instructions. Sharrock climbed high and cut the engine and they both strained their ears for the course to steer. When they decided they could both hear the same figure they turned on to it and eventually found *Vindex*, with their petrol running low.

Vindex had not yet got used to having an admiral and his staff on board. Captain's Secretary Peter Isaacson had lost his cabin again and was now installed on the bridge recording all the Captain's *ipsissima verba* as an insurance policy. The Admiral and his officers had crowded into the Air Direction Room, and messages were flying between the ASOs of the two carriers down the private line, with Dalrymple-Hamilton relying heavily on his young air officers.

Excitement rose in the crowded ADR as *Striker*'s two Wildcats closed their bogey. The R/T crackled and announced, 'Enemy in sight! A Bv 138.' Sub-Lieutenants Lucey and Dibben in the tubby Grummans could see the twin tail booms of the Blohm und Voss flying boat as it headed for cloud cover. This was the type of armour-plated snooper that had shrugged off the bee stings from the .303s of *Avenger*'s Hurricanes. The Wildcats had .5-calibre Brownings, but it would still be a very hard nut to crack.

Now the Bv was in the cloud. But he could not erase himself from the ship's radar screens. They held him, and *Striker*'s Air Direction Officer guided the fighters, and when he burst out into the open they were on him. He took a hammering from the Brownings, but went down enveloped in orange flame. Lucey had been shot down by a U-boat earlier in the year while serving in *Tracker* and this was his revenge.

The old firm of Bennet and Couch took off from *Vindex* on anti-submarine patrol to starboard of the convoy on the morning of 22 August in 825's Swordfish X, No. NR857. At half-past eight they were heading back for the convoy. The weather was bright but cloudy, with hailstorms, visibility about 15 miles. The nearest ship was HMS *Peacock*, 25 miles away in the outer screen of the convoy. Cloud base was generally about 2,000 feet. They were at present in a patch of bright sunlight at 2,200 feet, but more cloud loomed ahead of them. Holding his course of 120°, Bennett was just about to plunge into the cloud when he saw, about three miles off on their port bow, a lightish-coloured object. He immediately turned the aircraft towards it and recognised it as a U-boat. It was in fact *U344*, destroyer of HMS *Kite*. Pietsch's supercharger had broken down after his attack on the sloop, but he had been ordered by the *Führer der U-boote*, Norway, to continue in pursuit of the convoy.

The Air Direction Room in *Vindex* heard Peter Couch's loud 'Tantivvy!' as Swordfish X dived to the attack. As they closed, Bennett studied the submarine, which looked like one of the 750-ton type, sea-green in colour and very clean in appearance and design. Couch thought he could make out about four Oerlikon-type cannon mounted aft on the conning tower or on a 'bandstand'. She was making about six knots on a northeasterly heading. Bennett guessed that she had just surfaced and was steering for the convoy. He made his attack from astern, using his boost override to get every knot he could out of the slow Stringbag, weaving in evasive action. He released his stick of three Mark XII Torpex DCs, set for 22–24 feet, from a height of 50 feet, with the aircraft making 150 knots, still unhampered by any fire from the U-boat.

The three charges fell 150 feet apart. The first hit the water beside the sub's hull on her starboard quarter, the next alongside amidships, to starboard. The U-boat was now diving. The third charge hit the foc'sle, rolled down the canting deck and lodged under the jump wire or the mine guard at the bows. Ten seconds later, when the submarine's bow reached 24 feet, this charge went off, showing above the surface as a burst of black smoke as the stern of the U-boat rose above the surface. The other two charges raised columns of white water.

Couch was trying to make his report to *Vindex* and take photographs at the same time. Fortunately he had with him this time one of the good light American cameras and took five good pictures on the steep climbing turn after the attack.

When his news reached the ADR in *Vindex* there was a cheer. The Admiral said, 'Tell that Swordfish I want survivors!' Ken Mason told Couch on the R/T, 'Chuck them a life raft, we want survivors.'

Couch was pointing his camera at some small pieces of floating debris, one survivor swimming frantically and a dead body floating in a big patch of oil. He dropped a smoke float near the swimmer, partly inflated their K-type rubber dinghy and tried to throw it down, but the slipstream took charge of it.

His voice rang round the carrier's ADR: 'The bloody thing's lodged in the tail wires!'

Mason said, 'Well, shoot it away!' They heard the chatter of a Lewis gun.

Couch managed to puncture the dinghy, which had fully inflated itself on hitting the tailplane, but the remains were still stuck above the ailerons. Down below, the solitary swimmer had about 20 minutes to live in the cold sea, and just beyond him the tilted stern of the U-boat, propellers still turning, slid beneath the waves to take all his shipmates to their deaths in the depths of the Arctic Ocean.

It was the end of *U344*. *Vindex*'s plot had indicated, correctly, that this was the contact keeper, the submarine which had sunk the *Kite*, and her loss was now partially avenged.

Meanwhile Swordfish X was heading back for the ship with a dinghy wrapped round its fin. Stovin-Bradford said, 'Why not tell the ship's company?' When the aircraft landed on, the pennants of torn rubber streaming out behind it, there were hundreds of cheering men in the Goofers.

Sub-hunting Swordfish now had three alternative warloads—traditional depth-charges, rocket-projectiles, or the newer weapon which was known for security reasons as the Mark 24 Mine, but was in fact an acoustic homing torpedo, with which Avenger TBFs working from US Navy CVEs in the Central Atlantic had had great success. The Americans called it Fido or Wandering Annie, to the British it was Oscar, Hippo or the B-bomb. Oscar homed on the noise made by a ship's propellers as they churned the water, via a hydrophone installed in its head, shielded so that it did not home on to its own propeller effects. When it hit the water Oscar dived and levelled out at a pre-set depth, and could detect propeller cavitation up to a range of 1,500 yards. If no sound was picked up by the hydrophone, the torpedo made an upward circular search, maintaining it for 15 minutes.

Swordfish H of *Striker's* 824 Squadron, a Mark II aircraft, pilot Sub-Lieutenant T. G. Hounslow, RNVR, observer Sub-Lieutenant A. F. Hookings, RNZNVR, telegraphist/air-gunner Leading Naval Airman C. G. Horsley, was carrying a B-bomb as it shadowed a U-boat on the surface below, with the aircraft flying in sunlight and clear visibility about 68 miles south-east of the convoy and some 40 miles east of Bear Island when, at 11 a.m. he sighted a second U-boat about five miles to the north of the first.

Hounslow armed his 'mine', and Horsley reported their position. While they continued to shadow both U-boats, *Striker* flew off two Swordfish and three Wildcats in support. *Vindex* already had three Sea Hurricanes airborne under R/T directions, Bill John's H/NF732, Johnny Moore's F/DX126 and Pete Hellyer's Q/JS272, and vectored these to Hounslow's U-boat, while Messrs Talbot, Cooper and Durrant in *Striker's* Swordfish B, also up on a search, who had heard Hounslow's 'Tantivvy!', were also ordered by the ship to intercept. The nearest surface escort was *Keppel*, 48 miles away.

Meanwhile Hounslow and Hookings were studying their new target, which appeared to them to be a 500-ton boat, dark grey in colour, and was now about two and a half miles off. Hounslow thought she was probably going to dive, and closed her. Hookings took photographs as shells from the submarine's guns started to curve up towards them and burst on the surface of the sea ahead. The U-boat increased speed to about eight knots and began to zigzag, then turned hard-a-starboard, straightened up, and began to dive. Hounslow followed her round and in level flight at a speed of 105 knots dropped his Oscar 200 yards ahead of the swirl where the sub had disappeared a minute before. There was no indication of a hit. Swordfish H dropped markers and left to continue shadowing the southern U-boat.

Vindex's three Hurricanes found the position they had been given and were orbiting it at 3,500 feet when John saw the smoke float on his starboard beam. As the Hurricanes turned towards it they sighted the U-boat beyond it,

The enemy. Pictures of U-boat under attack, 22nd August, 1944, from the camera gun of Johnny Moore's Sea Hurricane F.

steering towards them. The fighters opened formation and flew up-sun of the sub, to come in out of the light on separate paths and divide the U-boat's aim.

Hellyer broke away first and made his attack from the submarine's port beam. The U-boat opened fire on him and began to turn to starboard so as to unmask all her guns on the bandstand aft of the conning tower. Shells, 40mm and 20mm, and heavy machine-gun bullets came up at him, but the aim was not very accurate and his cannon soon silenced them. The gunners left their guns and dropped down through the conning tower hatch as the U-boat reversed course and began to dive. Hellyer pressed his RP firing button, but nothing happened. He climbed away in frustration as Johnny Moore made his run in. Four RPs left his racks on trails of flame, and he was sure that one had scored a hit. The submarine's conning tower was awash now and she was almost under when John attacked from her port bow. His cannon shells hit the U-boat but Moore and Hellyer, as well as Talbot and Cooper in *Striker*'s Swordfish B, which was approaching, saw his RPs hit the water some 20 to 30 feet over. Both his and Hellyer's camera guns had failed to function, and only Moore returned with pictures of his attack.

The U-boat's periscopes and jump wire disappeared below the waves. Three seconds later Talbot dropped his B-bomb about 25 yards to port of the swirl. He dropped a marker in the swirl and circled the spot. Five minutes later he saw a patch of fresh oil spreading on the surface. He had not had a particularly good view of the U-boat, but reported her as being of 500 tons, 'painted white'.

Almost simultaneous with this attack another U-boat had been sighted by a *Striker* Swordfish 50 miles south-sou'-east of the convoy but she dived before an attack could be made. This and the attack on the other U-boats gave rise to a furious spate of U-boat transmissions, which were picked up by Huff-Duff in the JW59 escorts. At midday the convoy, with Bear Island 20 miles on its starboard beam, hauled round 35° to the north and stayed on that heading for a while. Another U-boat sighting was made at 2.50 p.m. by a *Striker* Swordfish, and two Hurricanes were scrambled from *Vindex* in support, but again the enemy got below before they could nail him.

Meanwhile the aircraft of Admiral Moore's Operation Goodwood were keeping *Tirpitz* far too occupied to make a sortie against JW59. In the forenoon of the 22nd, 32 Barracudas and nine Hellcat fighter-bombers attacked the battleship with difficulty through her very heavy smokescreen. Firefly fighters damaged two auxiliary vessels in Alten Fjord, and Seafires destroyed four Bv 138s, two Ar 196 and two Heinkel He 115 floatplanes at Banak, from which many attacks had been made on Russian convoys in the past. After another fighter-bomber strike on the *Tirpitz* in the afternoon, Seafires shot down two Bv 138 shadowers out at sea.

When *Trumpeter* and *Nabob* were refuelling escort vessels after this strike, *Kapitänleutnant* Hans-Jurgen Sthamer's *U354* hit and badly damaged *Nobob* with one of a salvo of orthodox torpedoes, and sank the sloop *Bickerton*, an old colleague of *Vindex*'s, with a Gnat acoustic torpedo. *Nabob* did not sink, though heavily down by the stern, but arrived at Scapa Flow on 27 August under her own steam.

Meanwhile *Striker*'s Swordfish B was airborne again, with a different crew: pilot Lieutenant C. G. Rowe, RNVR, observer Sub-Lieutenant R. E. Thomson, RNVR, TAG Petty Officer F.G. Storey, and had, with Swordfish L, been directed to search in an area to the east of the diving position of the two U-boats attacked four hours earlier. Just after 3 p.m. they sighted a U-boat about 12 miles away on their starboard bow, trailing a big oil slick five miles long and up to 100 yards wide.

Both aircraft turned to attack down-wind. Swordfish L led them down but was unable to get in an attack with its RPs, as the U-boat had started to dive when they were still three miles away, and there was nothing to fire at when they got to her diving position. Swordfish B dived from 1,500 feet, levelled out at 300 feet and dropped its B-bomb about 100 yards ahead of the swirl left by the submarine, which had disappeared about a minute before. None of the attackers had got a good view of the boat, but Rowe and Thomson thought she had been a 750-tonner, light grey in colour. They saw no evidence of any damage having been done by Oscar.

There was another sighting by Swordfish 50 minutes later, but this one too got away before anything could be thrown at her. After two hours and some 20 miles on their divergent north-easterly heading, CS10 decided that the convoy was getting too far off track for Kola, and swung back due east. U-boat transmissions became even more frequent during the dog watches, mostly originating in the south or south-east. Aircraft from *Striker* flying 45 and 60 miles from the carrier twice sighted U-boats, at 7.42 and 8.50 p.m.

Again it was the old story. The Stringbags could not get to them in time.

However, the transmissions plotted through the night of the 22nd/23rd indicated that the U-boats were falling back from their positions south-east of the convoy, ready to attack it when it was forced to turn south for Kola. But the far-ranging patrols of the carrier aircraft were keeping them submerged for such long periods that the convoy was beginning to leave them behind away to the south-west.

At 9.30 p.m. on the 22nd *Vindex* took over Controlling CVE for the night from *Striker*, and flew off four Swordfish, three to cover the area to the southward, one to search ahead of the convoy, where other U-boat transmissions had been intercepted.

At 9.58 Eric Johnson and Malcolm Piercy in *Vindex* Swordfish B/NR865 got a contact on their ASV 13 miles to the south-east, ran down the bearing and five minutes later sighted a surfaced U-boat, six miles off. She was too quick for them, and dived, but they marked the spot and orbited at 400 feet. Their patience was rewarded 40 minutes later when Piercy found another blip eight miles from the first, 42 miles south-east of JW59. He closed and saw another U-boat, making about ten knots. The sub had been under for some 20 seconds when Johnson arrived over the swirl but he dropped one DC as a scarer. This one had a dose of the old trouble and did not go off. Carefully Johnson marked the spot with smoke floats, then orbited the area between the two diving positions. While they were circling, Piercy got another contact eight miles from the second. This disappeared at four miles, leaving an oil patch. Johnson orbited his second and third markers.

Peter Cumberland and Frank Jackson had taken off in Swordfish L/NR857 at 10.25 p.m. and at 11.50 they reported sighting a surfaced U-boat 52 miles south-east of the convoy heading east, and approached the enemy to attack. This U-boat decided to fight it out on the surface, and two Hurricanes were scrambled from *Vindex* to help out.

At midnight Captain Bayliss looked in on the scene in the packed ADR. The staff had their hands full, with Swordfish orbiting the positions of one suspected and two known U-boats, Swordfish L fighting a surfaced submarine, Swordfish A investigating a contact 15 miles from the ship, two Hurricanes being vectored out to assist L, G being homed in distress with a broken piston and one cylinder wrecked, the destroyer *Whitehall* being vectored to assist G, three other Swordfish being vectored out to relieve time-expired searchers, two other searchers being homed, and *Striker's* Wildcats intercepting a bogey—which turned out to be Swordfish A. 'Apart from this,' Bayliss noted, 'peace reigned in the Air Direction Room.'

After firing at Swordfish L for about ten minutes, the U-boat, which had probably detected the approaching fighters on its radar, thought better of it and dived, and the Hurricanes were recalled. Cumberland went in and dropped his B-bomb in the swirl about 30 seconds after the submarine had disappeared. Dwindling fuel made Swordfish L return to the carrier 20 minutes later. When a relieving Swordfish arrived on the spot nearly an hour afterwards the crew saw a big patch of oil, some pieces of wood and a substance which they described as looking like 'large lumps of black horse manure'.

Bennett's Swordfish M was one of the four relief aircraft which took off, three to take over established searches, one to relieve the still orbiting Swordfish B. The lame Swordfish G reported that it might have to ditch, but the pilot persevered, and the Stringbag struggled on towards the ship, finally landing on after an agonising 45-minute flight.

At 2.15 a.m. on the 23rd the convoy and its escorts turned south, to leave Bear Island 35 miles away to starboard and head for Kola Inlet, hoping that if there were more U-boats lying in wait for them, the aircraft patrols would at least keep them down, as they were doing to the submarines south and south-west of Bear Island.

At this point the *Arkhangelsk* and her eight old destroyers parted company with the convoy and disappeared due east at 16 knots preparatory to swinging south again and riding the 30th meridian down to Kola. In fact three of the Trutz boats had managed to get ahead of the convoy. Two of these, Lange's *U711* and Wedemeyer's *U365*, contacted the *Arkhangelsk* group, and *U711* fired two torpedoes at the *Arkhangelsk*, and another, a Gnat homer, at her escorting destroyer, *Dersky*, but they all detonated prematurely. Lange claimed to have sunk the former HMS *Chelsea*, the latter, after some ineffectual depth-charging, to have sunk her attacker, which was wrongly identified as *U344*, the boat sunk the day before by Bennett and Couch from *Vindex*.

Sharrock and Murrant had taken off in Swordfish NF244 about midnight. In this area so far north there was light in the sky at this hour, and they sighted a surfaced submarine. Their attack was followed up with a depth-charge pattern from some of the escorts, and an oil slick ten miles long was seen, though a hit was not confirmed.

Bennett's Swordfish M flew on in fair weather, and at three minutes past three Couch suddenly got a blip on his screen, nine miles on their port beam and a few miles to the south-east of Johnson and Piercey's 9.58 p.m. contact. He and Bennett looked around them and in the clear light of the northern sun, which shone here like a bright lantern through the middle watch of the night, saw the U-boat almost at once, a long black shape.

Bennett closed. Five minutes later puffs of smoke rose round the submarine as she tested her guns. Then the Stringbag was within range and the enemy opened a continuous fire with pom-pom and several cannon. Salvoes of explosive shell burst near the wood and fabric biplane. The experienced Bennett continued to shadow, weaving between 1,500 and 2,500 feet, drawing in to not more than half a mile and turning away again, and most of the shells burst astern of them as the U-boat gunners overestimated the speed of the slow machine.

After about 20 minutes of this, when the enemy had lobbed some 800 shells at them, Bennett decided to make a medium level hit-and-run attack with one

Swordfish crew. Left to right: Sub-Lieutenant (A) Roy Jordan (pilot), Leading Naval Airman Agger (TAG), Sub-Lieutenant (A) Gareth Jenkins (observer).

depth-charge to try to make the U-boat dive. He had dropped down to 1,800 feet when he saw the submarine starting to submerge.

He immediately dived steeply and dropped three DCs alongside the complete length of the swirl, ten seconds after the U-boat's stern had disappeared. The depth-charges, as Captain Bayliss recorded, 'went off this time', and the explosions brought up a medium-sized patch of thick oil and scummy water about 100 feet in diameter, and more black 'horse manure', which was almost certainly clotted oil, with a few small strips of wood in the middle of it all. Then a light-greenish swirl of little bubbles about 10 to 15 feet in diameter appeared at the edge of the dirty patch and lasted about 20 seconds. The aircraft had to leave the scene five minutes later, as its petrol was getting dangerously low. When they landed on *Vindex* the weary Couch and Bennett had been airborne for just over four hours. Another Swordfish returning from patrol reported the oil patch in the position of Johnson's last sighting and 'what looked like a yellow football'. A *Striker* aircraft crew described the same phenomenon.

At 4.35 a.m. Roy Jordan and Gareth Jenkins in *Vindex's* Swordfish

The enemy. U-boat using evasive tactics, 23rd August, 1944, photographed from the attacking Swordfish of Roy Jordan.

A/NR861, having recovered from their brush with *Striker*'s Wildcats, were returning to the carrier on the last leg of their patrol. The sea was calm. The reception on Jenkins' ASV was very weak, but visibility was good. Jordan sighted a U-boat about eight miles dead ahead, steering for the convoy, 60 miles away to the south-west. The frigate *Loch Dunvegan*, 50 miles away, was the nearest surface escort. Jenkins sent their first sighting report to *Vindex*.

The U-boat was black and looked like a 750-tonner. Her duty watch seemed to be asleep as the Swordfish approached her. At about three-quarters of a mile she opened up with 20mm cannon and machine-guns, and started to zigzag. She fired an umbrella of ack-ack shells all round them, and in no time they were in the middle of dirty brown puffs of smoke with vicious-looking red centres. For 20 minutes Jordan drew their fire while he worked round to a position up-wind of the U-boat and Taff Jenkins reported the enemy's movements to *Vindex*. They heard him shout 'Tantivvy!' Then the R/T went ominously silent, and the conclusion in *Vindex*'s ADR was that the Swordfish had been shot down.

There were no more alarms for a while, and at 6 a.m. Jenkins' voice was suddenly heard again on the R/T, about five miles from the ship. The Swordfish was soon on the deck, to everyone's relief. A piece of shrapnel had fractured their aerial crystal just as they had started an RP attack. Then all the RPs had failed, and the U-boat had dived out of harm's way. Jordan had dropped smoke floats and orbited for 20 minutes before turning for base. When he got back he said, 'Bloody RPs. Give me depth-charges any day. Even an Oscar.' On landing, the two young subbies had to report to the bridge. Captain Bayliss and the Admiral were both pleased to see them back and sympathised with them for not getting the U-boat. The film in Jenkins' camera was developed and showed a new type of U-boat ack-ack gun aboard their target. 'No wonder they couldn't hit us,' said Taff, 'we're just too slow for all this sophisticated stuff.'

At half-past seven *Vindex* flew off two Hurricanes to chase a bogey, which turned out to be an ally, a Soviet-manned Catalina of the 118th Reconnaissance Regiment, the beginning of air cover from Russia. When *Striker* took over as Controlling CVE at 9 a.m. *Vindex*'s 825 Squadron had logged 127 flying hours in the previous day and night.

HF/DF was rich in U-boat bearings, especially around noon, and Captain Carne sent his Stringbags hunting. At 1.45 VR subbies Turvey and Lawrie and their TAG, D. C. Harris, were enjoying the bright sunshine at 3,500 feet, well to the east of Bear Island, when they sighted a slim black silhouette 15 miles ahead of them on their starboard bow. It was a U-boat on a similar course to the convoy, which had rounded Bear Island and was now on a south-easterly course heading for Murmansk.

The Swordfish turned towards the submarine, and as they approached each other head-on the U-boat opened fire with small-calibre non-explosive shells, then turned 90 degrees to port and opened up with heavier armament firing fused shell which burst short of the aircraft. Turvey turned to starboard

Convoy JW59. Vice-Admiral Dalrymple-Hamilton (centre) and Captain Bayliss (right) talk to 825 Squadron's fighter leader Jimmy Green in front of his Sea Hurricane Carol Anne, named after his daughter (Note the logo, of crossed baby's rattle and dummy beneath the name). Extreme left is Lieutenant Commander Vincent-Jones, the Admiral's Air Staff Officer, second left his Flag Lieutenant, Lieutenant Michael Chichester, RN.

on to a parallel course. The U-boat kept a heavy curtain of fire up between herself and the Swordfish, and when the aircraft turned in towards her, abruptly reversed course, and Turvey found himself flying parallel again in the opposite direction. The heavy firing, which had ceased while the U-boat was turning, opened up again. Turvey flew on ahead of her and turned to cross her bow, as he had guessed from the U-boat's reluctance to dive that she was probably the contact keeper, and he wanted to keep close enough to her to make an attack quickly if and when she did dive. But the U-boat skipper again matched his tactics and turned to starboard away from him, unmasking his heavy armament again, which recommenced its barrage. Then the gunfire abruptly ceased and in no more than another ten seconds the sub started to dive. Turvey immediately dived to attack down-sun along the fore-and-aft line of the U-boat's last visible course, although she was still turning as she dived. The old Stringbag's 130 knots was not enough for her to catch the sub before she could fully submerge. Her short periscopes had dipped under when he dropped his three DCs from 60 feet and they plunged in at 27-second intervals from 50 to 75 yards ahead of the swirl and across the curve of the U-boat's diving turn. Oil and brown bubbles came up two or three minutes after the explosions and the U-boat was cautiously assessed as 'probably damaged'.

U-boat transmissions thickened again between 4 p.m. and 5 p.m. and once more for some 45 minutes from seven o'clock. *Vindex* took over Controlling CVE at 6.10 p.m. and flew off four Swordfish, one of which returned with another case of the increasingly frequent engine trouble.

At 7.10 Bill McDonald in Sea Hurricane H/NF732 and D. R. Johnston in P/NF680 were scrambled and vectored out to 55 miles west of the convoy, where HF/DF had produced a fix on a probable U-boat. The sun was near the horizon but visibility was still almost perfect, with some scattered cloud. The two fighters flew over HMS *Caprice*, in the close screen of the convoy, then had another 40 miles to go, about ten minutes' flying time. They steadied on a course due west at 4,000 feet, and soon Johnston sighted an object just forward of his port beam, about 15 miles away. Minutes later the object separated into two surfaced U-boats. The Hurricanes turned towards them and gave the 'Tallyho!'over the R/T.

They opened formation, Johnston to starboard. McDonald was just getting into position up-sun of one U-boat when it dived a mile and a half away from him. This was out of cannon range, so McDonald immediately attacked with two rockets on the port quarter of the last seen course of the submerged submarine. His RPs hit the water about one U-boat length ahead of the swirl. Meanwhile Johnston was heading for a cloud to stalk the other U-boat, but as he was almost in it the sub began to dive, and he attacked with a full salvo of four RPs. The SAP heads smacked into the water about 15 seconds after the U-boat had disappeared, just over a sub's length ahead of the swirl, on the port beam of her course. There were still no signs of immediate results when the fighters left the scene five minutes later.

Vindex vectored Bennett and Couch in Swordfish M to the U-boat's diving

The end of a patrol. Note the wire crash barrier in the raised position.

position. As they approached at 1,000 feet, Couch got a very good contact on his screen at nine to ten miles, but at six miles this disappeared. The sea was calm and at four miles from the initial contact they saw a small black object below training a thin wake. It was too small to be a conning tower and was almost certainly a Schnorkel. This vanished at two or three miles. Bennett flew to the original position given and dropped one DC 'for luck' and a marker. The depth-charge threw up only the normal DC scum. Bennett orbited for 15 minutes, then returned to *Vindex*.

As relief aircraft, *Vindex* sent off a pair of Swordfish, a new kind of combination to cover all contingencies, one aircraft with RPs, the other carrying an Oscar and a depth-charge. At 10.20 F was 56 miles south-west of the convoy when it sighted two U-boats, which dived. Swordfish C dropped its Oscar in the swirl.

At 11 p.m. HMS *Keppel*, *Peacock* and *Mermaid*, which were acting as Starboard Bow Striking Force for the convoy, were sent to hunt down these contacts, two of three Trutz boats which had come up astern of the convoy. HMS *Loch Dunvegan* joined them later from the advanced Asdic screen. Ten minutes after the order had been received, Swordfish F regained contact with one of the U-boats, but found only a swirl at the spot.

The next patrol of Swordfish took off at 11.30 p.m. and flew for three hours without incident. Two more took off at 1.25 in the morning of the 24th, and Bennett and Couch's aircraft Z turned back with a faltering motor. At seven minutes past two, HMS *Keppel* was narrowly missed by a Gnat acoustic torpedo. At 2.35 Shaw and Drysdale in Swordfish W/915 from *Vindex* were flying at 1,500 feet when they sighted a trimmed-down U-boat five miles on their starboard bow, 54 miles north-east of the convoy.

The Swordfish approached the target, and Drysdale gave the 'Tantivvy!' on the R/T. At just over a mile range he reported that the enemy had opened a hot fire, and *Vindex* scrambled two Hurricanes to join in the fight. The U-boat was zigzagging by 90-degree turns, putting up intense fire. Shaw shadowed her, and Drysdale kept up a running commentary to *Vindex*'s ADR. A few minutes after three o'clock the Stringbag sighted *Keppel*'s foaming bow wave about ten miles away, and with this promise of support attacked with a ripple of six RPs, which straddled the U-boat as it dived, the last pair of rockets being aimed from a height of 300 feet at 200 yards' range to hit the water 100 feet ahead of the swirl. There were no signs of a kill, but the Swordfish crew estimated two possible hits. The Hurricane strike arrived but had nothing to attack.

The other escorts were racing up and now took over the hunt, while the Swordfish orbited the area. At 3.21 a.m. *Mermaid* had almost reached the markers when she got a good Asdic contact 500 yards on her starboard beam. Lieutenant-Commander Morse immediately reduced speed to seven knots, which was just as well, as the ship did not have her Foxers out, and 90 seconds later a Gnat from one of three Trutz boats which had managed to overhaul the convoy exploded close astern, followed by another one minute later, shaking the ship like a DC going off at 100 feet. The German acoustic torpedoes had a tendency to explode at the end of their runs or in the wake of a ship. Morse ordered a ten-charge pattern but there was a hiccup in the drill, and only one was fired.

At about four o'clock the Swordfish left to return to *Vindex*. By five o'clock 'Feelings of despondency were settling in,' Morse noted, 'when suddenly there was a roar from various parts of the ship that a conning tower had broken surface ...' *Mermaid* and *Loch Dunvegan* had been carrying out a slow, quiet, 'Observant' search, and the U-boat captain, unable to hear them, had assumed the coast clear.

Mermaid's Asdic operator picked up the U-boat at 800 yards off their port beam, diving. The submarine fired two SBTs, which were easily detected, and *Mermaid* dropped a ten-charge pattern, which produced a small patch of diesel oil. Asdic found the target again at 600 feet depth, astern of them. *Mermaid* attacked with DCs, *Loch Denvegan* with her Squid mortars. *Mermaid* made a third attack, and this time oil started to gush up to the surface and continued to spread out. The U-boat came up to 300 feet, and Morse made a fourth attack, following it up with another. Ten minutes after this there was a violent explosion from below. This could have been a delayed DC exploding on the bottom, but Morse signalled to the Admiral in *Vindex*, 'Still in contact. Oil welling up. Have carried out five attacks and will do more as fast as I can prepare depth-charges. Will stay here till I kill him.' His allotted time away from the convoy expired at 8 a.m., which gave him only another hour, but the Admiral now extended it by a further hour. Morse made three more attacks, and Asdic registered the U-boat crawling along at a speed of one knot between attacks, wriggling violently as the DCs were about to explode. Morse was anxious to drop as much explosive as he could before his time ran out, but the frequency of his attacks had got ahead of his DC party. While they were readying more DCs, he conned *Loch Dunvegan* in with her Squids, using his Asdic and radar. At nine o'clock Morse signalled to *Vindex*, 'U-boat very much alive and bubbling oil. It may take twelve hours to exhaust him.' He was given an extension till noon, and at once made a very slow, silent attack on the oil bubbles, then at 11.15 directed a DC attack by *Keppel*. He made two more attacks himself over the bubbles, which continued to rise more slowly. *Peacock* came up but could get no contact then had to return to the convoy. *Mermaid* and *Keppel* made a fast attack abreast. By one o'clock the bubble trail had come to a standstill, and the only echoes Asdic were getting were from them. His return now overdue, Morse expended his last DCs in three hurried attacks and suggested to Commander Jim Tyson in *Keppel* that they both remain, 'Would like to,' signalled Tyson, 'but we have to get back.' So the belligerent *Mermaid* left the scene. 'It was the worst thing I have ever had to do,' recorded Morse. He concluded that his Senior Officer must have 'some very strong reason indeed for not allowing us to remain. Perhaps enemy surface forces were known to be in the vicinity.'

The German squadron in Alten Fjord was too busy to make a sortie. That

'Secure from flying stations'.

afternoon Goodwood bombers struck at *Tirpitz* for the last time and Seafire fighter-bombers attacked the U-boat anchorage at Hammerfest. In all, they had hit the *Tirpitz* with two bombs, one of which did not explode.

Keppel and *Peacock* returned to the area of *Mermaid*'s dogged deeds at 4.30 p.m. All was as before. The bubbles had stopped and the U-boat had been submerged for 18 hours. A Russian aircraft reported a slick seven miles long in this area, and at half-past seven *Peacock* saw this river of oil and dropped DCs into it. Morse of *Mermaid* need not have reproached himself, as he did, for not having followed Nelson and disobeyed orders to leave his U-boat. Hans-Jurgen Sthamer's *U354*, his quarry, which had crippled HMS *Nabob* and sunk the *Bickerton*, never returned to port. The Russian Navy, in claiming wrongly to have sunk *U344* on the 23rd, actually sunk by Swordfish X on the 22nd, made their claim even more suspect by placing the 'kill' in the exact position in which *U354* was sunk by the *Mermaid* group on the 24th.

Meanwhile the convoy had altered course due south at 6.15 a.m. for Kola Inlet. More transmissions at night had shown that the U-boats were still dropping astern, but there were no more contacts or sightings. Four Swordfish took off for a final search at noon but sighted only two Russian aircraft. The fighters chased four other possible bogeys but they too turned out to be friendly.

At seven o'clock the local escort of the USSR flotilla leader *Baku* and four other destroyers and some small craft came up with the convoy near Kola Inlet. Then at last the British Liaison officer aboard *Baku* informed Commodore Creswell of the destinations of his ships. Seventeen of them, including his own *Samtredy* and the crane ship, as well as the rescue ship, were to go on 450 miles further east to the White Sea and the ports of Archangel, Bakharitza, Ekonomia and Molotovsk. Commodore Creswell was still worried, as his own particular destination of Molotovsk was only named on one of his charts. *Vindex*, *Jamaica*, *Striker* and the British escort force shepherded the other 16 ships to Kola Inlet. Some of the British destroyers moored at the wooden jetties of the Soviet naval base at Polyarnoe, near the entrance to the Inlet on its western side. The merchant ships anchored off Murmansk to await berths in the port. *Vindex* steamed on to Vaenga Bay, where she anchored in Berth 24A, opposite the Russian maritime aircraft base on Vaenga Island, half an hour after midnight.

7

Limit of Endurance

'HAVE YOU EVER BEEN EAST OF SUEZ?' Geoffrey Milner asked Jim Palmer.

'No,' said Palmer.

'Well, you are now.'

Vaenga Bay was not the best of anchorages for *Vindex*, with her inadequate merchantman's anchors. The water was deep and the holding ground poor. The smaller ships of the escort were better served by a pier at the head of the Bay where two destroyers could berth.

Everyone wanted to get off the ship as soon as possible and enjoy the delights ashore. In Vaenga these were sparse. Leave was piped, and the British were allowed ashore but had to keep strictly to the roads and not wander off them. There were armed guards, mainly women, at intervals along the roadside and four loudspeakers at the corners of the square broadcasting news bulletins. The town reminded some of the British matelots of the American backwoods settlements they had seen in Hollywood films, with log cabins and dirt roads. There had been some attempt just before the war to build some three-storey blocks of flats in brick. These had no floors, doors or windows, but there were families squatting on the ground-floor spaces.

Captain Bayliss, longing for exercise in the open, put on his tweeds and doggy cap and strode ashore but had not got very far into the countryside before he was fired on. There was very little to do and, with no shops, nothing to buy. There was ice on the streets but no wind, and Ken Mason and Don Moore strolled along without greatcoats. They found themselves walking past an army camp, where the Russian soldiers were having their mid-day meal over braziers, breaking brown bread into bowls of gruel. 'Look at those soldiers,' Moore said. 'They're all women.'

In Vaenga there was a camp of huts for survivors of ships sunk on incoming convoys, and a small Royal Navy hospital which cared for Merchant Navy as well as RN casualties. John Shaw and Ian Taylor went round its limited facilities. In some wards Russian patients were being looked after by their own medical staff, and to the two young British surgeons their methods seemed far out of date. They found a congenial colleague in Surgeon-Lieutenant Johnny Matthews, RNVR, an exile in this tiny isolated medical outpost in an unfriendly country.

The coldness shown by the Soviet authorities in North Russia towards the British sailors and airmen forced to spend time there reflected the general lack of gratitude for Allied aid. At a lunch given in the *Arkhangelsk*, ex-*Royal Sovereign*, for Vice-Admiral Dalrymple-Hamilton and five of his captains, including Temple Bayliss, Dalrymple-Hamilton asked Admiral Levchenko how he liked the new acquisitions to the Russian Navy. 'They are very *old*,' the Admiral said.

This was of course true, as the British admiral had to admit to himself while being plied with red caviar and vodka. When the time came to call the visiting party's boats back alongside, the interpreter said, 'Admiral Levchenko wishes to present each of you officers with a small token of this visit.' 'Expecting to receive something like the Hammer and Sickle in diamonds,' Bayliss recalled later, 'we were rather surprised to have bottles of vodka pressed into our hands.' The faces of his Commander and quartermaster as he was piped on board *Vindex* clutching a large naked bottle of vodka remained a cherished memory.

However, the party given for Russian officers in *Vindex*'s wardroom shortly after they had arrived at Vaenga was cordial enough. Most of the Russians had to be carried down the ladder afterwards. Peter Isaacson was impressed by the quality of their well-cut uniforms, with rings of genuine gold round their sleeves, unlike his own ersatz ones. And the company of dancers who visited the carrier and performed in the hangar wore chic fur and the women good make-up and silk stockings. He was told that the smartest ones were probably Party members. They had the inevitable NKVD man with them, though he was impossible to identify among the others. Hospitality was also available at the former Grand Duke Nicholas' hunting lodge, which had been turned into an officers' club.

A regatta was one way of making up for the lack of shore-going pleasures. A cutter from *Vindex* got becalmed in the lee of the *Arkhangelsk*, managed to get the wind again, then a passing Russian steamer set up a swell, and the boat's mainmast snapped. When the Admiral's barge, with Dalrymple-Hamilton acting as race officer, drew too close, a Russian sentry threatened it with a rifle. On 25 August a whaler crewed entirely by lieutenant-commanders—Stovin-Bradford, Percy Gick, Jock Kilpatrick, Jim Palmer, First Lieutenant Sargeant and Desmond Vincent-Jones, with Stovin-Bradford as cox and Percy Gick as stroke—won a pulling race round the ships in the anchorage.

Vindex and the other escorts which had brought JW59 safely to North Russia were in harbour for three days, during which time stores for the local Royal Navy staff at Murmansk were disembarked. At 1 p.m. on Monday 28 August, Admiral Dalrymple-Hamilton again transferred his flag to *Vindex*, and one hour later *Vindex*, *Jamaica* and *Striker*, escorted by *Milne*, *Marne*, *Meteor*, *Musketeer* and *Caprice*, sailed to overtake UK-bound Convoy RA59A.

The convoy had been steaming north with the 20th Escort Group (*Keppel*, *Whitehall*, *Peacock* and *Mermaid*) stationed ahead as the Striking Group, and the remainder of 20th EG as Close Screen. When the Admiral and his Heavy Escort joined them at 6 p.m. the Striking Group moved to a position on the

Vice-Admiral Dalrymple-Hamilton, CS 10, and Captain Bayliss during Operation Victual, the running of Convoys JW59 and RA59A between the United Kingdom and North Russia. Extreme left is Lieutenant Michael Chichester, RN, the Admiral's Flag Lieutenant.

The Lieutenant-Commanders' whaler crew who won their race round the ships anchored in Vaenga Bay, North Russia, between the sailing of Convoys JW59 and RA59A. Standing: stroke Percy Gick (Lt. Cdr. Flying), Desmond Vincent-Jones (Air Staff Officer to Vice-Admiral Dalrymple-Hamilton), V.L. Sargeant (First Lieutenant), Charlie Kilpatrick (Senior Medical Officer) and Jim Palmer (Assistant to Lt. Cdr. Operations, later Lt. Cdr. Operations). Seated: cox Freddie Stovin-Bradford (Lt. Cdr. Ops.)

port bow, and *Camellia, Loch Dunvegan, Cygnet, Charlock* and *Oxlip* formed an Outer Asdic Screen.

As on the outward passage, there would be little, if any, darkness on the return run. The duty of Controlling CVE was divided into 8-hour watches, with *Striker* taking over from the time of joining the convoy until 10 p.m., when she would be relieved by *Vindex*. As U-boats had detected hunting aircraft at long distances on the way out, the aircraft R/T frequency was altered and all the call signs changed, dummy traffic being maintained on the old frequency, using the old call signs.

It had been hoped that the convoy would be able to make $8\frac{1}{2}$ knots on the run, but RA59A too had a lame duck. This was the SS *Empire Elgar*. She had been in North Russia for two years. Her Master and officers had joined her a few months previously, but had never handled her at sea. She had carried out a speed trial in Kola Inlet before joining the convoy, but now her Master signalled to say that she could barely make $7\frac{1}{2}$ knots.

Fog also hampered progress soon after sailing, and no aircraft were able to fly until one Swordfish managed to get up from *Vindex* at 4.15 a.m. on the 29th for a patrol ahead of the convoy. The visibility grew even worse while it was in the air, and when it returned at 7.40 a.m. the pilot made a controlled landing by *Vindex*'s patent Morrison Method. Because of her unique blind landing technique, it was arranged that *Vindex* should maintain all routine searches until the weather cleared. It had improved sufficiently by 2 p.m. for two Swordfish to take off, and soon afterwards it was possible to resume the original carrier duty roster.

At 6 p.m. the Striking Group, *Keppel*, *Whitehall*, *Peacock* and *Mermaid*, was ordered to search through the position of *Mermaid*'s attack on a U-boat on 24 September. A Russian aircraft had reported sighting an oil stream seven miles long in this area and Thorold's group found an oil patch. *Mermaid* took a sample.

Just before 10 p.m. *Vindex* took over duty and flew off three Swordfish. One of these got an ASV contact at 20 miles ahead of the convoy, but it vanished at eight miles. *Keppel* and the Striking Group raced up and searched while the Swordfish orbited, but there was no more excitement until Eric Johnson and Malcolm Piercy sighted a floating mine, flew to the nearest escort, HMS *Marne*,

The *Vindex* Orchestra. Left to right: Surgeon Lieutenant-Commander Charlie Kilpatrick (top left, on trombone), Sub-Lieutenant (A) Al Martin (harmonica), Lieutenant (A) Gordon Bennett (trumpet), Sub-Lieutenant J.L. McGuire, Sub-Lieutenant F.S. Ellis (bassoon), at the piano Stovin-Bradford and Air Radio Officer Jock Morrison, Sub-Lieutenant (A) Norman Sharrock (flagiolet) and Chief Steward Charlie Arkell (violin).

and warned her by light. At 6.42 a.m. *Loch Dunvegan* got an HF/DF bearing indicating a U-boat on the convoy's port quarter.

Striker took over again at 6 a.m. on the 30th, and there were some U-boat transmissions in the forenoon. At 2 p.m. in *Vindex*'s watch, four Swordfish took off and got contacts at 12 and 36 miles south-east of the convoy. They flew through cloud and at 2.28 p.m. sighted a U-boat making about eight knots, six miles away. In the prevailing wind conditions the Stringbag took nearly five minutes to cover the distance, and the U-boat was long gone.

An hour later four Sea Hurricanes flew to the spot, in hopes that the enemy had come up again, but the Barents Sea was bare, and on their return one of them missed the wires and became so entangled with the barrier that the others had to land on *Striker*. While this was going on a Swordfish reported engine trouble. Ten minutes later its top cylinder blew off. Various navigational errors had also put it off course, but it eventually landed on with almost empty tanks at 5.15.

Other aircraft were failing to return on time because their crews were finding it difficult to steer accurate compass courses in these extreme northern latitudes. The merchant ships of JW59 had also had this sort of trouble. Both magnetic and gyro compasses had shown a disconcerting inconsistency leading to some erratic courses and general loss of faith in them. The local magnetic attraction, rapid change of variation and overcast skies preventing the chance of an azimuth, all contributed to error. Expert navigators like Geoffrey Milner had little trouble, and the three most experienced Swordfish crews in *Vindex* invariably navigated with complete accuracy, irrespective of which aircraft they happened to be flying in.

By the evening of the 30th Huff-Duff had found a U-boat on the convoy's port bow. At midnight the ships hauled round to port to miss this one, but there was another on their port quarter. Three Swordfish which took off from *Vindex* at 6 a.m. on the 31st had only clouds and Bear Island on their ASVs. Because of the peculiarities of the compasses they were restricted to a radius of 50 miles from the ship. *Vindex*'s three diverted Sea Hurricanes returned from *Striker*. The two carriers now reverted to 12-hour watches. Of the four Swordfish of *Vindex*'s evening patrol, one returned with a useless ASV, another with engine trouble.

Norman Sharrock, on his 107th overall, and 32nd night deck landing, crashed into the barrier, and at last joined the Sharp End Club. It was to be his last flight from *Vindex*.

At 8.45 a.m. on 1 September a Swordfish sighted a small oil patch. Huff-Duff had indicated a U-boat abeam and one astern. The Striking Group was shifted over to the convoy's starboard bow. At 9 a.m. *Striker* took over duty, and at 9.35 one of her Swordfish Mark IIs, pilot Sub-Lieutenant Comber, observer Sub-Lieutenant Bishopp, TAG J. R. Byrnes, was flying at 1,800 feet in a snowstorm, with visibility no more than two miles, when the crew sighted 'a black U-boat' on their starboard bow. Comber climbed into cloud, but the U-boat saw him and dived. He attacked and dropped three DCs about 300 feet ahead of the swirl, but the whirling snow spoiled Bishopp's photographs.

At noon the convoy once again altered to a more westerly course. More transmissions in the afternoon and the dog watches were picked up from U-boats trailing the convoy. *Vindex* took over flying at 9 p.m., but two Swordfish returned with ailing motors.

At five o'clock next morning three Swordfish led by 825 CO Freddie Sheffield in V/NR887, followed by Bennett's and Johnson's aircraft, took off from *Vindex* on an offensive anti-sub search. Cloud hid the sun, but visibility was good. At 6.10 a.m. Sheffield's observer John Vallely was given a vector to take them towards the position of an HF/DF contact off the convoy's starboard bow. At 6.18 Sheffield sighted a fully surfaced U-boat, and Vallely reported on R/T. The four ships of the Striking Group, searching in the same area 25 miles away, picked up the report and a few minutes later the order to close the spot at full speed.

Meanwhile the U-boat, coloured dark brown, which Sheffield identified as a 750-tonner, had opened fire on the Swordfish with two 37mm and three 20mm cannon and a machine-gun. Sheffield dived and fired an RP at her from 500 feet. The U-boat blew tanks to trim down, and Sheffield thought she was preparing to dive. But she continued to fire at the Swordfish, and Sheffield worked round to get up-wind for his next attack.

The U-boat turned so as to keep her stern-bearing full armament unmasked and continued to fire. Sheffield dived and from 800 feet at a range of 800 yards fired a ripple of RPs. At his approach the guns' crews cleared the submarine's deck and she began to dive. Holding his dive, Sheffield dropped two DCs from 50 feet into the sea some 15 feet ahead of the swirl where the enemy had just disappeared. They were correct for line but failed to explode. Vallely took some pictures with the clumsy big F24 camera which 825, still lacking the new equipment which they had been promised, was forced to use, but the spool jammed and spoiled the pictures.

Another Swordfish orbited the spot while the Striking Group of destroyers and sloops was homed to it. A relief aircraft, Bennett and Couch's Swordfish U, developed chronic engine trouble, and Sheffield ordered Eric Johnson's aircraft to escort it back to the ship. Bennett very nearly had to ditch, but just made it back to the deck. Johnson's aircraft had eight gallons of petrol left in his tank when he landed on.

Meanwhile the four hunters of the Striking Group were steaming hard towards the spot, Foxers streamed. At 8.50 *Keppel* sighted an aircraft marker and the four ships began a box search. They quartered the sea patiently for over two hours, and at 11.17 *Keppel* sighted a periscope and ordered all ships to close by hoisting the black pennant.

At 11.51 *Mermaid* got an Asdic contact at 1,450 yards and began a depth-charge attack. Her Asdic followed the submarine as she turned sharply to port, 400 feet below. One-funnelled *Whitehall* fired a shower of Hedgehog missiles from the for'ard launcher. *Mermaid* came hard in and dropped another DC pattern. Then the sub turned to starboard and Asdic lost her, then found her again three minutes later. *Peacock* attacked. Contact was lost, found again. *Mermaid* made her third attack. The U-boat turned hard-a-port as the charges were sinking through the water. Several times more the contact was lost and regained. *Mermaid* made another attack. The determined Morse was not going to lose this one. The two sloops followed the U-boat eastwards, and *Peacock* made what looked on *Mermaid*'s plot to be a very accurate attack. The sub turned south, then west, zigzagging all the time.

It was 4 p.m. now. The four ships pulled in their Foxers and prepared for a mass creeping attack. With *Peacock* directing them, *Keppel, Whitehall* and *Mermaid* switched off their main sets and eased in at seven knots, *Mermaid* in the centre, *Keppel* to port, *Whitehall* to starboard. Unable to fire charges from her side throwers, *Mermaid* rolled 18 DCs down her after rails. *Keppel* and *Whitehall* each fired 22 charges on the flanks, set to 500 and 850 feet. The sea erupted with geysers of white foam, then the contact faded.

There were one or two doubtful echoes, then the sub registered on the Asdics again, on a south-easterly course. *Mermaid* made ready to direct another creeping attack, but two loud underwater explosions were heard, followed by a third. The U-boat started to alter course to starboard, then stopped, at about 700 feet. *Mermaid* came in and dropped more charges. Still the sub showed no movement. *Peacock* reported big bubbles rising and 'unusual burbling noises'. The enemy seemed to be trying to surface.

Some splintered wood appeared on the sea. Then A-gun's crew in *Peacock*, corroborated by the ship's surgeon, reported that a human head had passed down the port side. Oil and wreckage were coming up practically alongside *Peacock*. Her seaboat was sent away. Over the next 20 minutes various things surfaced. The whaler picked up a pair of German trousers, a cushion, a glove, a check cloth settee cover, and a torn remnant of flesh, which was formally identified by *Peacock*'s surgeon as part of a human lung. These were the remains of U394.

After this, the threat from U-boats seemed to die away. The convoy rounded Bear Island and turned for home. Swordfish were in the air throughout the night of 2/3 September and at 7 a.m. four Hurricanes were scrambled in a hurry after the Trondheim Zenit. They actually caught a glimpse of him this time, a fast-moving Ju 88, but could not catch him. He had undoubtedly seen the convoy, and fighters were held in readiness to repel a dusk attack. But it never came, and just after midnight *Vindex*'s Swordfish resumed patrols.

The men and machines of 825 were tired now. Two Swordfish, one crewed by Johnson and Piercy, the other by Jordan and Jenkins, took off at 3 a.m. on patrol. As soon as they were airborne Eric Johnson called the ship to report oil pressure trouble, and was told to return and land on. Roy Jordan's engine did not sound very healthy either, and one cylinder was glowing red-hot. He requested permission to return also and was immediately told to continue the patrol, which was a local one, 20 miles from the convoy.

As it came in to land on, Johnson's aircraft drifted to starboard, hit the

Deck crash. On 4th September, 1944, Sub-Lieutenant Johnny Moore was landing his Sea Hurricane S when *Vindex*'s stern rose unexpectedly, hitting the aircraft, which missed all the arrester wires, lost its undercarriage on the crash barrier, and hit aircraft parked for'ard, breaking his own aircraft in two, and damaging another Sea Hurricane and two Swordfish.

The severed tail unit of Moore's aircraft in the foreground. Moore himself sits shocked and disconsolate on the wing of his broken machine.

The crane arrives to lift the wreckage clear.

Ready for action. HMS *Vindex*, Grumman Wildcat fighters and Swordfish ranged aft, before a Russian convoy operation.

bridge island and crashed into the sea upside down and on fire. Johnson bobbed to the surface but there was no sign of Malcolm Piercy. Confident of his pilot's landing abilities, the observer had had his straps loose and had been concussed by hitting his head on the radar screen. He came to under water but his foot was wedged in between the ASV and the bulkhead. He struggled free and rose towards the surface as Johnson dived down to look for him.

They both rose to the surface just as the M dinghy from the aircraft's upper wing bobbed up. Johnson climbed into it and found it already taking in water from a tear in the skin. He started baling, shouting to Piercy to keep clear for the time being in case he submerged the dinghy. When they were both aboard they had an argument as to who should sit on the drier side. The cold was bad enough, but the absence of wind probably saved their lives. A destroyer hove to close by, and Johnson shouted, 'Aren't you going to lower a boat?' The destroyer captain shouted back, 'No, the carrier's coming back.' *Vindex* had stopped and lowered her port whaler, and in 20 minutes from hitting the water the two men were rescued unharmed, apart from minor facial injuries to Malcolm Piercy, and the effects of the extreme cold. Both became eligible for membership of the Goldfish Club. In fact 825 Squadron sent in a block application to cover all those who had taken to their dinghies since joining *Vindex*.

Meanwhile Jordan and Jenkins were doggedly quartering the ocean in their ailing Stringbag. For three hours Jenkins sat in his cockpit with one eye on the engine and the other on the ASV screen. When eventually they returned to *Vindex* he went down to sick bay to see Malcolm Piercy. The observer lay in his bunk, clutching his RN Issue binoculars. 'Look what I've won, Taffy,' he said, grinning hugely. When they had crashed, all the equipment in the aircraft had been automatically written off, and whatever the crew had salvaged had become their personal property.

In the forenoon of the following day, 4 September, Kiwi Johnny Moore was in Sea Hurricane S, making a normal approach to the deck after a Viper patrol round the convoy, when *Vindex*'s stern rose just as he cut his motor over the round-down and smashed into the aircraft. Moore missed all the wires, caught the barrier with his undercarriage and crashed into the deck park for'ard, breaking his own machine in two just abaft the cockpit, damaging another Hurricane and two Swordfish and leaving himself with a very sore head jammed against the gunsight.

The heavy escort left the convoy in the forenoon of 5 September and at 4.30 p.m. steamed into Scapa Flow.

Norman Sharrock, keen to get ashore, suggested that he take some wardroom mess funds and go on a foraging expedition for food. The padre, the Reverend Pilkington, who was treasurer, gave him £25 and he was granted official permission for the foray. With him in the boat went the Captain's steward and the Met Officer, who had suddenly found that he 'wanted some maps' from RNAS, Hatston, Kirkwall. It was a one and a half hour run to

Kirkwall. There they ordered two sacks of lettuce and 50 chickens to be collected next day. On return to Scapa they found that *Vindex* had sailed for Greenock.

Although they had official sanction for their trip, missing one's ship in wartime was a court martial offence, and they spent an uneasy night aboard the depot ship *Dunluce Castle*. In the morning they rang the butcher ashore and had the chickens delivered, somewhat bloody, to the depot ship, and caught a boat for Scotland.

Meanwhile *Vindex* was heading for Greenock. When she was in the Pentland Firth she received a report that a U-boat was in the area. Two Swordfish were flown off, Gordon Bennett and Peter Couch in one, Roy Jordan and Gareth Jenkins in the other, to do a search/strike patrol. The crews were not pleased, as it now looked as if they would miss the party being organised for that evening in the ship. But they sighted nothing and were recalled just in time, as they thought, for the binge.

They arrived in the circuit, and Bennett landed first with no hitches. But as Jordan made his approach to the deck Jagger Mills waved him off. The ship called them up and told Taff Jenkins that their hook was not down. Roy Jordan threw the aircraft all over the sky in a fruitless attempt to dislodge the hook, and they were eventually ordered to make for RAF Stornoway, the nearest land base.

It was dark by this time. Jenkins gave his pilot a course to steer and switched over from R/T to Stornoway's W/T frequency. They found the airfield, and Jenkins requested permission to land. Back came the answer 'Wait'. They had now been airborne for over three hours and had passed the limit of safe endurance. Jenkins made repeated requests to land, but got the same refusal. Finally they were so low on fuel that he came in anyway, permission or no permission.

He made a perfect ADDL approach, but as they came over the boundary fence they saw a big Halifax at the other end of the runway, just getting airborne. They got down without hitting it, but were severely reprimanded at Air Traffic Control for landing without permission. The CO of the Naval squadron on Stornoway also gave them a tremendous bottle, threatening court-martial, and handed them a sealed envelope when they took off, to give to Percy Gick. As they approached *Vindex* the Squadron was flying off to return to Machrihanish. They landed, and Percy Gick ordered them through his loud-hailer to stay in the cockpit and follow the others off. Jordan waved the envelope at him and was summoned to FlyCo. Wings opened the letter, scanned it, roared with laughter, tore it in little pieces and threw them overboard.

Charlie Kilpatrick also made a report. *Vindex*'s Senior Medical Officer had served with the Squadron and the ship's staff through five hard round-the-clock operations, and he knew better than anybody just how much in need of rest they all were.

In particular he identified four aircrews who 'have throughout, by deed and

'Range three Swordfish'.

example, raised and maintained the standard of efficiency of the squadron at its recognisably high level. All of this group have now reached, or exceeded, the psychological limit of endurance ... For them an adequate spell of leave followed by a period of non-operational flying is considered absolutely essential.' A second group, he thought, could be kept on for one more operation with the ship, a third simply needed adequate rest and leave. In the event his recommendations were only partially implemented.

The Squadron flew its aircraft ashore to Machrihanish from *Vindex* on 7 September and many of them rejoined the ship via the Clyde Ferry for a final get-together. Norman Sharrock and his party rejoined the ship from Scapa with their bloody fowls, and chicken for dinner was a rare treat. On the 9th, after several farewell parties and speeches, Squadron members left the ship which had been a home for over eight months.

8

Trial

SHE WAS NOT THE SAME SHIP. A carrier always seems moribund when her squadrons have left her, but after 825, which had seemed part of the ship, had flown away *Vindex* felt dead. Footsteps rang through the empty hangar, the passageway flanked by empty cabins was silent. Worse still, both Freddie Stovin-Bradford and Percy Gick had left for other appointments. When Wings flew off he beat up the ship, and Bayliss shook his fist at him.

On 25 September the *Queen Mary* brought Winston Churchill back from the USA and berthed just downstream from *Vindex* in the Clyde. That night the wind got up and started to push at the carrier's high superstructure. This worried John Baker, who was Officer of the Day. He went up to the compass platform, took some bearings and called the cable party, but decided that the ship was not dragging, told the Officer of the Watch to keep a careful eye on the situation, and turned in.

At 6 a.m. there was a jarring crash. John Shaw leaped out of his bunk convinced that they had been torpedoed, thinking, in his torpid state, that they were at sea. Jim Palmer, recently appointed Air Staff Officer, whose whole cabin had shuddered like a room in an earthquake, rushed to his porthole— and found himself looking at the mighty stem of the *Queen Mary*.

Once again *Vindex*'s anchors had let her down. She had dragged steadily and stealthily through the night and finally scraped down the starboard side of the great grey liner. When John Baker reached the flight deck, Captain Bayliss was already up on the port after pom-pom platform with a signalman, passing helm orders to the Officer of the Watch on the bridge by semaphore. With no power on the engine these were not very effective. *Vindex* ended up across the *Queen Mary*'s stem, the latter with a long ugly scar down her side. The look on Captain Bayliss' face almost turned the chagrined Officer of the Day to stone.

With damage to her port gun platforms and walkways, *Vindex* went into dock for repairs. As a result, the working-up programme for her new squadron, No. 811, had to be cut to ten days.

This was particularly unfortunate, as the new faces did not seem to fit aboard ship. There was inevitable prejudice against them just because they were not 825, which the ship's company had come to regard as *their* squadron, as much a fixture in the ship as her guns. For their part, the person- nel of the new squadron became quickly fed up with being continually

Dawn. 'Start up Wildcats'.

compared with the apparently peerless 825, and always found wanting.

After over a year in HMS *Biter* in the thick of the Atlantic U-boat war, 811 had been re-formed, and during the three months prior to joining *Vindex* had worked ashore under No. 15 Group, Coastal Command, being twice complimented for its work with the RAF. But the junior members of the squadron had had very little sea time or flying at night. They had heard while still ashore of the awesome reputation of *Vindex* for flying her aircraft in conditions which would frighten off most aircrews, and they heard the news of their draft chit to her with some alarm. When they flew aboard her, the carrier's staff seemed dauntingly efficient. The latter found the squadron's flying ability up to standard, and there were no serious accidents or injuries during working-up, though as yet there was none of 825's enthusiasm or dash. But then there was only one 825 ...

It was to be hoped that the necessary harmony would be achieved soon, as *Vindex* was shortly going back to North Russia, to escort Convoy JW61 on Operation Trial.

On 21 October *Vindex*, with her squadron aboard, left the Clyde to rendezvous with the 21st Escort Group and proceed to Scapa Flow, where she arrived on the 15th.

CS10, Vice-Admiral Dalrymple-Hamilton, was again to command the escorting forces. For the very first time, this convoy was to have three escort carriers, *Vindex*, her British-built sister *Nairana* and the US-built *Tracker*. With him also he had the cruiser *Dido* and the ships of two escort groups: the 3rd EG's ex-US frigates *Duckworth* (Senior Officer), *Essington*, *Cooke*, *Berry* and *Rowley*, sloops *Lark* and *Lapwing*, and the veteran British W-class destroyer *Walker*; the 21st EG's former American destroyer-escorts *Conn*, *Byron*, *Fitzroy*, *Deane*, *Redmill* and *Rupert*. The Home Fleet destroyers *Nubian* and *Undaunted* would screen CS10 as far as the rendezvous with the convoy.

Nairana retained her Atlantic squadron, No. 835, re-equipped with 14 Swordfish IIIs and six Wildcat VIs. They were an experienced night-flying unit, though this would be their first Arctic trip. No. 853 Squadron in *Tracker* was a new squadron, formed to operate Grumman Avengers, with ten Avenger IIs and six Wildcat VIs. *Vindex* also had four Wildcat VIs aboard, strangers after the Sea Hurricanes, and very different in appearance with their big radial engines, tubby fuselages and narrow-tracked undercarriages. Biggest contrast, however, was between *Vindex*'s 12 Swordfish IIIs and *Tracker*'s big, bulky but sleek monoplane Avengers, with their enclosed cockpits and dorsal turret.

Having once again embarked the flag of CS10 in the forenoon, *Vindex* sailed from Scapa with *Dido*, *Nairana*, *Tracker* and the two escort groups at 1 p.m. on 21 October to rendezvous with Convoy JW61 and escort it to Kola Inlet.

Two Avengers took off from *Tracker* on a Cobra to locate the convoy. They found JW61 but got lost in bad visibility on their way back and eventually broke radio silence to request a homing by HF/DF. CS10 was late at the rendezvous, which was made at 9.30 a.m. on 23 October. The carriers took up their stations in the box.

There were 32 merchantmen around them, under the command of Rear-Admiral M. W. S. Boucher, RN, who had been a pilot in HMS *Courageous* in peacetime and the first Director of Air Material at the Admiralty. The convoy was predominantly American, with 24 vessels bearing unmistakably transatlantic names, including *Collis P. Huntingdon*, *Donald W. Bain*, *James M. Gillis*, *Andrew W. Preston*, *Eleanor Lord*, *William Wheelright*, *Joyce Kilmer*, *Abner Nash*, *Benjamin Schlesinger*, *Eloy Alfaro*, *Arold, L. Winslow*, *Henry Adams*, *John Harp Williams*, *Keith Palmer*, *Laurence W. Brengle*, *Nicholas Biddle*, *Park Benjamin*, *William Pepper* and *Winifred L. Smith*. There was even an SS *Stage Door Canteen*. The Commodore's own ship was the SS *Port Crevecoeur* and there were seven other vessels, *Port Yukon*, *Fort Romaine*, *Laurelwood*, *Syrian Prince*, *Lapland*, *San Venancio* and *Dolabella*. Also with the convoy were the Russian submarine chasers *1477*, *1485*, *1502*, *1504*, *1510* and *1517*.

The Arctic 'day' was now shorter than it had been on the JW59 run to Kola, and there would be more genuine night flying. The carriers were to work three watches of eight hours each, with the Controlling CVE flying standing patrols and searches, the Standby CVE ready to scramble extra searches or strikes if required, and the Available CVE resting her aircrews, command personnel and flight deck parties. This arrangement had not allowed for the fact that only *Vindex* and *Nairana* were equipped for night flying, and in the event each of the latter acted as Duty CVE for half the night, with *Tracker*'s Avengers flying daylight patrols.

On 26 October a Swordfish from *Vindex* wasted time carrying out a Cobra patrol on a rain cloud which was heading away from the convoy, and got itself lost. Captain Bayliss broke W/T silence to home them by D/F bearings. After four and three-quarter hours wandering the dark, cloudy skies the two shaken and exhausted young men landed on *Vindex*'s flight deck with two gallons of petrol left in their tank.

The weather was unusually good for this time of year, and there were no gale warnings, but it was treacherously fickle. The wind varied constantly from light airs to strong gusts, and there was a heavy, sullen swell which had greenhorns puking over the rail, and flight decks rolling awkwardly. *Tracker* lived up to her reputation for rolling on wet grass. 'I am reliably informed,' noted Captain Huntley, 'that, in a life not normally devoid of excitement, aircrews consider their senses are most acutely tickled during a journey from the after end of the flight deck to the accelerator when the ship is rolling 32 degrees each way. The accelerator being situated on the extreme port edge of the flight deck, the maximum thrill is obtained when once in position. At this moment a roll to port gives an uninterrupted vista of scudding clouds to starboard and an undulating sea to port.' In conditions like this *Tracker*'s deck handling parties found moving the heavy Avengers a hard struggle, and pilots had difficulty taxiing their big machines forward to the accelerator for launching.

But at least the Avenger crews were warm in their big glasshouses. For the

A Wildcat leaves *Vindex*'s deck, with ships of a Russian convoy on the horizon.

Gremlins! A favourite trick was to hold down the arrester wire just as your deck hook groped for it.

Swordfish crews the nights were long and bitterly cold. Though the crews now wore rubber immersion or 'Zoot' suits, they knew that survival in these icy waters depended on a very swift rescue.

Two of 811's Wildcats were scrambled from *Vindex* at 10.15 a.m. on the 26th to intercept a bogey which turned out, as did so many later alarms, to be a Catalina. Just before midnight HF/DF picked up U-boat transmissions, and the convoy altered course to avoid the area where they were concentrating, while the two escort groups were detached on a hunt. On the 27th an Avenger from *Tracker* on sector search off the convoy's starboard bow sighted a U-boat steering for the convoy and 40 miles away from it. The Avenger attacked and dropped an Oscar, which failed to work.

At five minutes past midnight on 28 October Swordfish H, piloted by Lieutenant (A) D. L. Walsh, RNVR, returning to land aboard *Vindex*, came in too low and was waved off. The aircraft flew up the starboard side of the ship, still losing height, and crashed into the sea just abaft the island.

Captain Bayliss was at once faced with an agonising decision. He well knew the danger of slowing his ship with U-boats in the vicinity, but he could actually hear his own men calling out for help from the water, and he feared the effect on his other aircrews if he did not try to rescue them. Dropping marine markers and informing the destroyer *Opportune*, their crash boat, he began a turn to starboard and lowered a whaler.

Opportune, which had been somewhat closer to the scene than Bayliss had estimated, came up as *Vindex* was completing the turn, and just as Admiral

Gremlins? Wildcat in The Goofers after hooking an arrester wire.

Able Seaman Jim Daymond was an inventive ship's safety equipment worker.

Dalrymple-Hamilton appeared on the bridge. He ordered Bayliss to leave the rescue to the destroyer and rejoin the convoy.

As one of the Swordfish crew, who was shouting for help from the water, was seen close by *Vindex*'s bows, with the whereabouts of the other man uncertain, Bayliss made a stern board to clear both them and *Opportune* before going ahead again to regain station with the convoy. The whaler was rehoisted with difficulty. At half-past one *Opportune* reported that Walsh had been picked up dead and that his observer, Sub-Lieutenant (A) W. E. Carr, RNVR, could not be found.

Both Walsh, an experienced pilot, and Willy Carr had been very popular in the squadron, and this tragedy crystallised some of the aircrews' fears of flying at night over Arctic waters where, they had been quite rightly told, the maximum life expectancy of an airman plunged into the icy sea was about 20 minutes. Deck landings grew more ragged.

However, there were few close U-boat contacts until the convoy reached the approaches to Kola, where the submarines had foregathered. With 50 carrier-borne aircraft, a swarm of Russian-manned Catalinas and two support groups, the escorts swamped the area and kept the U-boats down, and the convoy arrived in Kola Inlet at 9 a.m. on 28 October without loss.

The convoy escort force remained in Kola Inlet until 11.45 a.m. on 2 November. HMS *Duckworth*, the leader of 3rd Escort Group, remained alongside *Vindex* all the time, and the carrier kept all the ships of 3rd EG supplied with meat, bread and fresh vegetables.

It was thought that Walsh and Carr might have been lost because they could not operate their dinghies. In the darkness and freezing water it would have been next to impossible to tear open the press studs, then turn on the oxygen bottle, first removing the pin. The ship's Safety Officer suggested having an inflated dinghy ready on deck to drop over the side. On trials the oxygen bottle tore off and the dinghy filled with water. Able Seaman Jim Daymond, a staff safety equipment worker who had been in *Ark Royal* and *Formidable* before joining *Vindex*, suggested removing the oxygen bottle and substituting a nut with a blank end, the dinghy being inflated by bellows. This worked, and an inflated dinghy with someone in attendance was always ready whenever aircraft were taking off or landing on.

Shortly after clearing the Inlet to rendezvous with UK-bound Convoy RA61, *Vindex*'s Asdic cabinet reported hydrophone effect from a torpedo heading for the ship's port bow. Bayliss ordered 'Hard-a-port!', and the speeding fish was lost abeam.

A *Vindex* Swordfish reported an ASV contact just before 8 p.m. but it disappeared before the plane could reach the spot. There were some crashes and heavy landings on the flight deck.

At 9.20 p.m. on 3 November Swordfish G came in to land on with its port wing low. The batsman signalled a correction and the pilot swung his starboard wing over too violently, hitting the deck with it. He slewed over the starboard side of the ship, his deck hook snagging No. 3 wire as he went. The Swordfish hung over the side for about half a minute, until the hook was pulled right out of the aircraft, which fell away into the sea. *Vindex*'s swift rescue technique recovered the pilot unhurt, but the observer, Sub-Lieutenant (A) D. Evans, RNVR, who was very popular in the squadron, was never seen again, a search by the crash boat *Opportune* proving fruitless.

At 6.35 a.m. on 7 November Swordfish F, piloted by Sub-Lieutenant (A) A. D. Arcus, RNZNVR, left *Vindex* for a Cobra patrol using RATOG to get him off the deck. The launch appeared to go well, and the aircraft was lost to view ahead of the ship, but a few minutes later a marine marker was sighted in the sea about five cables astern of the ship, followed shortly by distress signals. *Opportune* at once closed the spot and rescued the crew of the crashed aircraft, only a minute and a half after it had taken off. Arcus reported that one of the RATOG rockets had failed to function properly and he had been unable to control the Swordfish.

At 11 a.m. on 8 November *Vindex* was turning into wind to fly off and land on anti-submarine patrols in the sort of long, low oily swell that is not always obvious, when the ship made a sudden exceptionally heavy roll. There were two loud reports, *pop ... pop*, from aft where two Wildcats, parked on the starboard after end of the flight deck, parted their standard lashings. One fighter went over the side, the other rolled forward and finally ended up on its back in the middle of the flight deck, out of commission for the rest of the trip.

Flying in *Vindex* was now reduced to a minimum, but there were two deck-landing crashes in succession in daylight, and night landings deteriorated, despite the fact that the nights were light, and the sea and swell moderate.

'Even by day,' wrote Bayliss, 'a safe landing became an occasion for relief ...'

It was clear, when the ship had returned to the UK, that 811's troubles stemmed from insufficient training in night flying. C-in-C Home Fleet made this point in a signal to Lumley-Lyster, Flag Officer, Carrier Training, and urged that training should be increased for any squadron allocated to a Russian convoy in the future, coupled with as few changes as possible in flying and deck-handling personnel during the winter.

Meanwhile FOCT had been visiting all the three carriers that had been on the JW/RA61 round trip. He found the squadrons in *Nairana* and *Tracker* 'in very good heart', but it was obvious to him that *Vindex*'s squadron had 'lost confidence in itself' and required 'further working-up to re-establish its morale'. The Squadron flew ashore for further night flying training.

9

'The stormy wind ariseth...'

VINDEX'S OLD AND BOLD 825 SQUADRON had gone, minus some of its time-expired crews, to Limavady, Northern Ireland, to work under Coastal Command. They operated against U-boats which were using their Schnorkels to work close to the western coasts of Britain and Ireland again, as German submarines had done in the early period of the war. On 7 November the Squadron was transferred to Mullagmore, about ten miles south of Coleraine, where their ageing Sea Hurricanes were replaced by eight Wildcats. There they flew convoy escort and continued to keep an eye open for snort boats in the North-Western Approaches. Christmas was coming. Many aircrew had bought poultry to take home, and they all had their leave passes signed and ready, when Freddie Sheffield came into the mess and said, 'Sorry chaps. We're going back to Vindex.'

The news was received by old Vindex hands with very mixed feelings. They had known that they would be going to sea again sometime, but now it looked like being a white Christmas in Murmansk. They flew aboard on Monday 11 December for two weeks working-up. Peter Cumberland and Frank Jackson, Eric Johnson and Malcolm Piercy got their old cabins back and began to feel at home. Cumberland, Peter Couch and Freddie Sheffield had been awarded the DSC, Piercy a Mention in Despatches. They were sorry to have missed the ship's commissioning anniversary party on 15 November.

They were met by Vindex's new Commander (Air), Lieutenant-Commander A. J. D. Harding, DSC, who had just joined the ship. 'Tich' Harding had been doing this job in Tracker since September 1942, and, with the ship due for a refit, had been expecting some long-awaited leave when he got orders to join Vindex forthwith ... 'I was not amused. When I joined her I found a very unhappy ship. They felt that no-one could replace Percy Gick. However successful one was at solving the different problems that arose it was always considered that Percy would have been even more successful, and maybe he would have been, but it did make life difficult.' Then one day there was a near-accident when a RATOG unit failed. Bayliss said to Harding, 'Well, who do I court-martial for this?' Without thinking Wings replied, 'Start with me, sir, I take full responsibility for my department.' This was considered to be the answer that Percy Gick would have given, and from then on Harding had no hassle.

They were exercising in the Clyde on Christmas Eve, and most of the ship's company and squadron personnel were expecting the Christmas leave which Captain Bayliss had promised them, especially the many Glaswegians in the crew. But at four o'clock in the afternoon the ship was groping her way through almost impenetrable fog at the mouth of the Clyde. Bayliss broadcast, 'I'm sorry, but you can see what it's like. I shall be forced to anchor off Rothesay.' *Ad hoc* arrangements were made for celebrating on board, but at 8.30 the engines were started up again, and the ship began to move. Bayliss had decided that, fog or no fog, he could not deprive the men of the comfort of their families at Christmas. Aided by Geoffrey Milner's skilful navigation, and using radar, he took the ship up-river. When Christmas Day dawned bright and clear, *Vindex* was found to be anchored 12 yards from her allotted berth.

From the Admiralty's point of view the choice of 825 Squadron was inevitable for the forthcoming Operation Greystoke, to escort Convoy JW63 to Kola Inlet and return with RA63. There would be very little daylight at all, with black darkness for most of each 24 hours. *Vindex* would be on her own this time and would have to provide all the air power. Bad weather too was forecast, sleet and snow, with a threat of gales. It had to be the night hawks of 825.

Vindex sailed for Scapa Flow, and on 28 December Commander John David Lewis Williams joined her there as Executive Officer in succession to Commander Archbold. Williams had been trained in the school ship *Worcester* and after service in the barque *Garthpool* had remained under the Red Duster until becoming Lieutenant RN in 1937.

Vindex had caused some delay in departure by getting her cables twisted, but finally embarked the flag of Vice-Admiral 10th Cruiser Squadron in the forenoon of 31 December in Scapa Flow, and sailed at noon with HMS *Diadem* and six ships of the 23rd Destroyer Flotilla to rendezvous with JW63, which had left Loch Ewe on the 30th, and escort it to Kola. Accommodation aft in the carrier was really crowded this time. In addition to CS10 and his staff, *Vindex* had embarked Mr D. H. Luna, technical adviser to the Norwegian Ministry of Reconstruction, and a 'Crofter' party of ten officers and 21 other ranks of the Free Norwegian Army and Navy to superintend the work of reconstruction in Finmark.

U-boats had been reported in the approaches to Scapa, and a Swordfish took off at 2.20 p.m. for a two-hour patrol ahead of the force. The convoy was sighted at 11.15 a.m. on 1 January and *Vindex* had taken station in the box by 12.45.

There were 36 merchantmen in JW63, including four munition ships, four tankers and two escort oilers, with Commodore Boucher in SS *Samaritan*. Some of his ships, like the SS *Henry Bacon* and *Crosby Noyes*, had been to Kola before, and the old faithful *Keppel* and the sloops *Cygnet*, *Lark* and *Lapwing* were veterans of the Russian run as well. With them in his close escort he had the old World War I destroyers *Westcott* and *Walker* and the corvettes *Alnwick Castle*, *Allington Castle* and *Bamburgh Castle*.

Vindex crossed the Arctic Circle on 2 January and Commander Williams was presented with his passport to the Arctic, originated by Commander Archbold, issued by Captain Bayliss as official representative of King Neptune, which proclaimed that the recipient 'embarked in HMS *Vindex* in latitude 66°33' North and in longitude 1°00' E bound for the Dark and Frosty Wastes of The Land of the Midnight Sun and did with My Royal Permission enter this Dread Region by crossing The Arctic Circle by virtue whereof, I, Neptunus Rex, Ruler of the Raging Main, do hereby declare him to be a loyal and trusty Bluenose and do call upon all Icebergs, Polar Bears, Whales, Narwhals, Sealions and other Creatures of the Frigid North to show him due deference and respect.' This essential document was signed by 'Neptunus Rex, Ruler of the Raging Main,' and by 'Aurora Borealis, Queen of His Majesty's Northern Provinces'.

At 10.5 a.m. on 3 January an unidentified aircraft was picked up approaching the convoy. It closed to 19 miles, then its range opened and shortly afterwards the blip faded from the screens. Another bogey registered at 11.45, 12 miles west-sou'-west of the convoy, and two fighters were scrambled. This snooper got to within six miles south-east of the ships, then flew away. *Vindex* did not see him but *Diadem* reported him as a BV 138. The Wildcats could not find him and landed on again at 12.10.

Wildcats were kept at readiness on the flight deck, as the convoy must have been sighted by now, and two of them went off again at 2 p.m. but came back in the twilight at half-past two with no score, though the destroyer *Scorpion* had done her best to shoot them down as they flew over her.

Much of the flying was being done in total darkness and patchy visibility. Even if every merchantman kept station, for the carrier to operate across a box two and a half miles wide, chasing the wind to fly off and land on aircraft, under such conditions, with only the aid of the Type 272 radar fitted in *Vindex*, would have been difficult, and with only normal straggling extremely dangerous. But to reduce the risk of collision to normal limits, *Vindex* had produced another of her unique inventions. On the suggestion of Navigating Officer Geoffrey Milner, Sub-Lieutenant (A) T. A. Mitchell, RNVR, the ship's Air Radio Officer, had very skilfully modified an ASV Mark XI aircraft radar set. This was installed on the bridge, and, despite limitations, gave a sufficiently clear presentation of the ships in the convoy to allow manoeuvring in the box with reasonable safety. Mitchell would have liked one of the American semi-portable SQ sets if a British Type 277 was not available, as these were also better for picking up low-flying aircraft than *Vindex*'s Type 281. Bayliss made a note to request the fitting of one of these sets.

In the forenoon of 5 January the convoy had reached an area of possible U-boat concentration, and 825 began patrols of two Swordfish, one searching ahead, one astern of the convoy. But the ships sailed on all day without incident, and patrols were called off at 4.30 in the afternoon. The sea was lively and one aircraft crashed and broke its undercarriage. Patrols were resumed at 7.45 a.m. on the 6th and maintained until 5.35 a.m. on 7 January, when bad weather stopped flying. The final patrol of the outward trip was flown off at 10.20 a.m. that day, and one of its Swordfish sighted the Russian local escort coming out to meet the convoy. Paravanes were streamed during the forenoon of the 6th as the ships approached the Murman coast, and at one o'clock on the afternoon of the 7th Vindex, escorted by four of the Fleet destroyers of 23rd DF, steamed on ahead and entered Kola Inlet, anchoring at No. 48 Berth in Vaenga Bay at 6.30 p.m.

It was a sign of the times, and of the progress of the war, that for the first time a Russian convoy had reached its destination without a single brush with the enemy. The seven U-boats of the Stier Group had actually been deployed, four south of Bear Island, three off the entrance to Kola Inlet, but none of them made contact.

Delay by the Soviet authorities kept the Norwegian party on board Vindex until the afternoon of 10 January, just over 12 hours before she was due to sail again. It began to look as if they would never get away, but remain to swell the congestion in the ship, now made worse by the addition of 21 Navy, Merchant Navy and Army men taking passage home. Eight officers of 825 Squadron were invited to Vaenga Air Station, and some of their hosts made a return visit to the ship.

At 9 a.m. on 11 January, the Norwegians having at last been put ashore, CS10 once more took his flag aboard Vindex, and in company with the destroyers Zambesi, Zebra, Walker and Westcott sailed to escort RA63.

Before the convoy had even formed up properly Huff-Duff was calling out U-boat bearings. Escorts made a DC attack, and the ships of RA63 executed a neat 90-degree turn in the darkness, led by the Commodore in the SS British Respect.

Vindex flew off one Swordfish on patrol at 10.40 a.m., soon after leaving Kola Inlet, which was relieved by two others at 1 p.m., and constant patrolling by a Stringbag pair was maintained until just before midnight. The arrester wires malfunctioned, and Cumberland's and Jackson's aircraft, the last one to land on, went into the barrier. Repair to the wires prevented flying until half-past five in the morning. After that the sea became ominously sullen and angry, the sky blackened, the cloud ceiling sank lower and lower, and with the reports of an imminent south-westerly gale, the aircraft were recalled. The CO's Swordfish was the last to land on, and Sheffield had to make his approach in swirling snow, the forerunner of a cold front stretching right across the path of the convoy from North Cape to Spitzbergen. Escorts carried out more DC attacks on U-boat contacts, but flying was impossible, with visibility down to groping distance at 300 yards.

Working with the aircraft on the flight deck when the ship was rolling and the deck slippery from sleet or snow was a hard chore. It was fairly easy to check the fore-and-aft movement of an aircraft with brakes and chocks under the wheels, but rolls and skids were trickier. Wildcats with their wings folded were especially awkward beasts, as they shifted about constantly on their narrow-tracked undercarriages and would often lift one wheel off the deck in a heavy roll. Vindex's metal deck became much more slippery than the

Safe arrival. HMS *Diadem* and escorts after Convoy JW63 has reached Kola Inlet, North Russia, without one encounter with the enemy.

wooden planking of an American-built CVE and many more permanent lashing-down points were needed than were fitted in the British-built carriers.

The flight deck was normally kept sufficiently clear of snow to operate aircraft. If the deck was steady enough, a Clarkat tractor with a steel plate on the back, adjusted to clear the top layer of snow, was used to save time, though this left a thin coating of very slippery ice which had to be cleared by hand, with all the shovels available, sand being quite useful on thin layers of snow to stop skidding. When the Aircraft Handling Party was at work with the ship rolling heavily they used life-lines secured to arrester wires and to a central jackstay, itself attached to the barrier and wires. What they really needed also were some boots or overshoes with a few heavy spikes.

Soon the full fury of a gale was roaring out of the south-west, battering at the tossing lines of ships. By 8 a.m. next morning, 12 January, its force had moderated somewhat, but the wind was now ahead. The blunt-contoured carrier butted through strong gusts, rough seas and a heavy swell. The Commodore reduced speed to allow stragglers to catch up.

There was no flying on the 13th, but *Videx* kept three Wildcats on deck to cope with emergencies. They were still there on the night of the 14th, and remained there undamaged, when a fierce gale fell on the convoy from the north-east, bringing rapidly thickening snow and high seas. The convoy turned beam-on to the rising sea, and *Vindex*'s engine room recorded a roll of $33\frac{1}{2}$ degrees. There was some damage to exposed fittings, and several minor injuries to men thrown off their feet, but the ship handled very well. Long icicles hung down from the bridge.

The ballast shifted in the American SS *Amasa Delano*. She took a list of 20 degrees to port and was in some danger of foundering as she rolled her heart out. The convoy altered course to leeward to help her and reduced speed by one knot, although this ran the ships too close to North Cape and the German torpedo bombers which had attacked, unsuccessfully, the previous Russian convoy, the first time this method had been used since PQ18 in 1942. But the vile weather had grounded them as well. By strenuous efforts the *Amasa Delano* corrected her list and regained her station in the convoy.

At 9 p.m. on the 15th HF/DF picked up a U-boat's transmission some 30 miles from the convoy. The weather moderated enough to allow two Swordfish to take off at 2 a.m. in the graveyard watch, but they returned after two hours in deteriorating weather with nothing to report, and flying was discontinued again.

During the forenoon a warning was picked up from Iceland forecasting a gale of up to hurricane force, likely to cross the track of the convoy. Everything loose or moveable aboard all the ships was secured or lashed down, and they plodded on grimly, waiting for the tempest to howl. In the afternoon the American SS *John Gibbon* dropped out with condenser trouble, and one escort stayed with her. The British tanker *Longwood* was also in difficulties. All her generators had broken down and one furnace had collapsed during the night. She held on doggedly, manoeuvring with difficulty.

Vaenga Bay.

It was during the last dog watch that the natural enemy, more savage than any human, struck them out of the west-nor'-west and quickly rose to great strength and ferocity.

The Admiral left the control of the merchantmen to the Commodore, and Boucher decided to stand on with the convoy. It was snowing and very dark. They were on a course they knew, with the wind abaft the starboard beam, and settled down, as much as any ships could ever do in a hurricane, to a speed of 8 knots, which Boucher thought best in the circumstances. It was his experience that this speed would keep a Liberty ship manoeuvrable with a gale abaft her beam but was not fast enough to allow her propeller to race dangerously. Thus an old Fleet Air Arm pilot guided his fleet into the gale.

But for the escorts there was no settling down. By 8.30 p.m. some of them could no longer hold on course and hove to. *Vindex* became unmanageable at 8 knots with the wind fine on the starboard quarter and proved impossible to steer, even with the aid of manoeuvring engines. Finally, at 9.20 p.m., she hove to. As she did so she rolled over 38 degrees, with the wind roaring at 80 knots. Waves broke over her catwalk, and several fish were left stranded there. Ton after ton of green water fell on her flight deck. Sea water flooded in through the fresh air system intakes, which had to be closed off. Peter Isaacson had been sent down to the wardroom to collect something and was there when the ship heeled. Sir Oliver Swan's grand piano, lashed down to the deck, broke loose and pursued him down the canting surface into a corner, where it stuck, lodged across the adjoining bulkheads. The ringbolts securing the long wardroom tables to the deck sheared off, and the tables were smashed against the bulkheads. For days the action ration sandwiches were eaten propped up in a corner somewhere.

During the night *Vindex* managed to maintain a course almost due north, putting the wind fine on her starboard bow, keeping up revolutions for ten knots, though her actual speed over the ground was more like three. Only occasionally did she tend to pay off from the wind, and Bayliss was able to bring her back without undue difficulty. The needle on the wind speed indicator on the bridge hovered constantly around 75 knots.

When a meagre, pale light signalled the dawn of the 17th the Commodore had only seven ships still with him. The rest were scattered over the Norwegian Sea.

In *Vindex*, with enclosed spaces virtually hermetically sealed by the closure of the fresh air system vents, the atmosphere was very thick, but had become gradually sweetened by the smell of rum. A cask of Nelson's Blood had broken loose in the spirit room and with the violent motion of the ship had breached several others. This apparent tragedy was paralleled by the smashing of case after case of whisky, gin and rum which had been badly stowed in the wardroom liquor store deep down in the ship.

By half-past nine in the morning the wind had dropped to 42 knots and Bayliss decided to turn again and try to overtake the convoy. Other escorts which had also hove to now turned as well, but because of damage most of

Goodbye to Russia for No. 825 Squadron, recalled to *Vindex* for Operation Greystoke, Convoy JW63 to North Russia and the return Convoy RA63. Here a Swordfish takes off on patrol shortly after leaving Kola Inlet to escort RA63.

them were unable to keep pace with the carrier. Destroyers *Westcott* and *Walker* had had their Asdics smashed and flooded, and *Keppel's* radio was out of action. *Vindex* eventually shaped course for Thorshavn in the Faeroes, screened by destroyers *Scorpion* and *Scourge*.

The spirit room was now opened, and a very long queue of volunteers formed up to clear up the mess, armed with buckets and other receptacles. The golden liquid swilling round the deck was eventually condemned by the Chief Medical Officer, as it had attacked and dissolved the red paint. It was claimed later that the lost ships of the convoy followed *Vindex* to the Faeroes by the scent of rum.

By the evening, 24 of Boucher's merchantmen had formed up again, but there were five stragglers from the leeward side of the convoy which had gone astray through the pain and difficulty of having to keep station by constantly looking to windward into a freezing hurricane and driving snow. There was plenty of individual damage, but no cracks in the welded Liberty ships, contrary to some gloomy forecasts. *Diadem*, which had hung on astern of the Commodore, had been pooped at least twice by huge following seas. Most of her boats had been smashed, her cables torn out and her hawsepipes ripped. A freak of wind had wrenched the foremost lifeboat, tightly griped-to, in Boucher's *Samaritan* round 90 degrees from its fore-and-aft position.

Forcing on through the night at an indicated speed of ten knots, *Vindex* overtook the convoy about 30 miles from Thorshavn. The dying gale had been succeeded by light winds and continuous snow with a touch of fog. At 9.40 a.m. *Vindex* flew off three Swordfish to search for the stragglers. Johnson and Piercy found one of them, the SS *Stephen Leacock*, and two corvettes, and flashed the signal to re-form at Thorshavn. A heavy snowstorm started while they were still in the air and lasted for two hours. It was miserable in the Stringbag's open cockpits, and there was some anxiety in the ship for their safety, but eventually the weather cleared, *Vindex* turned back east to find a clear patch, the tractor scraped the snow off the flight deck, and all three Swordfish were landed on safely in the lee of the Faeroes, where the carrier had put in to avoid a heavy swell.

She then steamed up Thorshavn Roads and anchored off the town at half-past two in the afternoon. The providential clearance in the weather also enabled 25 ships of the convoy to enter safely, followed by the five stragglers soon afterwards, but the return of heavy snow led to a collision, and the British freighter *Fort Highfield* was holed above the waterline on the port side. CS10 disembarked to *Diadem*, and at 5 p.m. on 20 January left for Scapa with *Vindex* and three Fleet destroyers, arriving at 9.30 a.m. on the 21st. As a result of the hurricane damage, there was a serious shortage of alcohol aboard *Vindex* and much moaning at the bar in the wardroom when they ran out of rum on the way down to Scapa, with MO John Shaw, as Wine Caterer, taking most of the stick for it.

The convoy was not yet quite clear of trouble. At 9.30 a.m. on 20 January, 22 ships of the Clyde and Barry Docks section left Thorshavn, having left the SS

Andrew Turnbull behind with her cables in a twist. A northerly gale with snow then struck them, and the SS *August Belmont*'s cargo shifted, leaving her in difficulties, with two lifeboats gone and a minefield to leeward. But an escort stood by her, and both vessels had rejoined the convoy by the morning.

Vindex was only in the Flow for a few hours before sailing again for the Clyde. From there 825 Squadron flew off to Machrihanish, and the ship docked at Greenock for a two-month refit. The ship's company had leave or went on courses. ASO Jim Palmer spent the third week of February at Machrihanish learning about the new anti-submarine sono-buoys with which *Vindex* aircraft would be equipped for the next sortie. On Friday 2 March the ship was moved into dry dock and became more like a cold, inhospitable hulk than an active vessel. Everyone was glad to get ashore. At Regano's in Glasgow Jim Palmer met Lieutenant-Commander Cooke, CO of No. 813 Squadron, which was to be the next to operate from *Vindex*. On Monday 12 March, Ian Taylor left the ship for Devonport. He was replaced in the ship by Surgeon-Lieutenant Dudley Heath, RNVR.

10

The last 'Tally-ho!'

WITH THE ALLIES DRIVING HARD through France and Belgium, the German armies were regrouped and replenished for an all-out counter-offensive to knock the Allies back on their heels and force them to concede more favourable peace terms.

This was the objective of the sudden push in the Ardennes in December, which for a short time was spectacularly successful, and was behind the unexpected attacks by torpedo bombers and U-boats upon Operation Acumen, the running of the convoys JW and RA62 at the end of November. *Campania* and *Nairana* had provided the permanent air cover, with the Swordfish IIIs and Wildcat VIs of Nos. 813 and 835 Squadrons. The escorting forces had beaten off the attacks, sunk *U835* with no loss to their own ships, and shot down two Ju 88s and one Blohm und Voss Bv 138 for the loss of two Swordfish aircraft and one Wildcat pilot.

But for the intervention of the common enemy, the weather, RA63 would almost certainly have faced renewed air and underwater attacks. The running of convoys JW and RA64, which followed *Vindex*'s Operation Greystoke, encountered both, and lived up to its code name Hotbed.

Rear-Admiral Roderick McGrigor with the cruiser *Bellona*, carriers *Campania* and *Nairana* and eight Fleet destroyers, joined the 26 ships of JW64 north-east of the Faeroes at dawn on 6 February. Shortly afterwards, Lieutenant Fleischmann-Allen from *Campania* shot down a shadowing Ju 88, but his wingman, Sub-Lieutenant Smyth, was shot down and killed. In the evening 12 Ju 88 torpedo bombers attacked from long range, hit nothing, and lost one aircraft.

Two of *Nairana*'s 835 Squadron Wildcats damaged an 88 on the 7th, then the weather closed in. An old Fulmar converted into a night fighter took off from *Campania*, broke down, and in landing put the flight deck out of action for a time. Two Swordfish smashed their undercarriages landing on in a snowstorm on the night of 9/10 February. In the forenoon 30 Ju 88s attacked the convoy. The old fighting *Whitehall* damaged one and shot down another with the help of the sloop *Lark*. Escorts and Wildcats made the bombers miss. McGrigor swung the convoy smartly out of harm's way. More enemy aircraft fell. *Nairana* jammed her rudder avoiding torpedoes. *Campania*'s Quigg and Davies shot down two 88s, then both were hit by the convoy barrage and ditched. On the 12th as the convoy groped its way into Kola Inlet through blinding snow the corvette *Denbigh Castle* was torpedoed and the same U-boat sank two merchantmen coming west from the White Sea for the return convoy.

By the time RA64 sailed on 17 February the U-boats had gathered around Kola. *Lark* and *Alnwick Castle* sank *U425*, then *Lark* was hit and disabled, and a merchantman torpedoed. In the afternoon, with the convoy creeping through cold mist, the dreaded 'Arctic smoke', the veteran corvette *Bluebell* was hit and blew up, leaving only one survivor.

The seas rose and the convoy was struck by a gale of hurricane strength. *Nairana* lost a Swordfish. As the gale died down four Wildcats scrambled off her slippery deck, and Armitage and Sargent set a Ju 88 from an attacking force on fire. Gordon and Blanco shot down another, the escorts two more. On the 22nd another gale battered the convoy. Then 20 Ju 88s attacked but sank only one straggler. Hotbed only cooled down when the ships reached the Faeroes.

In March *Campania* escorted JW65 to Russia with *Vindex*'s old 825 Squadron and its 12 Swordfish IIIs and seven Wildcat VIs aboard, accompanied by *Trumpeter* with eight Avenger IIs and eight Wildcat VIs. The convoy was routed beyond the range of enemy aircraft from Bardufoss and Trondheim, but two merchantmen and the sloop *Lapwing* were sunk by Schnorkel U-boats of the ten-strong Hagen group in the approaches to Kola. It was an unhappy trip for 825, who found no honour aboard the unfamiliar ship, and on 3 April 1945 the Squadron was disbanded.*

By that time the Allied armies were overrunning Germany, and the end of the war in Europe was in sight. It was in this atmosphere that the last Russian convoy operation, Roundel, was mounted.

Jim Palmer liked to get out into the countryside whenever he could, and was as much at ease on a bike or on Shank's Pony as he was in a boat under sail or oars. On a Tuesday towards the end of March the 8.46 a.m. train from Glasgow's Queen Street station took him north-west through the heather hills and lochs of Argyll, across the Grampians to Bridge of Orchy on the Orchy River. From there he cycled on north-west up to the Kingshouse Hotel at Glencoe. The following day he rode from the hotel along Loch Leven to Ballachulish and back in the rain, and part of the way down Glen Etive. It was snowing when he returned to the Glen on the Friday and walked up the slopes of Buachille Etive, very wet on Saturday when he walked from Glencoe to Rannoch Moor. He walked to Glencoe Gorge on Sunday in a downpour, and through snow showers to Curved Ridge and Crowberry Tower on Monday. The snow thickened on Tuesday 3 April, for the return cycle ride to Bridge of

---

*On 1 July 1945 it was re-formed at Rattray for the Royal Canadian Navy with 12 Barracuda IIs, re-equipped with Firefly Is on 1 January 1946, and embarked in HMCS *Warrior* on 3 March. With Firefly IVs it embarked in HMCS *Magnificent* on 22 May 1948, and was disbanded in HMCS *Warrior* on 12 December 1954 when its aircraft flew ashore to HMS *Daedalus*, Lee-on-Solent. For 28 years its unit number remained unused, but was revived in May, 1982, and allocated to a squadron of ten Sea King anti-submarine helicopters formed at Culdrose, Cornwall, to serve with the British task force off the Falkland Islands in the dispute with Argentina.

Orchy to catch the 11.15 for Glasgow. It had been Admiralty weather all the time, but the rigours of the bike and foot sorties made his always ruddy cheeks even rosier and set him up for the coming trip to the Arctic.

Vindex went on engine trials in the Clyde on Thursday, and on the Sunday No. 813 Squadron flew aboard. Working up began in the Clyde, with the ship anchoring at Lamlash at night.

At noon on Tuesday 17 April, *Vindex* embarked CS10, Rear-Admiral A. Cunningham-Graham, at Tail o' the Bank, and at 2.47 p.m. the ship went ahead in company with the escort carrier *Premier* and the destroyers *Zealous*, *Zest*, *Zodiac* and *Offa* to overtake Convoy JW66, which had sailed from the Clyde the previous evening, and escort it to Kola.

In the convoy were 22 freighters, a rescue ship, a tanker and two Norwegian vessels to take part in the anticipated relief of their country. Against the possibility of air attacks from Norway, *Vindex*'s 813 Squadron had altered its normal mix of aircraft. Three Swordfish were disembarked, and four extra Wildcat VIs borrowed from the fighter carrier *Searcher*, making eight Swordfish IIIs and 12 Wildcats. Aboard *Premier*, No. 856 Squadron had the reverse proportion, with 12 Avengers to eight Wildcats.

At 4 p.m. a Swordfish flew a pilot with appendicitis from *Vindex* to RNAS, Ayr, and returned in the middle of a practice close-range AA shoot by the two carriers. The convoy was met off Cape Wrath at 11.30 a.m. on 18 April and the carriers took up station in the box. Admiral Cunningham-Graham's flagship, the cruiser *Bellona*, joined at 8 p.m. *Vindex* assumed the duties of Fighter Carrier from 8 a.m. to 8 p.m., Anti-submarine Carrier from 8 p.m. to 8 a.m. daily.

At 4.30 p.m. on the 18th *Vindex* flew off one Swordfish and two Wildcats on a demonstration flight over the convoy to familiarise the ships with the aircraft types present and avoid if possible any self-inflicted wounds. One of the Wildcats slewed to port on landing, crashed into the walkway and was out of action for the rest of the trip.

The next four days passed without incident, except for radar contacts which turned out to be rain clouds, Coastal Command Liberators not showing IFF, and, at 7.30 a.m. on 20 April, the Trondheim Zenit passing about 50 miles astern. Anti-submarine patrols were begun at 10 a.m. on the 22nd by Avengers from *Premier*.

At 8 p.m. on the 22nd *Vindex* flew off her first Swordfish anti-submarine patrol, a machine piloted by Lieutenant-Commander Cooke, with observer Lieutenant(A) F. D. Baring-Gould, RNVR. As it left the deck its RATOG failed, and the aircraft ditched off the starboard bow of the ship. The crew were rescued after about 20 minutes in the water by the big Royal Canadian Navy Tribal-class destroyer *Haida* and returned to *Vindex* at 7 a.m. next morning unhurt.

The spirit of invention, initiated by Percy Gick, was always present in *Vindex*, and after this near-disaster Commander Williams came up with a method by which the ship could instantly mark the spot if an aircraft ditched immediately after take-off. He used available equipment, and the result was a marker buoy in the form of a small Carley raft and a dan buoy attachment fitted with light and radar reflectors. One of these was slung in quick-release gear from the after sponson on each side of the ship, with buzzers from the bridge to signal 'Let go' to the sentry. Captain Bayliss thought well enough of this ingenious device to send particulars to the Rear-Admiral, Aircraft Carriers, and Williams' original drawings and specifications appeared subsequently in an Admiralty Fleet Order.

On the evening of the 23rd, Huff-Duff spoke, and at quarter past eleven a Swordfish on a Cobra patrol astern of the convoy reported a contact. The plane dropped two sono-buoys, which were both heard transmitting in good voice and giving off the strong hydrophone effect of a Schnorkelling U-boat. Night patrols met increasingly bad weather, with frequent snow squalls. One of these fought its way along an HF/DF bearing but the sea was bleak and bare.

Fighters scrambled at 10.18 p.m. on the 24th intercepted a Russian Catalina on anti-submarine patrol, and there was another false alarm in the afternoon by another Cat not showing IFF. On the night of the 24th/25th a *Vindex* Swordfish and a Russian Catalina flew some distance together on patrol before parting company.

At half-past six on the morning of 25 April, the day on which Russian and American soldiers met on the Elbe, the convoy met the local Russian escort and split up, with *Vindex*, *Premier*, *Bellona*, *Zephyr*, *Zest* and *Zodiac* standing off to the north-east to cover the entry of the Murmansk portion into Kola Inlet. By this time 11 U-boats of the Faust group had formed a line across the entrance to the Inlet. Relays of Swordfish laid a series of lines of sono-buoys across the swept channel, keeping always 12 miles in advance of the convoy. Each line of buoys was patrolled by the laying aircraft for about an hour until the convoy had nearly reached it, then it would hand over to the next aircraft 12 miles ahead which had just laid the next line, then return to the carrier. The operation was named Sono-Cooke, after 813 Squadron's CO. At 7.40 air patrols flew from both carriers off the entrance to the Inlet. Three Avengers continued anti-submarine patrol 15 miles ahead of the outer screen from bow to bow until the entrance was reached, then patrolled to seaward until all the ships had passed inside.

The convoy got into Kola unscathed. One Swordfish lost its way in a squall returning to *Vindex* and was airborne for nearly five hours before landing on. When the convoy was safely inside, the Fleet destroyers which had escorted it returned to bring the covering force in. *Vindex* flew a final Cobra patrol round the force on the way in and anchored at No. 48 berth in Vaenga Bay at a few minutes past midnight on 26 April.

The escorts were in Kola Inlet for Easter. *Bellona*'s chaplain persuaded the Russians to let him have an empty go-down for the celebration of Easter Communion. All through the ceremony there were faces at the windows, and at a party in the evening the Soviet political officer said to Peter Isaacson, 'It

Gremlins? Wildcat of No. 811 Squadron which had parted its lashings after *Vindex* had rolled exceptionally heavily, 8th November, 1944. A second Wildcat was lost over the side.

was a strange party you were having this morning, very strange. Everyone seemed to have their glass of wine in turn.' *Vindex* provisioned the sloop *Cygnet* and the corvette *Honeysuckle*, which lay alongside her, as well as the frigate *Loch Shin* and the other corvettes *Alnwick Castle* and *Bamburgh Castle*. A total of 1,350 gallons of aviation spirit was delivered by *Vindex* to the Soviet naval air base at Vaenga, and a party given for the Russian air officers on the 27th was reciprocated by them at the base on the 28th.

The convoy was due to sail on the 29th. On the 28th a simulated sailing was staged to put the waiting U-boats off their stroke, and the 7th and 9th EG carried out a preliminary search. Sixteen U-boats were now deployed off the entrance to the Inlet, and *Oberleutnant* Westphalen's *U968* made an unsuccessful attack on the *Alnwick Castle*.

RA66 sailed at 7 p.m. on the 29th. The U-boats attacked. At 7.26 HMS *Goodall* got a contact. She was adjusting her speed for a Hedgehog attack when she was hit by a torpedo abreast the bridge. *Loch Shin* immediately turned towards her, picked up an Asdic contact, and a quarter of an hour later made a Squid attack. *Anguilla* followed this up with DCs. The *Cotton* then picked up the contact and also made a depth-charge attack, which forced the U-boat, *Oberleutnant* Dietrich's *U286*, to the bottom. Oil and wreckage came to the surface, and *Cotton* dropped another DC pattern in the oil slick. This probably finished off the *U286*, which was not heard from again. The *Goodall* sank, with heavy loss of life. *Oberleutnant* Gudenus in *U427* fired at HMC destroyers *Haida* and *Iroquois* and was lucky to get away after his targets had dropped 678 depth-charges on him.

Air patrols were stopped at 5 p.m. on May Day by thick fog which persisted until the end of *Vindex*'s anti-submarine duty at 8 a.m. next morning. At 5.15 p.m. a bogey was reported closing the convoy, and from then until 9 a.m. the convoy was shadowed more or less continuously by at least two Ju 88s at ranges varying from nine to 30 miles, from the port beam right through ahead to the starboard bow.

Fighters were scrambled three times from *Vindex* without success. When the enemy faded off the radar screens the fighters were recalled. The first Wildcat came in low, corrected too vigorously and went into the barrier. Now there were ten. Just after eight o'clock it began to snow heavily, making anti-submarine patrols impossible, but hiding the convoy from snoopers. The patrols were resumed at dawn on the 2nd, and an aircraft went searching for the ice line near Bear Island.

At 11.30 a.m. a memorial service was held in *Vindex* for those lost in the *Goodall*, and the colours were half-masted. The service had had to wait while Wildcats were scrambled to intercept bogeys. There were more fighter sorties at 1.15 and 6.55 p.m., but in each case the enemy escaped.

There was no flying on the night of 2/3 May, but at 5.55 p.m. on the 3rd two enemy aircraft were reported approaching the convoy. Two Wildcats, piloted by Lieutenant(A) D. E. Leamon, RNVR, and Sub-Lieutenant(A) W. V. Machin, RNVR, were scrambled at six o'clock and vectored towards the enemy. They

Sunset. 'Strike down the Wildcats'.

sighted a Ju 88, then lost it in cloud. At 6.21 *Vindex*'s Air Direction Room heard the 'Tally-ho!' as Leamon and Machin dived on the brown-camouflaged Ju 88 out of the clouds from 1,500 feet.

The 88 was making about 280 knots, flying from left to right. The Wildcats opened their throttles to match his speed as they swept in on his starboard beam. Leamon opened fire from 300 yards with a 9-second burst, Machin from 800 and again at 500 yards with shorter bursts. Both broke off at 100 yards. Their bullets hit the Junkers in its cockpit and starboard engine. Big pieces of the cockpit cover blew off, and dark grey smoke poured from the engine. He dived to sea level, turned to starboard and started weaving, then headed into cloud at reduced speed and faded off the radar screens.

After this final flurry of action, nothing was sighted by patrolling aircraft for the rest of the trip but oil patches and surfacing whales. *Vindex* and *Premier* screened by four destroyers left the convoy at 3 p.m. on 6 May and sailed for Scapa Flow, where *Vindex* dropped her hook at No. A3 berth ten minutes before midnight. Next day, 7 May 1945, came the news of the unconditional surrender of all German forces. Hostilities ceased at midnight on 8 May, and with them all hostile naval operations in European waters. *Vindex* stayed at action stations all night, as it was thought that fanatical German aircrews in Norway might attack the ships, but the night passed peacefully. Very lights made very good substitutes for VE Day fireworks, and one carrier even had a bonfire on her flight deck.

On *Vindex*'s return to the Clyde, two U-boats were seen in the Minches flying the black flag of surrender. The Admiralty were suspicious of the attitude of some U-boat commanders, however, and when convoys JW/RA67 were run to Russia later in May, they were allotted surface escorts and the escort carrier *HMS Queen* with 853 Squadron's eight Avenger IIs and eight Wildcat VIs.

But there was no war left in the Arctic. The operation was code-named Timeless, which seemed weirdly appropriate. It was certainly very strange to steam through the Norwegian Sea with Huff-Duff silent, to plough a Barents Sea empty of periscopes, and fly through skies devoid of the shadows of snoopers, which had come to seem as much a permanent part of the Arctic heavens as the Aurora Borealis.

11

'Sea getting bluer ...'

THERE WAS STILL WAR in the Far East, where British escort carriers were supporting the flank of the Allied armies driving the Japanese out of Burma. On 16 May an Avenger from HMS *Shah* sighted and bombed the cruiser *Haguro*, one of the last few Japanese major warships left in the East Indies theatre, and Captain Power's destroyers finished her off.

Other Royal Navy escort carriers were working with the Fleet Train supplying the British Pacific Fleet, which was supporting the United States Third Fleet and its Fast Carrier Force. In the hard fighting for Okinawa, the biggest island in the Ryukus chain south of Japan, the Allied ships had suffered severely from kamikaze attacks. Of the three British Fleet carriers serving with the Pacific Fleet, *Indomitable* and *Formidable* were both hit by suicide planes, the latter twice, though their tougher construction saved them from the scale of damage sustained by American carriers. Allied troops were well enough established on Okinawa for the British force to be withdrawn temporarily, and its ships were on their way south to Australia for repairs and replenishment. Heavy bombers flew into Okinawa to begin raids on Japan as a preliminary to the invasion of Kyushu. On 13 June the Third Fleet anchored in Leyte Gulf in the Philippines, having been at sea continuously for 91 days, thanks to the regular supply missions by the Fleet train.

There was nothing left in European waters for escort carriers to do. In late May, Captain Bayliss returned from a visit to the Admiralty and told Commander Williams that *Vindex* was to join the British Pacific Fleet as a replenishment carrier, and that Williams was to succeed him in command. On Monday 28 June, after a final dinner with his officers on the Sunday, Captain Bayliss left *Vindex* to command HMS *Vulture*, the RN air station at St Merryn in Cornwall. Commander (F), Tich Harding, left on the Tuesday, and on Wednesday Jim Palmer handed in the keys of the Ops Room. He left the ship a week later. Chief Engineer Weir remained on board.

With Commander Williams as Captain, and a virtually new ship's company, *Vindex* lay in the Clyde storing and preparing to go east and join the Fleet Train. A young seaman radar rating, Eric Clark, going out to join her in a puffer steamer from Greenock, though the carrier 'a shapeless heap'. He found that there were just enough men aboard to work the ship as a transport.

Vindex sailed for Belfast at 1 p.m. on the bright and breezy day of 3 June 1945 and arrived there at ten o'clock in the evening. The next three days were

Replenishment carrier. HMS *Vindex* passing under Sydney Harbour Bridge, after the end of the war in Europe.

spent loading a deck cargo of Seafires and Barracudas for the BPF, storing a large number of bunk beds, and filling up to capacity with drafts of men for passage to Australia. While this was going on the 12 Fireflies of No. 1790, the first Royal Navy front-line night fighter squadron to be formed, flew in to the airfield at Sydenham, fresh from working up at HMS *Ringtail*, Burscough, Lancashire, and a brief spell aboard the escort carrier HMCS *Puncher* for day and night deck landing experience. From Sydenham they were taxied to the nearby wharf alongside *Vindex*, hoisted aboard by dockside crane and struck down in the hangar, where they remained until off-loaded at Sydney just in time for the end of the war. *Vindex* returned to Greenock for final storing before sailing for Australia on Sunday 1 July. Also being transported was the entire T124X Drafting and Pay Office, from Liverpool.

For the Captain, and any old *Vindex* hand, it was a strange trip. *Vindex* had aircraft on deck and in the hangar, but they were not for flying, merely being transported for some other ship to operate. The Air Direction Room, for so long a busy, crowded place, was empty, the transparent perspex plot clean save for a few traces of coloured chinagraph pencil. The 293 set was the only radar used at sea, and the five radar ratings found that there were so many vacant radar offices that they were able to organise their own private cabins.

'Sea getting bluer' Eric Clark wrote in his diary, 'make and mend on deck . . . Tropical rig.' On 5 July porpoises escorted the carrier through the Straits of Gibraltar into stormy weather. In the evening of the 7th they passed Pantellaria and saw the film *Lady Let's Dance* in the hangar. On the 10th they stopped briefly at Port Said and sailed through the Suez Canal and the Red Sea. On the 13th the sun passed overhead. Next day Aden passed abeam and as they entered the Arabian Sea a flight of locusts landed aboard. Clark also saw his first flying fish, though the Barracudas stayed firmly lashed down on the flight deck. The Indian Ocean was unwelcoming. 'Sea rough. Very sick' he wrote. Two days later he had found his sea legs, and on the evening of 20 July was on watch when an echo of the Camel's Hump in southern India appeared on the radar screen. Next day *Vindex* put into Colombo, Ceylon, and the watch ashore bought souvenirs, mostly elephants. On the 24th they were in Trincomalee offloading a cargo of bombs, before crossing the Indian Ocean. Clark learned that he had spent enough time in South East Asia Command to qualify for the Burma Star, and on 27 July met King Neptune and was ducked when *Vindex* crossed the equator. The film that night was *Flight From Folly*.

On the 28th the carrier was off the coast of Sumatra, and the Southern Cross was seen shining in the tropical sky. They had forgotten there was a war on, but on 30 July the ship entered the Danger Zone, and 'Darken ship' was piped. On 4 August the coast of Australia came in sight to starboard, and *Vindex* steamed through the Timor Sea, passing the mouth of the Gulf of Carpentaria for the Torres Straits.

Vindex passed Cape York to starboard as the Flying Fortress *Enola Gay* was dropping the first atomic bomb on Hiroshima. She sailed through the Coral Sea, where the first great carrier battle of the war had been fought. 'Saw whale,' recorded Eric Clark on 9 August. That day the second atomic bomb was dropped on Nagasaki, after which there could be no more war.

When they anchored off Brisbane on the afternoon of the 11th Clark had qualified for the Pacific Star. Next day they went alongside and offloaded the Barracudas and left at 4 p.m. for Sydney, enjoying the film *Broadway Rhythm* en route. *Vindex* arrived there next morning. The great bridge and the famous harbour were truly spectacular. The carrier tied up at 13 Berth, Pyremont, and various passengers were put ashore. VJ Day, 15 August 1945, was celebrated beerily ashore with friendly ockers.

There was clearly no role for *Vindex* now as a Fleet replenishment carrier, but there was urgent need for ships to carry people and stores. At 5.15 p.m. a Naval draft of over 300 men reported to *Vindex*, now berthed alongside at Darling Harbour embarking Red Cross stores, first-aid equipment, food and clothing for Hong Kong. The work was being done on the double, but the crowded quayside was still jammed with all kinds of stores, from bulldozers to toilet paper. Having stowed their gear, the draft were put to work. Army trucks roared up with more stores as gaps opened on the quayside. A blue-overalled chain passed cases up the gangway. Messdeck passageways and spare cabins soon filled up. Big crates of machinery were jammed into the hangar. Ten million cigarettes alone were loaded. As the stores were for prisoners of war in Hong Kong, all hands slaved willingly through the night, and there was no pilfering.

Vindex sailed at 11 a.m. on Monday 20 August. The great steel bridge rumbled with traffic as she steamed underneath it. Half an hour later she was out at sea, the day fine though cloudy, and a heavy swell running. Men who chose a billet on the flight deck found themselves breathing diesel fumes from the carrier's exhausts. On the 22nd the ship called at Brisbane for yet more stores, which the hands loaded stripped to the waist in the town's hottest weather. In the hangar the temperature reached the nineties. Ashore there was ice-cold Aussie beer, fried oysters and chips. The ship sailed again next day, and by 8 p.m. 'only the deep blue Pacific Ocean lay around us,' wrote Petty Officer Ronald Sired '... only the occasional splashing of flying fish, the swirl of water as large fish raced after prey, and the rarer sight of shark's fin protruding above the calm surface could be seen.'

On Sunday afternoon, 26 August, *Vindex* was off the Louisiade Archipelago, with the reef-bound islands of the Coral Sea well to port, 'and often the aroma of flowers was brought by the light breeze'. Across the green Solomon Sea to the Bismarcks she sailed, still alone on the sea. As she neared the equator the ship became a floating oven to the hands re-stacking stores for ease of off-loading at their destination. At tea time on the 28th the saw-toothed hills of Manus Island were sighted, and an hour or so later *Vindex* steamed into the vast lagoon, dropping her hook in the clear waters. At least 50 ships lay at anchor. Recognisable were the British carriers *Colossus* and *Unicorn*, the cruiser *Manxman*, one of the saviours of Malta. Stores were exchanged for mail, and the ship left for Leyte in the Philippines. Landing parties detailed for

Hong Kong were instructed to handle the Japanese 'correctly and in accordance with British traditions'.

Shortly after noon on Monday, 3 September, the blue hills of Leyte rose over the horizon, then the green forests fringing the steep coastline. Anchored in the great Gulf, with the bright sails of Moro outrigger canoes flashing about between them, were scores of warships, including the British cruisers *Bermuda* and *Euryalus* and the light Fleet carrier HMS *Vengeance*. A sudden squall drenched the ship, then as quickly vanished, and the hot sun dried the decks.

Vindex sailed again next day, and at midnight entered the San Bernardino Straits between wooded Samar and Luzon. Morning found the carrier threading her way between the thousand islands of the Sibuyan Sea. A Japanese 'Mavis' flying boat, still with the Rising Sun on wings and fuselage, crossed their path, a grey *Hubuki*-class destroyer passed them close on the opposite course, flashed some enigmatic morse, and was gone. By evening *Vindex* was in the South China Sea and on course for Hong Kong.

At dawn on 8 September she altered course round a fleet of Chinese fishing junks, and an hour later the dark mass of Hong Kong Island lay ahead. Soon *Vindex* was steaming into the great harbour, full of ships. There were the mighty *Anson*, flagship of the BPF, carriers *Indomitable*, *Venerable* and *Vengeance*, cruisers and destroyers, and eight submarines clustered round their depot ship, HMS *Maidstone*. Off Stonecutters Island lay the Japanese destroyer *Sumire* and a consort. Sunken ships near the quays showed their masts and funnels.

As soon as *Vindex* had anchored, she was surrounded by dozens of sampans, with the half-starved boat people begging for food. Half-loaves were thrown down to them, and the hysterical delight of the lucky ones, the despair of those who had missed out, touched the soft-hearted matelots, who swarmed round the ship's canteen buying up bars of chocolate, tins of fruit, jam and condensed milk to throw to the sampans.

The harbour had not been fully surveyed for wreckage, and *Vindex* was given a foul berth alongside the stone and wooden quay at the Kowloon docks next to the troopship *Empress of Scotland*, which was discharging men, and the carrier's port propeller was ruined. Her spare propellers were at Durban, there was no shipping available to fetch one, and until the ship could collect one herself she would have to run on the starboard engine only. There was no lighting for discharging cargo at night, but *Vindex* used her four generators to flood Kowloon with light.

The ship shifted to the Navy dockyard at Victoria next day. Hong Kong, between occupation and revival, was in limbo. *Vindex* had brought men and stores for its rehabilitation. Shots were heard ashore in the evenings, and on the 9th the duty watch aboard *Vindex* opened fire on a sampan crewed by suspected looters, after a bullet had pinged off the bridge island. There were few people in the city yet. Food was scarce and expensive. Naval patrols marched through the streets at night.

On 14 September the second reason for the ship's visit to Hong Kong, and the bunk beds in her hangars, was made heartrendingly clear when the first of some 300 Australian prisoners of war began to come on board. They were emaciated and in rags of clothing, all suffering from beri-beri, pellagra or some other result of their brutal treatment by their Japanese captors, and all so far gone in malnutrition that they could not cope with the comparative banquet which was served to them on the mess tables of the British carrier. They were kitted out with jungle-green uniforms and slouch hats, and quartered in the hangar.

On 17 September British and Australian men, women and children from the Stanley Civilian Internment Camp made their way aboard *Vindex*. They were all in poor health too, though not in such a bad condition as the Australian POWs. For nearly three and a half years they had formed a self-contained community of some 3,000 people totally confined behind barbed wire in half an acre of space on the Stanley Peninsula, on the south side of Hong Kong island, existing in crowded squalor in school buildings, bungalows and flats, with no proper sanitation, a near-starvation diet, and the rare Red Cross or family parcel which the Japanese did not keep for themselves.

Mrs Jean Gittins was Secretary of the Faculty of Medicine in the University of Hong Kong when war broke out in the Pacific. The University was at once turned into a relief hospital for men wounded by the advancing Japanese, and Jean became Secretary of the hospital. Her husband Billy was a Hong Kong University Engineering graduate and a member of the Hong Kong Volunteer Defence Corps.

The Stanley Peninsula had been the scene of a last stand by Allied troops who had not heard of the surrender, and afterwards drunken Japanese troops had shot the medical officers at the St Stephen Casualty Hospital, raped the nurses, and bayonetted the patients in their beds.

Stanley had been a quiet holiday resort for the people of the colony, but the Japanese had chosen it as a convenient place in which to segregate enemy aliens from the rest of Hong Kong. The buildings were soon grossly overfull, with as many as 30 people to one small flat. There was a serious shortage of furniture of all kinds, beds and cooking utensils. Meagre rations of rice, vegetables and bad fish were issued. The rice was cooked in dustbins.

Jean Gittins lived with friends in the smaller of two rooms in an upstairs flat with no furniture and bare concrete floors. The only redeeming feature was the view of the open sea. She suggested making a roof garden, and in soil brought in bucket by bucket they were soon growing tomatoes, shallots, and mint for its vitamin A value. They made sure that the only way up to the garden was from inside the flat, as thieving was rampant in the camp, even to the extent of stealing a blanket from a sleeping child. They could swim, if they were strong enough to make the long walk to the beach. One of the worst things was the invasion by bed bugs, fat and gorged with blood, while the humans became day by day weaker and more anaemic. Some senior civil servants in the camp, suspected of being involved in a projected break-out, were executed.

In October 1942 they received their first Red Cross parcels. There were two each, and over a period of some six months there was a monthly issue of tinned meat, sugar, cocoa, tea and dried fruit. As they had no way of preserving all this, it was eaten in one big blow-out. Cardigans were made into windbreakers and trousers. In January 1944 the Camp administration changed from civilian to military, and the internees were put on army rations, receiving an extra four ounces of rice per day instead of flour, and the meat ration which they collected every ten days was replaced by four ounces of peanut oil and a dessertspoonful of sugar each, adult and child alike, though the soldiers did organise communal gardens.

The health of all the inmates of Stanley deteriorated seriously. Professor Byrne, a friend of Jean's, died of a heart attack, and Jean herself was sent to hospital, her weight down to under 90 pounds. Bill Faid, from Jean's flat, slipped and died from a fractured skull, but Captain Horner Smith, former master of the Yangtse river steamer *Sui Wo*, helped her with the garden and carried the water which they had to fetch from the sea for the toilets.

Billy Gittins had been captured, and was in a prison camp only ten miles from Stanley, but the Japanese allowed no contact. She heard from him twice, then in December 1943 all communication ceased. Eventually she heard that he had been moved to Japan.

In 1944 they were given their second Red Cross parcels. The hospital received urgently needed drugs and vitamin tablets. For 12 weeks, while the supplies lasted, they were each given a quarter of a thiamin tablet a day for four days, followed by a vitamin capsule every two days, but by January 1945 the health situation was grave, with everyone suffering from beriberi or pellagra, and starvation threatening. Determined efforts to organise an educational programme paid off in the uplift given to morale. There were lectures for the adults on engineering, mathematics, economics, psychology, languages, history and English literature, and some of the children reached University of London matriculation standard.

This drab, debilitating existence dragged on until, on the wonderful evening of 15 August 1945, came the news that the war was over. At last, after days of suspense, on 29 August British planes flew overhead dropping food and medical supplies. Then the Navy arrived. Jean left Stanley by bus, walked into the Gloucester Hotel and sat unbelieving on a big bed with a spring mattress in a large room with a private bath. But 'Sleep was a problem: the brain, accustomed to doing no work at all, remained over-active at night; mosquitoes, owing to Japanese neglect of the town's drainage, were plentiful, and the sounds of a city, albeit one just faintly stirring from death, were more than enough to shatter sleep.' Converting to more civilised food was also a problem. 'To adjust one's digestive tract from a diet of spinach and rice to one of bread, milk and tinned meat was not easy.'

Worry over the fate of her husband was temporarily soothed by the arrival of a friend with news and photographs of her children Elizabeth and John in

Australia. Then she was told that passage home had been arranged for her aboard a British aircraft carrier.

She saw HMS *Vindex*, grim and grey, with mixed feelings. Painful though internment had been, there had always been the future to dream about. Now the suffering and starvation were over, and that future, with all its uncertainties, was here.

Mrs Olive Burnett felt much the same. In her case, although this big solid ship 'looking every bit like the dock itself in her wartime camouflage,' was to take her to her family in Sydney after the long years of internment, she was also taking her away from her husband, who had to remain behind to get his newspaper restarted.

Nervous, fearful and uncertain, still demoralised from over thirteen hundred days and nights of captivity, the thin and shabby survivors walked shakily up the gangplank. Some of them, struggling with precious possessions, tended to treat the sailors detailed to help them as servants or stewards from the old POSH P & O days. The matelots did not take kindly to being called 'boy' and ordered about. *Vindex*'s First Lieutenant was forced to gather their civilian passengers all together and remind them gently that they *were* after all guests aboard one of HM ships, and that his men were not coolies.

Both Jean Gittins and Olive Burnett were lucky in their accommodation on board the carrier. Duncan Sloss, Vice-Chancellor of the University, arranged for Jean to have a single-berth officer's cabin. Olive was allotted a two-berth cabin. Most of the passengers shared six-berth or eight-berth cabins, but most of the other 50 women internees were quartered in the hangar. Other internees had camp stretchers set up on the mess decks. Jean was also fortunate in having Captain Smith from the camp aboard to look after her. Because he had been a ship's master, *Vindex*'s Commander Williams made a special fuss of him. He loved being on the sea again, instead of just looking at it as he had been forced to do for three and a half years, and radiated cheerfulness. 'You'll arrive in Sydney,' he said to Jean, 'to find Billy waiting for you. Now do cheer up and come and have a drink. We must show some appreciation of all the attention the officers are heaping on us.' The ship's officers, 'so big and healthy,' Olive Burnett thought, were certainly attentive. They ate with the internees and made sure that they did not have more food initially than their shrunken stomachs could cope with. Gradually the servings were increased as they became more accustomed to the wholesome food that had been only a memory while in Stanley Camp.

The sea was calm when *Vindex* left Hong Kong at 4 p.m. on Monday 18 September, two hours later than scheduled so as to take on board a pathetic looking batch of POWs from Ambon Island, but Olive was a poor sailor and went to bed at eight o'clock. She awoke at midday on the following Wednesday, had a shower and made her way to the wardroom for lunch. There the ship's medical officer told her that he had looked in on her but had decided to let her sleep on. The long sleep did her so much good that she even forgot to be seasick when the ship ran into the back half of a typhoon.

Jean Gittins went down with malarial fever but a course of quinine soon revived her. They were given free cigarettes and drinks and a token fiver in 'real money', and were shown the technicalities of the diesel engines and the radar equipment in a conducted tour of the ship. There were films and concerts in the hangar. 'So I set aside my fears,' Jean wrote later, 'and lived for the present.' She was asked to type up records kept by the Australian Colonel W. J. R. Scott, whose sick and emaciated men were now languishing in *Vindex*'s hangar. As she worked on this in the Captain's suite, for so long the quarters of Temple Bayliss, she became familiar with the sufferings of those whose captivity had been so much worse than theirs.

The cinema showed Abbott and Costello in *Money for Jam* on the 22nd. Next evening there was a concert in the hangar, with internees and POWs doing turns, followed on the 24th by the film *Uncertain Glory*. They called at Manus Island, and the passengers were taken ashore to stretch their legs for a short time. The Officer Commanding the RAF there was a friend of Commander Williams, and he arranged for Jean Gittins to make her first-ever flight in an aeroplane. It was only a little ramshackle machine which the RAF had swopped with the Americans for a case of Scotch but the joy ride was a big thrill for her.

Between the Admiralties and Australia the ship ran into a storm which became a howling gale. It was still blowing on 2 October. The ship's generators cut out, and she drifted for half an hour. Next day they were in Sydney.

Vindex entered the Heads and steamed up the Harbour with cheers and sirens sounding all around her from the fleet of small boats which had come out to meet her, and the bridge and the 'Wooded hills and blue waters sparkling in the spring sunshine,' as Jean Gittins wrote years later. The ship berthed at 14 Berth, Pyremont, Woolloomooloo, with a band playing on the dockside and relatives and friends behind a barrier some distance away. The actual reunion had to wait until the internees had all been issued with ration books and appointments at the Dental Hospital. They trooped down the gangways, 'gaunt, without money, two cane baskets for luggage and wearing Red Cross clothing handouts,' Olive Burnett was to recall in later years. Jean Gittins was reunited with her children, only to be told that her husband Billy had died in Japan.

Vindex shifted to Sirius Cove, and dockyard mateys came aboard to make improvements to the ventilating systems. Then the ship took on stores, including the first beer for the Fleet Club at Hong Kong since the Japanese surrender. For security reasons the crates were stowed in the magazines, though most of the ship's company had managed to try a bottle by the time they reached Hong Kong, where the rest filled a standard sized junk.

On 22 October Commander Williams was temporarily relieved in command of *Vindex*, though remaining as Executive Officer, by Captain Jamie Armstrong, Royal Australian Navy, whose appointment, made locally in the

BPF, was to enable him to complete 12 months' service in RN carriers preliminary to appointment to the RAN's first carrier.

Later in the year *Vindex* brought over 500 Australian soldiers from Melbourne to Hobart, Tasmania. They were overcrowded but made no complaint, as they were about to be demobbed and were coming home for Christmas. Also passengers, but travelling in greater comfort and dignity, were the new Governor of Tasmania, Sir Hugh Binney, and Lady Binney. When she left again for Sydney *Vindex* carried 1,000 cases of food which Hobart had contributed to the Food For Britain drive, as the result of an appeal by the Lord Mayor, Mr Soundy. This was the second consignment to leave on a British warship, the first having been lifted by the battleship *Duke of York*. The food was transhipped in Sydney, and *Vindex* spent the Chinese New Year in Hong Kong where the ship loaded up with Spitfires and vehicles for the air base at Iwakuni in Japan. There the aircraft were offloaded into lighters, and *Vindex* sailed to the naval base at Kure across the bay, from where there was a sightseeing trip to the blackened wasteland that had been Hiroshima.

Then it was out through the Bungo Channel again and back to Hong Kong for a few days before shuttling back to Sydney. They took what was by now a familiar route, picking up and discharging various cargoes, including deck loads of aircraft. The route took them down through the South China Sea to the Philippines, across the Sibuyan Sea between Mindoro and Luzon, and through the San Bernardino Straits into the Philippine Sea and the broad Pacific. Thus they traversed the path Kurita had taken with his battleships just over two years previously when the two great battlefleets had clashed in the fight for Leyte Gulf and the possession of the Philippines, a time when *Vindex* had been making her unhappy passage with JW61 to Kola. Through this strait the Japanese battleships had debouched and come down upon the brave bantams of the American escort carrier squadron. The volcanic peaks of Luzon, the green jungle, the clear blue seas off Samar, were so peaceful now. *Vindex* was still running on her starboard engine only, and Captain Armstrong would have been glad of the other one, in cross winds or currents, navigating narrow channels between coral reefs, or berthing without tugs.

There was a brief call in the Bismarcks, then they were ploughing the Coral Sea once more among the ghosts of *Shoho* and the mighty *Lexington*.* There the ship answered a call from a merchantman with a sick crew member. *Vindex* rendezvoused with her and hove to while the man was transferred to her sick bay, and he was put ashore at Sydney, where the ship was given a refit. The ship's main cold store had broken down on passage, and an urgent job was to get rid of the decaying meat and poultry which was stinking up the ship. A new laundry was also installed in the lower for'ard washroom.

One of the many *Vindex* plank owners who had left her shortly after VE

---

*The Japanese carrier *Shoho* and the American carrier *Lexington* were both sunk by carrier planes in the battle of the Coral Sea, 7/8 May 1942.

Day was Junior Engineer Peter Humphreys. He then passed his 2nd Class Board of Trade examination, becoming RNR instead of RNVR. He requested a steamship to widen his experience, but was appointed to *Vindex* again, and joined her when she was refitting at Sydney. This time round he was a Senior Watchkeeping Engineer, receiving reports on the control platform, with periodic rounds of the engine room to talk to his machinery and check the work of *his* Juniors.

Captain Armstrong handed back command of *Vindex* to John Williams, and there was a strong buzz that the ship was going home. It had been decided to transfer HMS *Golden Hind*, the headquarters of the British Pacific Fleet, from Warwick Farm, Sydney, to Colombo, Ceylon, and it was transhipped as a complete working administrative unit, desks, files, papers and staff, in *Vindex*'s hangar, to be re-sited at HMS *Mayina*, which had been a transit camp for the Eastern Fleet just outside Colombo.

All the office furniture was embarked in the ship at Garden Island in Sydney Harbour and set up in the hangar as complete working units as though they were ashore, from the Commodore's office downwards. It was hoped, vainly, that work would continue uninterrupted, but some of the staff were layed out with seasickness, and all were half-cooked in the hangar. *Vindex* was ill-suited to the tropics. There were some nasty moments, especially in the Australian Bight, when *Vindex* reacted in her usual lively way in a swell and several Swordfish radial engines still attached to the hangar bulkheads swung out over the heads of the penpushers as the ship rolled. They were glad when *Vindex* docked and they could set up the firm on land again.

In Ceylon there were numbers of now redundant American aircraft on loan to Britain. The Lease-Lend agreement specified that at the end of hostilities these aircraft were to be either returned or destroyed. In this case the US authorities had asked for the machines to be written off. *Vindex* loaded many aircraft which had never flown, and dumped them out at sea. It went against the grain.

From Colombo *Vindex* sailed for Mauritius, where no ship had called for years, for civilian passengers, thence to Durban to pick up her spare propeller, to Simonstown to fit it, and finally homeward. At Simonstown the ship also embarked five tons of gold and, carried aboard unguarded in two tatty suitcases, the Greek Crown Jewels. The gold came down to the dockside in heavily escorted armoured cars. The boxed ingots were carried down below between lines of hard-faced guards, and both rich cargoes not only locked but welded into a magazine. In Britain the whole treasure house was taken away in the back of an unescorted truck.

At every port of call on the way back to the UK they picked up and disembarked scores of passengers, civilian and military, and arrived home with over 80 civilian wardroom guests, with many others quartered on the lower deck, as well as an immense number of Hostilities Only officers and men due for demobilisation. Men ashore with low demob numbers were exchanged for men in the ship with higher ones, and when the ship docked at Plymouth, all *Vindex*'s ship's company except a few regulars were due for discharge. Within hours of their arrival there were too few hands to man the ship, and she went into reserve, finally anchoring in the Firth of Forth.

12

Port Vindex

V*INDEX* REMAINED SWINGING ROUND THE HOOK in the Forth for some months, forlorn and gathering barnacles. While she was there the Port Line, her original owners, bought her back from the Admiralty. She was taken to Rosyth for partial de-storing and towed to the Tyne in August 1948 for conversion by her original builders, Swan Hunter, to a refrigerated cargo-liner for service between Britain and Australasia.

De-storing was then completed. A total of 23,500 buoyancy drums were removed from the ship, as well as 3,000 tons of pig iron which had been put aboard as ballast. Practically the whole of the bridge island structure, flight deck and gallery deck were dismantled and removed, involving the cutting away of hundreds of tons of steel, and the petrol storage tanks, which had been built into the ship, were cut out. The exhausts, which vented from the sides of the carrier, and their silencers were removed. The flight deck was removed, the hangar deck cut away fore and aft, and what was left ultimately formed the bridge deck, foc'sle and poop decks of the new ship. Light steel bulkheads fitted as subdivisions were cut away, and only the main bulkheads left in the ship. Owing to the large number of holes which had been cut in the plating for ventilating and access, a certain amount of new shell plating was necessary. Some of the generators were taken out of the ship, and two new generators were fitted.

Electric welding was used extensively in the construction of the new bulkheads, deckhouses, casings, deck plating, tank top plating, tunnels and butts of shell plating. The ship was of normal three-island type, with three complete decks, and foc'sle, enclosed bridge and poop rising above the upper deck. There were six holds, five of them, together with their lower 'tween decks and No. 1 upper 'tween decks, to be insulated. Compartments were arranged at the sides of five of the remaining upper deck spaces to carry chilled cargo, while the centre was to be available for general cargo. General cargo was also to be carried in No. 6 hold and 'tween decks, in foc'sle and poop. Large cargo hatches were served by 16 electric winches and a three-ton electric crane between Nos. 4 and 5 holds, with derricks of lifting capacity varying from seven to 15 tons fitted at the fore-mast and at derrick posts. A heavy derrick of 60 tons' working load was fitted on the after side of the foremast at No. 2 hatch.

Single and double-berth cabins were built at the sides of the bridge 'tween

'That one, Ma'am, was called the "For Christ's sake" wire.' Commander Dennis White, RN, Director of the Fleet Air Arm Museum at Yeovilton, Somerset, shows a model of HMS *Vindex* to HRH Princess Anne at a London exhibition, 15th October, 1974.

The Fighting *Vindex* (after Turner). HMS *Vindex* enters the Tyne for re-conversion to a merchant ship, 4th October, 1947.

decks for the crew, including petty officers and stewards. This accommodation was fitted out in accordance with the latest requirements of the Ministry of Transport, each man having a reading light over his bed, facilities for writing, and ample drawer space. A crew's laundry, washplaces and a hospital were constructed aft, as well as a recreation room lined with solid oak panelling from the saloon and captain's cabin of the *Port Melbourne*, sold in 1948 for breaking up. Galley and cold stores were located for'ard. The galley was fitted with an electric range, ovens, grill, and water boilers, and adjacent compartments were fitted out as a bakery, butcher's shop and servery.

Above the bridge deck a long deckhouse contained the engineer officers' and junior officers' accommodation, ship's offices, and a laundry for passengers' use, as well as the dining saloon for the use of both passengers and officers. The top of this deckhouse formed the boat deck, and at the forward end of this was the bridge house containing two double-berth staterooms and eight single-berth cabins with shower and washroom attached. A lounge/card room, writing room and cocktail bar were all lined with English cherrywood or limed oak. At the after end of the boat deck was a deckhouse containing the engineers' lounge and accommodation for four cadets, including a study. The Captain's rooms, senior officers' cabins, officers' lounge, chart room and wheelhouse were all located in the navigating bridge.

The reconstructed ship was re-named MS *Port Vindex*. This was really a departure from the Line's normal naming of its ships after ports in Australia or New Zealand, in honour of the ship's wartime service, although there was at least a sheep station in Australia called Vindex. Her Royal Navy ship's bell engraved HMS VINDEX, was also bought from the Admiralty and hung at the top of the gangway, and the old *Vindex* crest was displayed on board, together with photographs of the ship in her wartime form.

With Mr J. R. Rooper and Mr B. P. Arrowsmith, directors of the Port Line, and their Superintendent Engineer, Mr W. R. Cromarty, on board, she completed successful sea trials on 1 June 1949. Gordon Bennett, late of No. 825 Squadron, attended the trials, on Swan Hunter's invitation, 'went all over her and could recognise nothing. Even the bar had become almost TT, but she was a beautiful job.'

MV *Port Vindex* sailed on the early morning tide the following day, commanded by Captain H. Hamilton Smith, with Vernon 'Ben' Battle, who had been torpedoed in the Altantic in the SS *Port Auckland*, as his Chief Officer. She left Wallsend with the insulation in the holds and 'tween decks only partially completed, taking general cargo outward. She started her homeward loading at Melbourne with wool, tallow and general cargo which included large quantities of specially packed cake for a Britain starved of such luxuries. On completion there she sailed down to Hobart, Tasmania, to load canned fruits, jam and other local produce.

After a few voyages carrying general cargo in all spaces, the refrigerating machinery was installed and insulation completed. When fully loaded MV *Port Vindex* had a deadweight tonnage (displacement less the weight of the ship herself) of 12,010, a gross tonnage (total cubic capacity of enclosed spaces at 100 cubic feet/ton) of 10,704.

For 22 years she sailed between British and Australasian ports, carrying general cargo outward, which included machinery, manufactured goods, heavy lifts, power station components and car parts for assembly in Australian factories, and returning to the United Kingdom with wool, canned goods, frozen lamb and dairy products, mainly butter and cheese, from New Zealand.

On retirement from the Navy, John Williams, HMS *Vindex*'s last captain, emigrated to Australia. With his record of maritime service, not the least important being his earlier Merchant Service time with extra-master's certificate and square-rigged endorsement, he was given an appointment with the Australian Department of Shipping and Transport. After seven years in various jobs relating to ships and seamen he came to Tasmania in July 1959 as

Between sword and ploughshare. *Vindex* at Wallsend, 1948.

You can't make an omelette . . .
The removal of *Vindex*'s flight deck structure prior to re-conversion.

'A beautiful job'. MS *Port Vindex.*

Regional Controller of Shipping there, and remained in this post until he retired in 1972. MV *Port Vindex* sometimes called at Hobart to fill her holds with the Tasmanian spring apple crop for Britain, and on one visit her Master, hearing of his connection with the wartime carrier, invited him on board. The seam welds of her side plating recalled an earlier profile, and her non-cambered decks, but otherwise the only reminders of the old ship were the bell and badge.

On the Australasian run with *Port Vindex* was her original twin, HMS *Nairana*, which had become the Royal Dutch Navy's carrier *Karel Doorman* for a brief spell, then had been also bought back from the Navy, for £50,000, and converted into the MV *Port Victor* at a cost of £1,000,000.

On 23 August 1971 MV *Port Vindex* arrived at Kaohsiung, Taiwan, for breaking up. John Copland-Mander, Works Superintendent for the Port Line, had served at sea in World War II as a ship's carpenter and had two ships sunk under him, the *Somersby* by U-boat, the *Gemstone* by surface raider, and had ended the war as a prisoner of the Japanese. In January 1950, then a senior shore carpenter for the Port Line, he had gone down to Devonport to help take over the Dutch carrier *Karel Doorman*,* formerly HMS *Nairana*, which was to be reconverted to the MV *Port Victor*. The history of this ship and her twin *Port Vindex* interested him, and when he heard years later that the latter was to be scrapped he asked the board of the Port Line if he could have the ship's main bell, which was the original used in her carrier version and still inscribed HMS VINDEX.

In warships other than carriers this bell would have been hung by tradition aft on the quarterdeck. *Vindex* had no quarterdeck. The after end of the main deck, covered by the after part of the flight deck, was called the After Working Space, from which two alleyways led forward, one on either side of the ship. To starboard, in accordance with merchant ship tradition, was the Engineers' Working Alleyway with workshops for ship (as against aircraft) repairs and the cabins of the junior engineers. The alleyway on the port side led to the wardroom, then on past the Captain's day cabin to the Embarkation Space, open on both sides of the ship, which was where gangways were rigged in harbour and where such ceremonial as the ship ever performed took place. Amidships on the bulkhead at the forward end of the Embarkation Space was the usual plaque, commemorating the time and place of the launching of HMS *Vindex*, and immediately above and in front of this hung the ship's main bell. It was never struck for the hours, but Sea Hurricane fighter leader Jimmy Green's little girl Carol Anne, the name which had also adorned the nose of his aircraft, was christened in it.

This bell was subsequently delivered to John Copland-Mander's office in the Royal Docks, London. There it stayed for about a year until he also obtained the big bell, marked HMS NAIRANA, from the MV *Port Victor* when she

---

* This name was transferred to the Light Fleet carrier HMS *Vengeance*, acquired by the Royal Dutch Navy from the RN, which subsequently became the Argentine Navy's *Veinticinco de Mayo*.

too was scrapped. He presented both bells to the Fleet Air Arm Museum, Yeovilton, Somerset, where, at the time of writing, the only flying Swordfish is also kept.

HMS *Vindex*'s former batsman John 'Jagger' Mills wrote to the Port Line also requesting the old ship's bell. In due course he was given a smaller bell marked HMS VINDEX which had hung in the wheelhouse in the traditional place immediately abaft the wheel, adjacent to a microphone connected to the ship's tannoy system to broadcast the time at sea (and on which at New Year the youngest member of the ship's company rang sixteen bells). Mills hung the bell outside the front door of his house in Kent. Surgeon Ian Taylor, another ex-*Vindex* man, often visited him there, and always admired the bell. Mills died shortly after this, and his widow presented Taylor with the bell, which he hung at his home in Norfolk.

HMS *Vindex*'s wartime form is preserved in the model made by Swan Hunter and loaned by them to the Fleet Air Arm Museum.

In July 1979 Lieutenant-Commander John T. Leech, RN (Rtd), who had spent much of his working life maintaining Naval aircraft and aero engines, including the battle-worn Swordfish of No. 830 Squadron in Malta, as well as ships' engines and machinery, was choosing a name for his new Aquastar twin-screw motor cruiser, which he had bought as a fibre-glass hull in 1976 and fitted out himself in his spare time. He wanted one not already in the British or Lloyds Registers, not a made-up name, but one with some meaning to it. He was leafing through a Latin dictionary when the word 'vindex' stood out, meaning 'protector, maintainer, deliverer'. He also remembered that he had collected a draft chit to HMS *Vindex* in September 1944, only to be given a pierhead jump to the Light Fleet carrier HMS *Perseus* instead.

After the usual exhaustive check on details of craft and owner, which took six weeks, the name was accepted by the British Register of Shipping, there being no other vessel so recorded, and on 8 October 1979 his boat was registered *Vindex* in the port of Bristol, thus keeping the name afloat for at least a few years longer.

Index

210